ONE LIFE

ONE LIFE

The Free Academic

Max Kaplan

Madison • Teaneck
Fairleigh Dickinson University Press
London: Associated University Presses

© 1998 by Associated University Presses, Inc.

All rights reserved. Authorization to photocopy items for internal or personal use, or the internal or personal use of specific clients, is granted by the copyright owner, provided that a base fee of $10.00, plus eight cents per page, per copy is paid directly to the Copyright Clearance Center, 222 Rosewood Drive, Danvers, Massachusetts 01923. [0-8386-3737-X/98 $10.00+8¢ pp, pc.]

Associated University Presses
440 Forsgate Drive
Cranbury, NJ 08512

Associated University Presses
16 Barter Street
London WC1A 2AH, England

Associated University Presses
P.O. Box 338, Port Credit
Mississauga, Ontario
Canada L5G 4L8

The paper used in this publication meets the requirements of the American National Standard for Permanence of Paper for Printed Library Materials Z39.48–1984.

Library of Congress Cataloging-in-Publication Data

Kaplan, Max, 1911–
    One life : the free academic / Max Kaplan.
    p. cm.
    Includes bibliographical references (p.)
    ISBN 0-8386-3737-X (alk. paper)
    1. Kaplan, Max, 1911– . 2. College teachers—United States—Bibliography. 3. Sociologists—United States—Biography.
4. Musicians—United States—Biography. 5. College teaching—United States. I. Title.
LA2317.K26A3   1998
378.1'2'092—dc21   97-26170
                                                                                               CIP

PRINTED IN THE UNITED STATES OF AMERICA

With love
Terry, Marcia, Charlotte, Philip

Contents

Prologue: The Campus and the World ... 9

Part One: Life

Introduction ... 17
1. Maturing ... 18
2. Teaching ... 37
3. Consulting ... 50
4. Writing ... 64
5. Modeling ... 74
6. Fiddling ... 84
7. Ending ... 90

Part Two: Vision

Introduction ... 99
8. Roles: Prophets, Activists, Scientists ... 103
9. Flexibilities: Lifestyle, Time and Place, Work ... 115

Part Three: Realization

Introduction ... 125
10. Leisure and the General Process of Theory/Policy ... 128
11. Leisure and Ethics: Connections and Judgments ... 144
12. Apostles of Accuracy, Exploration, Significance ... 160
13. Sociology and Music Education ... 170
14. Las Colinas: Plans for an Experiment in Puerto Rico ... 183
15. Leisure: Toward a Theory and Policy for Israel ... 195
Epilogue ... 213

Notes ... 222

Prologue: The Campus and the World

AMONG the broad lifestyles that are the core of social psychology—business, agriculture, military, the professions, entertainment, etc.—the academic has its uniquenesses. The "academy," going back to the Greeks, eventually led to the college and university as we know them, as well as to teaching, research, and service centers ranging from permanent institutes to workshops and momentary conferences.

Academia is a vast enterprise. Its essential ingredients are separateness, relative isolation, self-sufficiency, protection from the outside, and a configuration of faculties and students. Its essential creed is freedom from pressures and special interests. Its hopeful goal is growth in the body of general and specialized knowledge, and development in the skills and maturity of the student body.

I had the privilege of serving the academic community and sharing its lifestyle for over four decades in institutions of Wisconsin, Colorado, Illinois, Massachusetts, Maryland, Florida, and Alabama. Amidst these positions in both major and minor institutions, there have been visits, lectures, and consultations in many parts of the world, among many cultures, political systems, and educational traditions.

And that is one of my points: the immense variety of environments in which the academic lives its purposes, yet within the singular traditions suggested above. Of course, the *academic* is not an abstract, but a community of students and scholars in the flesh. They share a general vision of society, of life in general, and of themselves.

Even since my earliest membership in this community, as a music teacher in a small Colorado junior college, I have been aware that among the transformations, this community has become less isolated, less independent. This applies to every interest and specialty, including the physical and social sciences, the arts, the service agencies, the humanities, and the administration itself. Direct relationships have increased, even with the military and with foreign governments. This has happened to every institution, not only to the more prestigious.

Such studies might move in many productive directions:

What is the nature and objectives of the many outside or special interests of these nonacademic forces?

To what degree do they affect the "purity" of academic pursuits?

How can we estimate or specifically measure the impact of the academic partnership on the "clients?"

How do these outside forces contribute to the selection and execution of research and teaching programs?

How independent have outside sources of funding reflected on higher institutions as a whole?

It must be immediately apparent that a full career could be devoted to such questions and their many subissues. The inquiry might be centered in the fields of educational administration, educational ethics, political science, or in something amounting to "cultural interlocking." For those seeking a brief introduction to such issues, I recommend an essay by Eric Trist. "The organization and financing of research" in *Main Trends of Research in the Social and Human Sciences*[1] I note one paragraph:

Most professors assume non-academic responsibilities in voluntary associations, political and religious movements, and other sectors of public life, including government committees. These engagements constitute a considerable portion of their regular activities. Much of the work is done on an honorary basis . . .

In the United States, however, much of the interaction with such agencies as governmental in nature are for a consulting fee. Some universities place a limit on how many hours or weeks per year may be devoted to such outside activity. Others welcome these external activities as good for prestige of the institution, and in many cases, good for the teaching transaction. I have known scholars at MIT who considered every potential grant from a military or commercial contract to see whether, aside from pragmatic results, "pure" research might also emerge; contracts with the dual potential were, of course, preferable. Many situations in this country include graduate students, especially in the natural and physical sciences, who obtain valuable experience as associates to their professors in such consulting or research projects.

In eastern Europe, even after the demise of Communism, the "academies of science" are continuing, that is, special research groups set up by the government for studies connected with public policy.

The conjunction of the campus and the world comes about in various ways: direct communications between persons, impersonal channels such as written documents, impersonal contacts through reports, and more recently, through the internet. An illustration of the first is the faculty member who lectures or consults in such a live situation as a corporate environment; a printed economic forecast illustrates the second. Of course, these channels overlap. In the first, perhaps more than in the second, the faculty may be expected to work according to a body of theory in that field, as well as to make recommendations. Again, these objectives may explicitly overlap; however, it is the theoretical approach that is generally the more permanent and valuable to the client.

Yet at this point we are confronted with the fact that even in such a democratic culture as the United States (especially in reference to the social scientist) he/she is a product of a cultural condition or system of values. Professor Dror notes in his pioneering presentation of "meta-policy" that "a distinction must be drawn between the moral responsibility of individual policy scientists as a community . . . concrete findings and detailed recommendations will vary with the underlying values accepted by policy scientists and dominant in their culture." Writing before the Communist demise; Dror notes that "within the democratic society, terror, mind control and single-party leadership will be excluded from the domain of policy and metapolicy alternatives. But the basic orientations and methods of policy sciences are value neutral. . ."[2] He raises the crucial question, should we try to combine knowledge with "safeguards against misuse through much attention to the moral characteristics of the scientist?"

In approaching this criterion, no one has written more pointedly than the Swedish sociologist Gunnar Myrdal in the first of three volumes on the *Asian Drama*.[3] In direct reference to biases of the Western approach to poverty in Asia, Myrdal finds deep-laden *a priori* judgments in both cultures. In the universities of South Asia he finds economists who are strongly anti-Western in their sympathies and politically far to the left; in the West he finds bias toward "unwarranted optimism, or what George F. Kennan called the 'great American capacity for enthusiasm and self-hypnosis.'" Noting the inevitable *a priori*, Gunnar concludes that "In strict logic . . . every theory contains the seeds of an *a priori* thought. . . . This is the crux of all science: It always begins *a priori*, but must constantly strive to find an empirical basis for knowledge and thus to become more adequate to the reality under study."

Myrdal administers another blow to the wish for value-neutrality, for in his stark judgment " . . . every study of a social problem, however limited in scope, is and must be determined by valuations. A 'disinterested' social science has never existed and will never exist. Research, like every other rationally pursued activity, must have a direction. The viewpoint and the direction are determined by our interest in the matter. Valuations enter into the choice of approach, the selection of problems, the definition of concepts, and the gathering of data. . ."

Hence the importance of the first section of the present volume, which lays out the life and directions of the "free academic" before us; he may have comparative freedom from a highly organized and integrated institution known as the university, but he is not free from his culture and personal history.

ONE LIFE

Part 1
The Life

Introduction

I<small>N</small> other writings I have raised the specific question about my life and career: what has been the relationship between the two? From an essay "An approach to leisure studies, origins and influences," I reproduce only one paragraph to illustrate some connections.[1]

> Music and sociology—what of that juxtaposition? Of course, each contributes to the other: even a concert of the worst kind can afford one an intellectual preoccupation of observing the audience; the string quartet, my favorite type of music making, also represents one of mankind's supreme models for integrating the group and the person; my major hypothesis in *Leisure Theory and Policy* is based on *crescendo-decrescendo* continuum, representing a move toward increased specialization of social roles and then a gradual fusion of work-nonwork in the nonprimitive or cultivated social order. The book's major theoretical instrument is the model of four "string quarters," one within the other. Technically, I have long felt that sociologists could find in the arts a remarkably accessible set of laboratory situations suggested in T. W. Adorno's work, Mukerjee's unique *Social Functions of the Arts*, Max Weber's writings, or Burke's analysis of dramaturgy. Above all, the study of art from either a social-aesthetic or institutional level reminds us that the social sciences cannot afford to assume that their "value-free" stance is the only legitimate road to the typography of a culture. But just as leisure studies can serve to remind the aesthetic and art purists that audiences as a whole and creators/performers in large part are engaged in leisure pursuits, and subject to comparable analysis as publics to other tastes and events.

This section of the present volume sets forth a narration of the life, followed by observations of teaching, consulting writing, theorizing, fiddling, and ending. Modeling and consulting lead to essays of the third section ("realization"), but all of the first part has some relevance to the central theme.

1
Maturing

THE FAMILY

Rocky, the oldest of my three great-grandchildren, is seventeen—"going on twenty-seven" as the family says. Assuming I have another seven or eight years in me, I could end up being a *great-great-grandfather.*

I will not be alone, for while in 1900 those of us in the United States over eighty numbered almost 375,000, we will double that number by 2030. Of course, I will be gone by then, but like many of my peers—contrary to the popular myth—I am perfectly well. I have no beard; I do not rock on the proverbial porch; only occasionally do I need a Bufferin. I'll meet Bill Clinton for junk food anytime he cares to drop over, at any McDonald's. My teeth are my own. No allergies.

One cannot become a great or a great-great-grandfather without first having gone through preliminary steps, from son to father to grandfather. I know all of these roles or experiences. What I know hardly at all, sad to say, is the backwards progression: my father when he was a son, his father, *his* father, and back to the man who was my great grandfather in some *shtetl* in Lithuania. I know more about Mother's kind of life from reading such writers as Sholem Aleichim and Isaac Singer, and studying pictures of daily life in such volumes as *The Old Country: The Lost World of East European Jews,* by Abraham Shulman.[1] Further, in the mid-1970s I had driven several times through the villages of Romania, Bulgaria, and Czechoslovakia, and had encountered in their streets not only peasants but also chickens, cows, horses, and sheep, and had been in homes very much like those of my parents. It was not until 1962 that I had sense enough to sit Mother in the yard of our Newton Centre home, tape recorder between us, to pursue such basic questions, "What was your home like in the suburb of Vilna, Who were your playmates, What did your father do for a living?" "Living?" she smiled, "No one made a living." It was then that I learned that as a counterrevolutionary, she had spent several months in jail. Why, I asked in surprise, had you never told your sons about this? "You know," she replied, "I have a good pension in California. If they found out that I had been in prison. . ."

Henry, my father, arrived in the Golden Land about 1905; Sarah, my mother, two years later. The home in Milwaukee was psychologically part east-European, part mid-west American. We spoke to Mother in Yiddish, Father in English.

Family friends in the neighborhood were for the most part their landsman, all going through the experience of assimilation intermingled with tradition. Their children sought to play down the old, often embarrassed by European accents. One mark of emancipation, soon after marriage, was for the first generation to move to a mixed part of the city, sometimes even to modify the last name. Irving Howe has brilliantly portrayed the life of immigrants in New York City.[2] On a smaller scale, it was much the same in Milwaukee.

To be part of the immigrant milieu was to attend the Yiddish theater, much like Shakespeare's audience with its informality and dialogue with those on the stage; to become a faithful reader and believer in the Jewish *Forwards,* similar to the *Christian Science Monitor* in its breadth; to grow up in the educational and recreational atmosphere of a settlement house; to gather every Saturday evening in the home of one of the landsman, children all huddled in one bed before the era of baby-sitters; to invite, then insist, that every talented son play his fiddle; to argue politics, national and international.

Like the families around us, education was a basic value, with high school graduation a major attainment. Two of us, Frank and I, went through the teacher's college, at fifteen dollars per semester. It was, by any measure, a lower-middle-class family.

We had no car, most years no telephone; I read my fill of classics as a boy by the light of a coal stove in the living room. Sam built our first radio on an oatmeal box, with a "cat's whiskers" from Woolworth, a telephone receiver that had its first home in a nearby drugstore, and a large glass fruit bowl to amplify the sound. Sam worked after school in a bowling alley at the rear of a barbershop, setting up pins. Frank and I "owned" a downtown corner to sell newspapers for our daily profit of ten or fifteen cents. Our street gang put on theatricals for neighborhood kids in our basement for a penny admission; before the age of guns and drugs, our most violent activities included the stealing of candy and trinkets from the dime store on Saturdays. Like the first shave, long pants were our rite de passage to manhood. Girls were talked about in boasts, but from little experience. Some of our earnings went into the war effort, while the profit from dances organized by our parents went to relief of prisoners in Russia. We knew of the gulags long before Solzhenitsyn's writings came along.

There were family rituals, such as journeys downtown on Sunday afternoons to watch "greenhorns" arrive at the train station, followed by a climb to the top balcony of the Majestic theatre to see eight acts of vaudeville, Pathé News, and a film comedy. At home, we enjoyed fires and horse-drawn fire engines, which might overturn on an icy day if we were lucky.

This was Mother's life in the New World. What was she like?

In 1961 the Greater Boston Youth Symphony played for President and Mrs. Kennedy and several thousand guests on the East Lawn. Mother crossed the country by bus from Los Angeles to meet the Kennedys. After the concert, our group of one hundred players went inside for lunch. I had not known far enough in advance for security clearance that would provide a formal invitation for her. She promised to remain in her seat until I returned. She was gone when I came out. In due course she appeared, accompanied by a handsome military guard. He told me the story. When I left, she had approached him. In her Lithuanian accent and a smile, she asked, "Mister soldier, who owns this big house?" "Why, madam, you do and I do and everyone owns the White House." "That's what I thought," she replied, "I came by bus from California to see my house, and now they won't let me in." He took her by the hand, and gave her a private tour that covered more than we had seen.

That was Mother.

During our stay in the Washington area, the Army arranged a tour of the sights, including Mt. Vernon. Mother enjoyed the home where Washington had lived. Viewing the old landmark with great interest, she turned to me and in a voice heard by everyone, "Max, was the President a poor man or a rich man?" I said he was a rich man. She looked carefully around the living room and said, "Then why couldn't he buy new furniture?"

That was Mother.

The Holocaust was often a topic of conversation. During those days I had been starting a music department in a tiny junior college in Pueblo, Colorado. I never was sure as to how many of my cousins were still near Vilna, nor how many had been destroyed in the concentration camps. I had heard the number twenty-one, but doubted that high a number. Nevertheless, had Henry and Sarah not come to the United States, their children would undoubtedly have, in their early adulthood, found their end in Auschwitz or a similar hell. An opportunity came to visit this camp in the early 1970s during a visit to Warsaw with my wife, Barbara. I had been with her for several days in Budapest, where she was spending several months observing the Kodaly pioneers in their remarkable music program. She came with me to Warsaw, where I addressed the Polish Academy of Sciences and completed the consulting that I will discuss later in this volume. I then took a bus to Oswiceim, where Auschwitz-Birkenau had been built to kill millions of Jews, Catholics, gypsies, political dissenters, and Jehovah's Witnesses. It was a rainy Sunday afternoon when we got to the camp. Several hundred school children were also there. The tour started with a film documentary; we visited many buildings that were barracks, and the crematoria where the murders had taken place. There were walls with thousands of pictures taken of prisoners by the meticulous bureaucracy. I went down many names, to see if I could recognize any of our family. Among the deepest impressions of the visit was a blown-up photograph—a mural on an outside wall—of the symphony orchestra that had been formed by prisoners. We saw piles of clothing gathered from six barracks—348,820 suits of mens clothing, 836,525 dresses, plus thousands of spectacles, combs, and other personal articles. Much of this can now be viewed in the Holocaust Memorial Museum that opened in April 1993 in Washington.

Seven years before Mother's visit to the capital and Boston, the Hitler period had taken on a very close family meaning through Riva, a first cousin. She, her husband, and three daughters had been seized in Poland, sent to a labor camp in Siberia, and there the youngest daughter had died. Somehow they had escaped via some underground group and after the war found themselves in an officers' camp built by Hitler near Munich. In my first overseas trip with Betty, my first wife, we visited Riva, who by then had spent seven years in a hospital with tuberculosis; by then her husband and two daughters had been sent to Milwaukee by HIAS, a Jewish agency. Yet, through error or intention (using her papers to send another person to America) the U.S. Consulate in Munich had no record of Riva; at my urging, they examined her; the German hospital refused to readmit her. My early efforts then were to get her into Canada, but the officials there refused to admit her to Canada as a way station to the States. Months of correspondence and visits to Washington followed, and I succeeded in having a special bill passed by Congress, signed by Eisenhower. Now she would be permitted to be with her family for ten days, to be followed by an indefinite period in the county hospital. She arrived, saw her family, went to the hospital, and was released (law or no law) in several days. Riva now lives in Milwaukee, and her daughters are married. One of the problems I found in the extensive correspondence with German officialdom as I tried to get her out of Munich was that she constantly referred to her "mother," in reality my mother. Riva had grown up in the same home as Mother, near Vilna, but Sarah had already joined her husband in the New World. They met for the first time in Milwaukee.

Not long after that, Mother fell while chasing a bus as she followed her daily schedule. This usually included a stop in one of her favorite cafes, shopping in the farmer's market, visiting a Lutheran missionary for an English lesson (as the sisters played the game of trying to convert her), and on occasion, going to a funeral. She did not need to know who was being buried. Her first concern was age; the younger the person, the more she cried. Mother died only a few days before Barbara and I arrived in Los Angeles, on the way to her summer teaching at the University of Washington. We were in time for the funeral. Barbara and Sarah had talked on the telephone; they would have liked each other.

There is a great sociological classic, *The Polish Peasant in Europe and America* (1927) by W. I. Thomas and Florian Znaniecki, which reproduces many letters by immigrants. The letters that Mother wrote to her sons invariably began in the pattern found throughout those volumes. The coauthors called this the "bowing" letter form. Following a religious greeting, they note, "There follows the information that the writer, with God's help, is in good health, and wishes the same for the reader and the rest of the family. . . . Finally come greetings, 'bows,' for all the members of the family. . . . These elements remain in every letter, even when the function becomes more complicated . . . a manifestation of solidarity."[3]

Within her "bowing" letters, Mother often mentioned her love for America, in spite of her economic worries. What would this woman have been, if she had been raised in our culture, or given a full education in her own land? In addition to her natural curiosity, her energy was unbounded.

Father was an expert tailor, and had begun this trade in his native village, as well as later in the military. In the United States, even after technology had made pressing machines available, he continued to press with his hand iron. This kept his income down, and if he paid the rent on his shop for the month, it was a successful month. His shop was near downtown Milwaukee, near the stately courthouse. Either Frank or I would go home at noon, pick up a basket of warm food, hop a street car, and return to elementary class by 1:30 P.M.

One impact of having a tailor for a father was to make us conscious of clothes. He also made us politically conscious. Weekly discussions took place in our home during evening meals, on Sundays, and every Saturday evening in the home of friends. We were exposed to extended talk and debate on issues that affected Jews in Europe and the United States. Agitation for the establishment of a Jewish state was a constant matter of debate; my folks were anti-Zionist, always arguing for less nationalism in the world. Strongly anti-Communist, they were also anti-capitalist and responded to such leaders as Norman Thomas on the national level, Victor Berger on the Wisconsin stage, and Dan Hoan, for many years a remarkable Socialist mayor of Milwaukee.

Even social dances were semipolitical, raising money for political prisoners in Russia, and awarding prizes for displays in mime on the dance floor. Every Sunday, Father read aloud to the family from the *Forwards;* the feature we enjoyed the most was the Bintel Brief (a bundle of letters), addressed to the Ann Landers of that time. These covered a variety of problems familiar to the immigrant community: love entanglements, poverty, loneliness for home in Europe, citizenship issues—"letters that gave vent to the hope and frustrations they had formed as they tried to build new lives in these strange and forbidding yet at the same time wonderfully exciting 'Golden Land.'"[4]

Another dominant factor that had direct influence on the Kaplan home was the Workman's Circle (WC), or Arbeiter Ring, begun in 1892. In his classic work, *World of Our Fathers,* Irving Howe draws the conclusion that in the course of time the WC transformed itself from an instrument of Socialist politics into a "sentiment tended with affection and respect but no longer from the premise that the will or even heroism of an immigrant generation could change the world."[5] Yet in its beginnings the Circle did, indeed, have serious political goals. During the time of Father's activity in the very young Milwaukee chapter, politics was giving way to an emphasis on social and educational objectives.

It sponsored many lectures, it provided for the children of its members the rudiments of a secular Jewish education, "some middle path between a complete break from Jewishness and a lapse into faith."[6]

Father was buried in Denver with funds from the Workman's Circle. For many years he had occupied the honored post of "hospitaler," visiting members who were sick, and in a pre-social work setting, arranging for the needs of families in crisis. Before moving to the West for its climate, a lodge had been named for him.

The oldest son was Sam, then came Frank and me, with eighteen months between each of us. They are still alive as I write. Aside from genes, our longevity may in part be due to a family pattern of no smoking, no drinking, and incidentally, no cards. I don't recall a "rule" or any discussion of these matters. (On Sundays we sometimes got a mug of beer for Father from the nearby saloon.)

Sam attended what we call today a "magnet" high school, for students skilled with their hands and intent on a trade. He would occasionally come home with wood-carved patterns or molds to be used for pouring metals in the manufacture of mechanical parts. He came under the influence of Uncle Sam (Mother's brother), who was cross-eyed, exaggerated everything, and wandered the carnival routes throughout the country with his homemade cameras, weight machines, and fortune-telling devices. Sam, my brother, eventually obtained the concessions in several Chicago dime stores for pictures. Most of his profit came from the sales of frames. He hired a number of his in-laws to run the store operations, while he made the rounds to check on chemicals. Later he opened a studio in Los Angeles, and went out for more business to parties, weddings, and school events. During the Korean War he was assigned by the draft board to take identification pictures among workers in war plants. As a person, Sam has always preferred to work alone; he is excellent in talking with strangers; his lifelong passion has been to watch television.

Frank and I attended college in Milwaukee at the same time. While I majored in music education, he studied special education, and became an expert in serving young people in prison situations or in special classes for the mentally and physically impaired. Over many years in Los Angeles, he developed a mastery in the teaching of reading skills. Even now, long retired, he is in constant demand as a substitute teacher by the county school system to deal with knotty problems. Frank has always had a unique ability to get quickly to the heart of an issue. He is faithful to his physical workouts, especially swimming, contrary to either of his brothers.

Well, that was the Milwaukee family. Like millions of other immigrant families with parents of the Old World and children of the New, we were dual-cultured, committed both to the home and to the street.

One connection between the culture of the parents and that of their children was Lincoln Center, only a few blocks from home. It was one of the many institutions across the country modeled after Hull House in Chicago, which in turn had been based on the Booth House in London. In the heart of what we now call the "inner city"—usually ethnic in character—they served a variety of purposes for all members of the family, going beyond the YMCAs and the emphasis on physical activity. Lincoln Center was directly programmed for immigrants: English lessons, legal and financial counselling, lectures, concerts, a drama program, art and music lessons. We had a community chorus and band.

As these "settlement houses" outlived their assimilated clientele, many of them turned to other objectives. In Cleveland and Chicago, for instance, they turned largely to the needs of black girls who came to the north for jobs. Many turned entirely to programs of adult education and to the arts. As music schools, they offered topflight instruction, charging whatever the family could afford, and often, providing lessons for nothing. In the mid-1960s, when the Guild of Community Schools of Music and Art had reached a membership of about forty schools here and in Canada, I was invited to visit many of them for a social-philosophical evaluation in respect to current trends of class, family life, and musical institutions. As I entered such schools in New York, Boston, Cleveland, Hartford, Los Angeles, and San Francisco, I was often reminded of my experiences in Lincoln Center more than half a century earlier. They had the same neighborhood atmosphere, the same spirit of helpfulness. They supplemented, and in some ways exceeded, the structure and quality of the important public school music movement that had also played a vital part of American life in the same decades.

Unity and Diversity

The neighborhoods of our ethnic families were building blocks toward the blending, and eventually, the elimination of neighborhoods as physical places and psychological realities. The one where we grew up has long been replaced by a highway; our elementary school is not to be seen; apartments have replaced the two-story homes in our part of town. This was part of the national unity that was becoming the core of American aspirations.

Max Lerner has written of the aspirations that would eliminate the differences among us, in food, in entertainments, in the criteria of personal success, even in class distinctions.

> In addition to the British, the Scotch Irish, the French Huguenots, the early German settlers from the Palatine and the later Germans who left behind the abortive German revolutions of 1848, many other strains came to America. There were Irish Catholics driven by famine and an inner restlessness, there were Norwegians, Swedes and Danes, Hungarians, Austrians, Bohemians and Moravians, Spaniards and Portuguese; there were Swiss, Italians, Serbs, Greeks, and Armenians; there were Russian and Polish peasants, Lithuanians and Finns; there were Jews, hoping that America would be the last stop in their history of wandering; there were Mexicans and Canadians, crossing not a sea but a border; there were Latin Americans; there were Chinese, Japanese, Filipinos. . . . Thus the bundles of Old World memories, jostling each other in the New World, have enriched the American tradition.[7]

Indeed, as our generation grew up, the American Dream was on the way to realization through the mixing of populations across the states, the growth of suburbs, mass education, and assimilation of national values. Intermarriage across ethnic lines soon became common. It seemed that Mark Twain's observation, made at the beginning of the century, had become prophetic.

> There isn't a single human characteristic that can be safely labelled 'American.' There isn't a single human ambition, or religious trend, or drift of thought, or peculiarity of education, or breed of folly, or style of conversation, or preference for a particular subject for discussion, or form of legs or head or face or expression or complexion, or gait, or dress, or manners, or disposition, or any other human detail, inside or outside, that can rationally be generalized as 'American.'[8]

This change in values became part of the social fabric as we moved to the top of our careers. By now, World War I had been fought and won. We entered an era of growth, in numbers, in gadgets, in longer weekends, in mass media, in the size and price of our cars, in launderettes, in packaged foods, in the circulation of *Reader's Digest* and *Life*, in such national treasures as Bob Hope and Jack Benny, in adult education, in country clubs and municipal tennis courts. FDR was followed by Truman, then came Kennedy and Johnson . . . and on to Reagan and Bush. On the one hand, through this history, we had evidences of a national unity that feeds on disasters, triumphs (space explorations), and wars; on the other hand, as presently into the Clinton presidency, national divisions based on differing interests, competing power groups, and searches for self-identity among ethnic and other groups.

Also in our time, the young rebelled against everyone, without a clear agenda of their own. Later I will note this struggle on our campuses. At the other end of the age spectrum, the elderly found their collective voice, and maintained their growing political power even against the "great communicator."

This alternating rhythm—unity and diversity—has become dramatic in recent decades. Unity will emerge, given the next international crisis, earthquake, or the death of a great movie or sports hero. Confrontation will also continue, on new issues as well as such present items as abortion, race relations, crime, homosexuals in the military, national budgets or national health plans. These and many other developments are not to be seen as isolated areas for policy or disagreement, but as Alvin Toffler wrote in 1980, "part of the new civilization bursting into being in our midst" that challenges "old ways of thinking, old formulas, dogmas, and ideologies, no matter how cherished or how useful in the past. . ."[9]

In a more recent challenge, *Preparing for the Twenty-First Century,* the Yale historian Paul Kennedy speaks of the consequences of the disappearance of the U.S.S.R., the possibility of regional conflicts in its wake, the further rise of Asian power, nuclear-armed China and India, our own economic problems, the population revolution in the North and South imbalance, and environmental dangers.[10]

My own concerns for tomorrow also include the growing wealth and political challenge of the political right joined with the religious politicians of the Robertson-Falwell type, ongoing use of drugs at all levels of society and of related crimes. Since Clinton may be my last president, there is in my mind a certain visceral satisfaction in coming to my end under a leader with a mind, a conscience, and a vision. There may be hope along the way.

TECHNOLOGY

A second transformation has colored the maturation of my generation. This time it is not a polarity—unity, diversity—but a one-sided phenomenon that we call technology. The major issue that technology once again raises is the one that Plato argued, that philosophers like himself should run the world and define its values. Much later, St. Simon argued the case for leadership by sociologists. Toward the end of the 1920s there was a group of activist engineers, calling themselves Technocrats, who actually began a political movement on their own behalf . . . God, after all, was an engineer-mathematician. Some two generations later, Ross Perot, the billionaire, self-styled problem-solver, has become a master of the mindless sound bit on behalf of the businessman as national manager. The most esteemed critic and interpreter of technology, Jacques Ellul, has no political formula to peddle; he provides analysis and perhaps a note of hope. Along with such analysts as Toynbee and Spengler, perhaps Ellul puts most trust in the clergy—using that term in its noninstitutional sense.

La Technique, writes Ellul, has always been present to some degree, even in primitive and preindustrial society. In earlier periods, however, it existed only in limited areas, among men who also held other values. Now the society is characterized by an *automism*, so that we accept the mechanical as superior to the nonmechanical; by *self-augmentation*, in which anonymous accretion of invention replaces the inventive genius, and by *monism*. With monism, technical phenomena becomes a whole. No one element can be grasped in isolation. The whole is objective, having no end; technique creates the automobile but does not define its precise use. No purpose or plan is progressively realized with the new combination of techniques. "There is not even a tendency toward human ends." Thus, the phenomena is "blind to the future. The only choice man has is to use it according to technical rules or not at all."[11] Indeed, the destructive possibilities are preferred by the state, with easier criteria for efficiency. In such a milieu there is an expanded appetite for things; work by persons is not necessarily the ideal. If we assume that the mission of the humanistic community is to break through the technological Frankenstein, we must raise the issues of man's relation to things and to humanistic values. Since Ellul is a theologian, he holds that such values can prevail.

Like all of my contemporaries, for me the spread of technology was a fact of everyday life. We accepted at face value such obvious products as cars, telephones, electricity. There were other miracles that came along—laser, for example—that most of us hardly understand, but became part of the larger picture, along with increasingly sophisticated computers, VCRs, superconductors.

As time went on, nothing surprised us in newspaper reports, including the possibilities of life spawned in the laboratory. The future had become part of our lives.

To those like my brothers and myself, some of the Dream came through in our childhood, as Sam made our first radio out of an oatmeal box and other found objects. Mother, never, to her dying days, believed that airplanes could fly even as she watched them in the air; more immediately, she knew that no dishwasher could substitute for old-fashioned hand effort. Seeing no wires beyond the wall plug, she enjoyed TV—although she was sure that it could not work. Her dependable broom was always nearby, even after she owned a Hoover. By then, along with others, she was unaware that she had already captured much of that Dream with a built-in energy factor equal to ninety-five full-time male servants.

In my case, I became intellectually involved with technology through my professional interest in leisure. Changes in work were a prime element in the democratic spread of "free time." In my writings and lectures I was drawn into discussions on the meaning of technology for our sense of values, for the changes in home life and for the growing "popular culture" that led to a dramatic consumption of gadgetry. Lewis Mumford, Jacques Ellul, David Riesman, Alvin Toffler, and many others became colleagues in person or friends across the printed page. Emanuel Mesthene, director of the Harvard University Program on Technology and Society (1964–74) during my stay in Boston, is a good flutist, and on a number of Sunday afternoons we would play violin-flute duets (mostly baroque material) and discuss his challenging assignment. After the first atomic bomb was dropped in Japan, I attended secret discussions in the mid-west, convened by a federal agency, together with scientists, clergymen, philosophy professors, and others.

Finally, let me reproduce a series of letters to suggest an amusing aspect of technological change on a personal level. On 3 December 1965, I wrote to my publisher, John Wiley Company, for several copies of a new book, subtracting the cost from forthcoming royalties. The following letter came from the firm's assistant comptroller.

Dear Dr. Kaplan:

This will acknowledge receipt of your note jotted on the bottom of our invoice, requesting that the charge be deducted from your royalties. We are returning herewith this invoice and are asking your assistance concerning this type of transaction. The charging of purchases against royalties requires a completely manual operation. It requires a special handling by the Accounts Receivable Section, the Royalty Section, and also the Tax Section. Special handling ordinarily would not be a problem, except that our royalties are prepared by data processing. Thus, for our system this type of transaction becomes what we call an "exception." Naturally, we can handle any exception, but we are asking you to help us to eliminate this type of exception wherever possible. Unless we wrote this type of letter explaining to you that this type of transaction was in fact an exception you would have no way of knowing our problem. Therefore, if at all possible, can you remit the amount of this invoice directly to the attention of the undersigned. In the future we would appreciate all purchases paid direct rather than applied against royalties. Your cooperation and assistance is appreciated.

I replied:

I bow to the complication of data processing and all the other forms of automation and technology. Enclosed is my check for the books. Already I can visualize the new subversive of the Great Society. Who would dare stop to add a column of figures on paper or to record the result in his hand in an old-fashioned account book? There used to be an old problem in logic when we were young: Is God powerful enough to create a rock that He cannot move? Now there is a new issue: Can the machine create the formula complicated enough that even the machine cannot remember or resolve?

Our assistant comptroller replied:

Thank you for your letter of December 8, but most of all thank you for understanding our problem. It appears that you have a very good knowledge of machine problems, and I can't help but agree with you. Your check is appreciated and has been applied against your outstanding invoice of $13.39. I certainly wish others would be as cooperative as you were, and also as prompt in their reply.

Beyond such personal experiences, it became apparent to all of us that technology was now a dominant factor in the military. Eisenhower's reference to the "military-industrial" complex and its potential dangers became one of his major legacies in the American mind. National defense and huge profits were the twin stimulation for enormous advances in research. It was a recent development. I believe it was as late as 1935, when I was already twenty-four, that a distinguished chemist wrote to the military to suggest the addition of more scientists for pure research. A high navy official replied that they already had "one chemist." That same year, Princeton had obtained a grant of something like five thousand dollars for biological studies. At its high point, 1987—a half century later—the budget for research and development in the U.S. military came to 33.5 *billion dollars*. In addition, the budget for the NASA program alone was over 7.5 billion. As never before, TV brought the level of war technology to the American public in the Desert Storm attacks over Iraq in 1991.

Medicine was another area in which, in our adult lifetimes, technology took hold. Good health, always a goal, has become an obsession among us, and thereby, a major objective for advancements in technology. Robert S. Morison, for twenty years the director of medical and natural sciences for the Rockefeller Foundation, notes that the recent attention to technology in medical sciences began with the attempt to observe the negative aspects of technology itself, as in air pollution. On a wider level, this weighing of costs and benefits led in 1962 to the Office of Technology Assessment by Congressional action. "Assessment" presupposes some criteria. "What, after all," Morison asks, "is a benefit? Who gets it? . . . Are all lives equally valuable?" Such questions enter into the signing of "living wills," denying the use of technology to keep us alive beyond our wishes.[12]

Dr. Kervorkian of Michigan, in my view, will in later years be widely honored for his legal-ethical struggle to counterbalance life-preserving techniques. The vast bulk of technology in medicine is welcomed, if not its outlandish costs, by Americans; about 10 percent of our entire consumer expenditures go to keep us well and alive. This, says Morison, is evident even visually. "In most communities of moderate size the local hospital or medical center outclasses the structures that house the local library, the art gallery, or the church, just as in the national capital, the National Institutes of Health outspread the National Cathedral, the National Gallery, and the Library of Congress combined."

It may be that my great-grandchildren will profit from a new balance between the medical traditions of East and West, or between the mental and the biological. John Naisbitt's observed balance between "hi-tech" and "hi-touch" may be most appropriate in the medical area. He notes that transplants and brain scanners led to a new interest in the family doctor and neighborhood clinics, and that the development of the pill by chemists led to a revolution in lifestyles.[13]

Even as technology was evident on these fronts, its daily incursion into every home was through television. TV came to us in Champaign-Urbana in 1953. Fortunately, our daughters were by then addicted to Gilbert and Sullivan; their superb university high school provided a creative program of extracurricular activities. I like to think that the books and music in our home had something to do with shaping their values. The television of that time has been many times multiplied in its impact since that time, for aside from electronic games, videotapes, and VCRs, the violence of our time over the airwaves seems to have multiplied many times over the 1950s. Only a fool can be oblivious to the nature and quantity of sex and violence that now comes to us on behalf of profit. The industry has for years spewed the paradoxical nonsense about how successful was their commercial segment of every program but that violence had no impact on the minds of their viewers. Study after study makes mincemeat of this claim and sham. My concern is especially with children.

Writing in the *Daedalus* of winter 1993, Professor Condry of Cornell reminds us that in preindustrial society, children acquired a knowledge of their world as it existed in their family and community.[14] The advent of schools supplemented such learning by direct participation. Then along came TV, taking as much as forty hours of the child's time per week. Yet beyond the number of hours, the writer notes that heavier viewing results in more aggressive behavior by children—a fact that emerges from hundreds of studies. Modern television, writes Condry, is primarily a marketing device that ignores or subordinates information, education, or curiosity. In his studies, for every antidrug message in a study of thirty-six hours over a two-day period, six were pro-drug; for alcohol, the ratio was one to ten. He concludes:

> Many children are troubled today . . they spend too much of their childhood watching television. Television is a thief of time . . . it is a liar. . . . For the little truth television communicates, there is much that is false and distorted, about values as much as facts.

Perhaps there is hope, for three years ago the TV and movie industries began a self-study on the issue of violence. I have been involved in one such effort, many years ago, when the movie moguls decided to study their product to raise its standards and (I was sure at the time) their profits. Among others, I advocated an educational program over a matter of years, in which their theater facilities, unused most of the day, would become community centers devoted to creative efforts, including community theater; thus a potential audience might be developed and the movie house would be looked upon and used as a useful creative tool. The final decision made in Hollywood was to produce more movies featuring sex. . . .

Of course, violence on the screen is both a cause and a reflection of violence in the society as a whole—an American value that can be traced far back in our history. Rationality, as Mark Twain reflected, is less a characteristic of a society than its public opinion, which he calls "corn-pone opinions."[15] Hardly a man anywhere in the world has an opinion upon morals, politics, or religion which he got otherwise. Broadly speaking, there are none but cornpone opinions. The result is conformity. So today our children grow up in a time when violence is generally approved, over half of their homes have guns, the NRA grows in membership and arrogance, and both TV and motion pictures have a ready audience already developed and millions of small children to mold.

And that is how our generation also grew up. Whether on the matter of ethnicity, or the potential of technology, we picked up our cornpone ideas from signals everywhere in the streets and institutions, including the press, our entertainments, our attitudes toward law and order, and the less-evident presence of "white collar" crime in corporations, banks, savings and loan institutions, and in halls of legislation.

Yet it was a mixed society that matured us, with the kaleidoscope of feelings and ambitions and values that came with our move into the suburbs, our migrations across state lines, changes in our family lifestyles, the changing nature of work in the new sea of electronics and robotics. What changes have taken place in my lifetime in the schools; including an expansion in the arts! Shopping took on revolutionary changes, for in my childhood we still told the grocer what we needed, and he went back, selected the items and that was that; Piggly Wiggly, I think, changed all that with its open shelves, starting a remarkable change that is still going on with the evolution of the shopping mall. If malls were our new recreation complexes, the home was a new consuming and entertainment center, and our comfortable cars—with their heating controls, radios, telephones, computer units—became magic carpets that soar over the landscape.

The question arises, what influence did this childhood and young adulthood have on the choice of leisure as the unifying issue for the last forty years of life? I had occasion to consider this at the request of my colleagues in the field. For the November

1980 issue of *Loisir et Société*, edited by my good friend and colleague, Phillip Bosserman, I was asked to examine my career from the view of "origins and influences."[16] From that essay I take the liberty now of extracting some paragraphs. I noted that young sociologists from immigrant families did not go into such peripheral specialties as art and leisure: there are more "fundamental" issues crying for analysis: group relations, adjustments to a new culture, poverty, alienation, crime. . . . I was interested in those issues. My writing drew on them, as in the essay "We have much to learn from the inner city," or in a chapter of the 1975 book on Jewish and black attitudes toward leisure. The real influence goes deeper. In early years, as social worker, city planner, researcher with a tuberculosis agency, adult educator, student of music, junior-college instructor during wartime, I had the opportunity to develop priorities of man's needs. Housing, health, economic maintenance: all are basic to survival. But David Riesman put my question into words: survival for what? The conviction came early, if in cloudy form: we need to know more about our purposes, meanings, anticipations, hopes. An understanding of art and nonwork experience became, for me, not only a legitimate objective of social science, but, perhaps only for me, the study itself symbolized the success over our material growth.[17] As my mother sent her three sons to learn the violin as a celebration of opportunity in America, so now my studies of such symbolic actions were an affirmation and celebration of the life these thirty million immigrants had undertaken in the 1880–1910 period from all corners of Europe. I did not need to study something like anti-Semitism as a sociologist: I preferred to observe the victories of a society where our Polish, Hungarian, Italian, and German parents had come to find gold in the street, then found that they first had to build the streets; then we, their offspring, could ride over them to our parks, friends, libraries, schools, and concerts. The arts and leisure were more than sets of activities; they were national goals, heaven-brought-to-earth, triumphs over material goods and instruments, statements of opportunities for what I later came to call the "cultivated society."

From my residence at the University of Illinois came a first-hand familiarity with Spencer, Simmel, Weber, Comte, Parsons, Sorokin, and other sociological giants of yesterday and today. Florian Znaniecki was the most modest of men; one could sit in his seminar on methods of sociology without hearing him mention his book by that name. He was the major formative influence on my work, not about the arts or leisure *per se* but his elegance of mind, his depth of philosophical and historical reading, his concept of social role (the basis of my 1979 volume), his concern with macroscopic analysis, the freedom he permitted his students, and his gentleness as a person in company with his brilliant scholar-wife, Eileen. It was a time when the doctorate in sociology at Illinois could still be earned without one course in statistics (but so rough was it to earn that only three had been granted in the twenty years before our generation); yet, as in Albig's seminars on public opinion, we could develop a sense of quantitative verification as well as of statistical pitfalls. Gallup and other pollsters turned to him to improve their techniques; we saw in Albig's publications a scientific beauty in their blend of the quantitative and interpretative temperament. From Max Weber, always present in our reading and conversations as graduate students, the "ideal constuct" provided a major tool in building the elements of leisure, when I got to that point in a 1960 book, as well as in understanding the arts (helped by Gurevich and his concept of polarities) for a 1966 volume.

Music and sociology—what of that juxtaposition? Of course, each contributes to the other: even a concert of the worst sort can afford one the intellectual preoccupation of observing the audience; the string quartet, my favorite type of music-making, also represents one of mankind's supreme models for integrating the group and the person; my major hypothesis in *Leisure: Theory and Policy* is based on the *crescendo-decrescendo* continuum representing a move toward increasing specialization of social roles and then a gradual fusion of work-nonwork in the nonprimitive or cultivated social order. The book's major theoretical instrument is the model of four "string quartets," one within the other. Technically, I have long felt that sociologists could find in the arts a remarkably accessible set of laboratory situations, suggested in T. W. Adorno's work, Mukerjee's unique *Social Functions of the Arts*, Max Weber's writings, or Burke's analysis of dramaturgy. Above all, the study of art from either a social-aesthetic or institutional level reminds us that the social sciences cannot afford to assume that their "value-free" stance is the only legitimate road to the typography of a culture. But just as leisure studies can see in the arts a major prototype of human experience in which utilitarian means give rise to qualitative ends, so leisure studies can serve to remind the aesthetic and art purists that audiences as a whole and creators/performers in large part are engaged in leisure pursuits, and subject to comparable analysis as publics to other tastes and events.

In his *The Act of Creation*, Arthur Koestler has something to say about those who bring two fields into an integrative relationship.[18] What merged for me was to become a *holistic* attitude toward leisure: through a comprehensive conceptual model I was freed from wasting future years on the dichotomy of work/leisure.

Let others, if curious enough, draw further connections, more objectively than I can, of the links from early influences to theoretical results. The more important question is whether from even one case we might extract some clue for such a search. Among the propositions to be explored, then, might be these: the selection of interests, indeed, the choice of a profession; the values brought to the work, including the criteria of success; and the techniques brought to bear as a consequence of the preparation. Also affecting the selection of work or interests might be the factors from the life narrative that includes the social circles (friends, family, classmates, etc.); particular events, such as moves to a new environment; the "temperament" of the person; and matters of pure chance, including one's health.

2
Teaching

CONVERSATION

He was afraid. Now he came to my office. It was in Champaign-Urbana, between the North and the South. Tom, a handsome, light-skinned black man, had never been to the deep south. He was about to graduate with a degree in criminal justice. Tom felt guilty as a black man, for he had never participated in the civil rights struggle. His conscience told him to go to the real south and become active. His mother wanted him home in Chicago, get a job, marry, and produce grandchildren.

Marvin was a fine violinist, a gentle, pacific person. He had just received a letter from his draft board. As nonmilitary as anyone could be, he asked whether he should join some of his friends in Canada.

Judith was a theater student at Boston University. Even in that milieu, she had managed to remain a virgin until last night. She insisted that her only motive in giving in to a comparative stranger was to "make a statement to my father." I gathered he must be a strict disciplinarian. Had she called her father with the news before telling me? Not yet. That was her problem: should she call him?

A friend came to my office in the Sunshine state. About forty years of age, her husband had been killed by a car only a few weeks before as he sat on a Tampa street waiting for the lights to change. His widow, sitting before me now, had known that the man was doing "quite well" as a manufacturer of clothing. But now she was dumbfounded to learn from the family lawyer that she had become a millionairess many times over. With her grown children at Harvard, she could go anywhere to live, do anything. Her question to me: "In your travels abroad, do you know any eligible men, especially from English royalty?"

There was the case of the lovely junior in one of my classes at the University of Colorado. We were about to take a class trip to something or other out of town—overnight. With a cup of coffee in hand in the cafeteria, she finally came to the question, "How many nights would it take to get an 'A' in the course? (at the time she was, generously judged, worthy of a 'C')."

Bennett College, now defunct, was a good junior college for very rich girls (and some scholarship students). For a year I served in Millbrook as its Academic Dean. Missy was one of those who came to the office quite often. Once it was to get my advice on the purchase of a small recording machine to play records required in her music appreciation course; should she get a machine by going to Poughkeepsie, or pay a few dollars more in the college bookshop? On a school trip to New York City, I heard Missy argue with a gateman in the subway (her first subway ride) for change in coins after she had purchased the subway chip. Today she appeared in my office after a visit to the school by the family lawyer. Her father, an oil magnate, had changed his will, and the lawyer came to inform her that in a year Missy would hold the deeds to three blocks of property in downtown Houston. Her question to me, for she knew of my interest in the arts: should she use some of the income to build an art museum that she would design? She had about twenty million in mind. . . .

Jane was a beautiful sophomore who lived in a sorority just across Lincoln Hall at the University of Illinois. Lincoln Hall was where sociology was taught. Every known sorority and fraternity could be found on that campus, with great social and political power in terms of campus politics. The Greek groups all kept well-organized files on every instructor, and copies of any examination that could be obtained one way or another. The Greeks, of course, held real power over the lives of their members, such as to whom they could or could not date. Jane came with what to her was a tragedy. She had been accepted and initiated by a high-ranking sorority, but shortly after moving into the house, was convinced that she had made a mistake. She should have joined sorority B instead of A. She was willing to move to another university and start all over again in search of the right group. But Jane had just learned that there is a tight national, inter-sorority rule in this regard. What should she do now, for the matter was interfering with her studies, her choice of men. . . . At the moment, she was in one of my classes and not doing too well.

Perhaps the most fateful visit to my office was by Gene Shalit. Gene had been a student of mine, but now was working in New

2: TEACHING

York for *Look* magazine. He was always a good student and writer, and "street smart." He had heard that the Prince of Monaco would prefer a wife who was an American. Gene got permission from his superiors to move on that assumption by contacting the prince and volunteer his help in the quest. The arrangement was that Gene would select the young lady, pay all of her expenses to Monaco, provide her with appropriate clothes, jewelry, etc. and that the prince would agree only to see the young lady in his garden for a few hours. The understanding was reached. The magazine, of course, would publicize all this with the prince's permission. Now Gene was in my office, devising a way to select the right girl.

We visited a photographer near the campus who took pictures of the university graduates, as well as social events and engagements. Purely on the basis of "wholesome appearance," we selected a dozen girls, and Gene began the task of tracking down each girl for the qualifications he had in mind, including permission from the parents.

Everything proceeded well. The girl who was finally selected by Gene came from a rural home in the state. A former student of mine, I could testify as to her intelligence.

Joy (her real name) met the prince in his garden. She had been fully covered by the *Look* reporters every step of the way. However, to our surprise, the prince was charmed by Joy, kept her for more than the allotted time, and began a serious correspondence after she left. Joy would come to my office to let me read his correct, but very personal, correspondence on royal stationery. Some months later the prince wrote that he was coming to the United States for medical work, but also to meet Joy again and her parents. Everyone was delighted at the possibilities.

On the way, the Prince of Monaco stopped off in Cannes for the annual film festival. He ran into Grace Kelly . . .

Conversation on the campus of every college goes on everywhere, in corridors, living quarters, on the street, in eating places. Between student and student, student and faculty, faculty and faculty. This living "organism" that is set up for teaching, research, and service—the institution for higher learning—thrives on gossip, exchange of information, personal advice-giving, and commentary *ad infinitum* on courses and teachers. Informal therapy and amateur counseling is built into every campus, every sorority and fraternity, every dormitory, and alas, into many library hours.

Among the faculty, the smaller institution lends itself better to conversations among those from different areas of scholarship. The faculty club, lounge, or restaurant—as well as social visits—bring together the biologist and the literature specialist, the physicist and the psychologist. In Pueblo, my first campus position, we had only fifteen faculty members; in a middle-sized university, such as Colorado, there were several hundred; the University of Illinois, several thousand. In the last of these there were three or four Nobel-prize winners. I never knew any. We read about them, and on occasion could hear one in a public appearance.

That is the ever-present miracle of a campus, that it is a miniaturization of all major, legitimate interests: the hard sciences, the social disciplines, philosophy, literature, and the professional schools. Government, industry, commerce, the mass media, agriculture, the military, international affairs, space exploration, the arts, sports, recreation, family matters—all, all have roots in the theory or the science that is a concern to theorists and thinkers and laboratories and experiments in the "artificial" world of the institution that brings the young and the old together, sometimes the wise and the eager, the novitiate and the experienced. It is not a place for the arrogant, the lazy, the seeker of degrees in name alone. Those come. Sometimes they seem to succeed. It is a place for the inquisitive, the contemplative, the curious. They, too, come. In such systems as grading and counseling, the faculty is there to distinguish one from the other. In this way we provide some guidance to the future of the society. Thus the campus lives in the past and the future, a crucial institution.

Classroom

It is a privilege to teach persons of any age, but the responsibility of influencing young minds in their twenties is one that has a tradition going back to the seminaries of the ancient rabbis, the academies of Greece, and more specifically, the universities of sixteenth-century Italy. Among the three purposes of the contemporary university—to transmit knowledge, create knowledge, and serve the society—teaching supposedly stands first, for there are other institutions that can create knowledge, and others that can translate knowledge to the needs of society.

On my part, the responsibility has never been a light one. Even with the masses of students in large institutions who may take education lightly—too many—everyone must have the opportunity to fulfill the Dream that was a major force in the settling and development of our nation. I have on occasion cringed when I have heard young instructors refer to their students as "bodies." I have had little sympathy with other faculty whose open time for students in their offices is severely regimented. Over the years, my classes have ranged in number from 8 to 450. When I sit in a sports arena that holds 70,000 to 75,000, I have a fairly accurate view of those whom I have taught. Where are they now? What has been the impact of our association? How many would even recognize my name? (Even when using a textbook written by me, some students never really knew the name, or could spell it correctly.) One day in Illinois, a call came to my home from a lad whom I immediately recognized as a great football hero. It was the end of the term, and he asked politely if I had yet turned in his grade for the course. I responded that to my recollection he had not been a student of mine. A pause at his end, then, "Well, I wondered myself whether I had your sociology course, and just thought I would check."

In teaching my first class at the University of Colorado—after the tiny junior college in Pueblo—I recall that my hands shook as I taught from a page of notes. Confidence comes, but even the giants of the field must be cautious in their teaching. I recall sitting in a seminar led by a guest professor, the eminent anthropologist, M. J. Herskovitts. This world authority on African culture was describing the tradition among tribes where multiple wives were permitted, and yet, jealousy among them and their children was "not evident." A lad in the back of the room put up his hand. "Professor," he began, "I grew up in such a family. Let me tell you how it really was."

Sometimes the naivete of the students is amazing, and yet the instructor cannot show his incredulity. There was the girl in a class at Boston University whose father owned a textile mill near the city. She told us that about three hundred employees were employed in the factory. When asked what she thought her father earned per year, she guessed "about ten thousand dollars." There was a young man at another university who entered into a discussion of tenant farmers in the South. I had told the class that the average income of a tenant farmer was about nine hundred dollars per year. This chap objected, since they "must have other sources of income." I asked what those sources might be; his answer, "stocks and bonds."

I prize the memory of one class of thirty students who, on the last day of a class on "leisure," handed to me a petition asking me to teach another class on the subject, without credit.

The most ambitious course in sociology developed by itself at Illinois during the Truman presidency. It was while I was still pursuing the doctorate, and four groups of sophomores were under my care. We were all equally bored by a textbook that had been selected by a previous instructor. When President Truman delivered his "bold four-point program" about bringing aid to developing nations, I put a proposition to my 175 students: how would we proceed if Truman had come to us as a team of consultants, to submit reports on the social implications of such technical assistance as dams, roads, and other improvements?

The four groups agreed to scrap the text, and created five committees in each class to deal with family, religion, economy, education, and government. Thus we arrived at twenty committees across the board, four dealing with each issue. All formal classes were canceled, each committee chose a chairperson, each class had one coordinator. Committees met on their own schedules, each student was a member of one committee, chairs reported weekly to the coordinator, who kept in close touch with me. I also met regularly with each chairperson, and any student had access to me in the office.

Thus the assignment for each committee was simple and complex: if dams or other technical aid were to be brought to this nation, what likely impact might it have on religious beliefs . . . or other areas as suggested above?

With each student writing a portion of the committee report, the full document at the end of the exercise came to many volumes. All this was submitted to a professor in political science who had actually served as a technical advisor to the United Nations. For the final "examination," we all met together in a church basement near the campus—with refreshments—to hear a professional evaluation of our work. His general response was that a professional group of consultants to the President would not have come up with a more complete set of conclusions and recommendations. We allowed for his generosity, and yet. . . . The common observation of the students at the end was, why had we not started the project sooner? This was one of the high points of my teaching career, but it almost cost me the doctorate. The colleague in charge of all the sophomore introductory course in sociology wrote a scathing indictment of my project, addressed to the department, as he argued that our business was to "prepare students for advanced classes," rather than to "experiment."

Campus

As a young man I idealized the university campus as the natural habitat for rationality. To some extent, after four decades, I still cherish that view. Along the way one learns that the presence of many kinds of departments or "colleges" and many types of administrations—from the president down—can play havoc with rational decisions or attitudes outside of technical expertise.

Every college or department has its own character. For example, along political lines, conservatives find a more congenial atmosphere in business, engineering, agriculture, or medicine. Liberals find their way more in the humanities and arts. Economics students are close to businessmen in their values, while journalism and marketing divisions have no values except the creation of more consumers and profits. Recreation and sports rank low in the academic pecking order, and intellectualism to any degree is not expected by others: however, those teachings have risen considerably in recent decades, with their contemporary activity in theory and research.

Over the years, such simple categories, my own construction, of course, have softened. In part, some changes emerged with the seriousness that veterans from the Korean and Vietnam wars brought to the campus, along with many wives and children. Those older students had a deep impact on the campus and the greater responsibilities that confronted every faculty. As job objectives became more central, the humanities began to lose out to heavy enrollments in schools of business. The social sciences were especially hurt.

Within the humanities, sociology has always stood out as the most ambitious and least identifiable one in its proper content. Further, the very nature of sociology provides a built-in danger to the campus and to the society as a whole. Indeed, my colleagues and I were aware in the 1970s of spies in sociology classes, or of regular students quite willing to serve in such activities. Reports were made to Senator McCarthy, to veterans' groups, to churches, and to other department of the university. The evangelical groups were especially interested whenever religious topics were discussed. Discussions of nationalism, or the "relativity" that is the fiber of studies of culture, was most interesting to outsiders. This could have been no surprise to any knowledgeable observer, for sociology has the responsibility of analyzing the culture concept—culture as the totality of social institutions to which we subscribe in thought and behavior. This includes the nature of family, government, church, education itself. The discipline deals therefore with the obvious that is all around us, at least in the beginning of such studies, and therefore many students quickly assume they understand society. It is, at first, less dramatic than the new material in the biological sciences, or the experiments of psychology.

And therefore, students of sociology are willing to accept the clichés that pertain to such issues as sexual preference, and less willing to accept the importance of environmental factors. The "sociology of religion" can be especially troubling, in spite of its history rooted in anthropology. Young people from churchgoing, middle-class families are exposed to such irreverent observations that gods come in many forms, and that the concept of myth does not imply its "truthfulness" to the society in explaining the processes of life itself. This cannot make for light conversation during a Christmas break with the family.

When Galileo went against established wisdom, he argued that the earth and its satellites revolved around the sun. In *The Discovers*, the historian Daniel Boorstin recounts how, to save his neck, the scientist "began marshalling arguments for the simultaneous truths of the Bible and the Copernican theory."

> There is only one Truth, he said, but it is communicated in two forms—the language of the Bible and the language of nature. Both are God's languages. In Scripture, God wisely spoke the vernacular, while in Nature He spoke a more recondite tongue . . . 'two truths can never contradict one another.'[1]

We have no current Galileos, but the present university could easily hold its own against all critics by noting that many truths can, indeed, be found on the campus: those pragmatists in pharmacy, engineering, and agriculture, whose Truth is that the bridge stands, the patient lives, and the corn grows. The campus has Truth among those who cherish tradition, whether codified in legal-historical documents or in the great treasures of literature. Those whose Truth centers on beauty are to be found in the arts, music and dance.

When Allen Bloom devoted a book to a brilliant criticism that the contemporary university has lost sight of the Truth, he left out too many parts of this total picture.[2] Thus in recent years there have been attempts in some leading universities (among them Columbia and Harvard) to provide a common core for all students, whatever their special fields may be; or, at least, they create a survey course that seeks to integrate some basic views of value to all students.

Sociology, like Galileo, consists of two truths: (1) that the culture concept rests on evidence from many societies of a variety of basic values and codes of behavior, and (2) that every society can achieve order only on the basis of firm beliefs in its own value systems and customs.

Taken separately, each statement can be acceptable to anyone. Taken together, this is difficult for the believers in one Truth, their own. Yet the first has a large body of anthropological literature, and indeed, much primary evidence from the journals of missionaries. To those who argue that the variety of customs merely provides an upward climb in which their own has become the final achievement, my favorite reply is an invitation to put this argument before the 800 million Muslims, the 656 million Hindus, or the 310 million Buddhists. These combined—not to mention Sikhs, Confucians, Baha's, Shintoists, Jains, and Jews—exceed the Christians by several hundred million.

Every textbook that studies societies can provide examples of cultural differences, and such comparisons are not limited to recent or contemporary scholars. As long ago as 1580, the essays of Montaigne presented hundreds of examples. I select only a few at random:

> There are nations where no one save his wife and children speaks to the king except through a speaking-trumpet . . . where husbands can repudiate their wives without cause, but not wives their husbands for any cause whatsoever. . . . The law-maker of the Thurians decreed that whoever should desire either to repair an old law, or to introduce a new one, should present himself before the people with a rope around his neck, so that, if the innovation were not approved by everyone, he might be instantly hanged . . .[3]

Over many years in the classroom, where "relativity" has often been considered a dirty word by those who would ignore cultural differences or who assert their own superiority, I have found several reactions:

1. Some students were shaken, and reported the subversive professor to their leadership in the religious community;
2. Some students saw this as a newfound freedom for themselves, and used it in relationships with the opposite sex;

3. Some became confused, took the tests, and stayed away from the social sciences for good;
4. On most students, perhaps, there seemed to be no impact, either because they did not grasp the implications, or because they followed the pattern of simply taking notes and moving on.

I turn to my sociological colleagues. By that time in their lives, the biggest fallout has already occurred, back in graduate studies. Some graduate students are more vulnerable than others; as my mentor, the great Florian Znaniecki, boasted that in Poland he had once made a credible sociologist out of a priest; with me, he had a musician to deal with. The young scholar, as he advances in his studies, finds his area of confusion not in the culture concept, but rather in the proliferation of interpretative schools of thought within the scientific community. That is quite a different matter, concerned with scientific method. For example, Pitirim Sorokin summarizes such "schools of thought" in sociology as the mechanistic, geographical, biological, selectionist, hereditarist, sociologistic, psychological, and psychosociologistic.[4] Since his time, other schools or scientific fashions have no doubt made headway. In my own case, I carefully progressed through my doctorate by limiting my professors to only three who were compatible in their outlook. Thus, I avoided the danger of falling "between the cracks" among a faculty where often the fundamental theoretic difference could be catastrophic to the powerless student. My last vivid memory of the doctorate process was of the oral examination that followed six days of intensive writing. My committee consisted of several major professors and two scholars who represented my "minor" fields, political science and anthropology. As a courtesy, the two latter were given first crack at me for questions. The political scientist started with the question, "From a sociological point of view, would you say that Hitler was an evil man?" Before I had a chance to reply, the distinguished anthropologist Oscar Lewis took it upon himself to criticize the question, and then proceeded to formulate his own position. The argument between the two eminent scholars went on for two hours, while the rest of us provided a privileged audience.

The "two truths" debate applies, indeed, to the scholar's analysis of leisure. On the one hand, following Znaniecki's dictum of the "human coefficient," he is obligated to accept the values of the participant. If drug-taking or gang behavior are the free choice of many, we cannot, *as scholars*, deny that this is leisure. These are entered into our statistics of expenditures and time use; they can accurately describe the behavior of real persons. As Znaniecki wrote, "to realize any philosophical ideal, nonevaluative scientific knowledge of culture is indispensable."[5]

On the other hand are those like the Swedish sociologist Gunnar Myrdal, who wrote that "every study of a social problem, however limited in scope, is and must be determined by valuation. A 'disinterested' social science has never existed and never will."[6]

My own writings are Galileo-like, accepting both "truths." I admit the polarity of *constructive-destructive* into my theoretical system on the impacts of outcomes, but leave it to the judgment of segments or of persons within the society. I object strongly to the practice among some scholars of eliminating some behaviors such as sex, drugs, or alcohol from their tabulations of leisure. Strangely, these were all eliminated in the mountain of statistics collected by the late Alexander Szalai and his international team in a twelve-nation time-diary study.[7] In spite of the difficulties of what the late psychologist John Neulinger called the "objective/subjective dichotomy," this omission was inexcusable, for it implied that only "good" leisure should be studied. Neulinger's position, following his injunction of leisure as a state of mind, was that "sex is probably the most ideal joint activity and perhaps the only one that will ever lead to pure leisure."[8]

As to teaching about leisure, the first task is to convince young people that the topic merits the attention of a university. This is easy to do if the scope is accurately portrayed as going far beyond "fun and games" to include a vast array of arts, mass media, tourism, adult education, social life, personal hobbies, recreational reading, gardening—and, of course, games and sports.

Introduced to the large concept, the student is led to see examples of leisure everywhere, starting with his own actions, roommates, family, friends, and in places he/she frequents (theaters, parties, night clubs, etc.).

Among the techniques we pass on to students are the familiar tools of direct observation, casual conversations, pointed interviews, the construction of questionnaires, and the less familiar technique of time budgets.

I have always assigned interviews of families, to discern and try to explain the leisure actions of individual members and the family as a whole. Explanations may include such matters as income, health, education, equipment in the home, location in relation to community facilities, personal taste, and attitudes, and so on. Family interviews are always in pairs. For the first family, explanations are proposed by the student in a written report, always ending in the form of a hypothesis, such as, "In a family where the father works at night, the probable impact on leisure of other family members will most likely be. . ." A second family is then sought in which father works at night, to see if the leisure picture is about the same or different from the first family. Thus the student experienced an elementary field exercise in scientific method.

In such studies, students are generally inclined to form judgments as to "good" and "bad," leading to ofttimes heated discussions in the class of moral values, suggested above in the discussion of sociology as a discipline.

Over many years, I was impressed with discernable impact of such teaching upon individual students. I recall the dramatic case of a married graduate student who was presenting an oral report on the interview with his grandfather. It had been a highly critical judgment, when suddenly this young man burst out, "My God, that's exactly what my own family is doing!" That took place at the University of North Carolina. One summer at Boston University one of my students was interviewing a family on Beacon Hill. The family had consented to let him make notes on such equipment as radios, books, instruments, and sports items in each of the rooms. During the interview, one member of the family called the police, suspecting that the "student" was "casing" the home in preparation for a subsequent burglary. After that I provided my students with an identifying letter on university stationery.

Aside from these uniquenesses in courses on leisure, the situation at the University of South Florida—my last ten years—provided still another factor in that the courses were an integral part of the Leisure Studies Program. Aside from the researches that were going on among the staff, and the wide travels for lectures and consultations within the United States and abroad, we were often visited by scholars from elsewhere. Thus our students were exposed to an ongoing, exciting enterprise of international dimensions. Among our visitors—who often stayed for days at a time—were Joffre Dumazedier of Paris (the acknowledged pioneer of the field), Anna Olszewska of the Polish Academy of Sciences (who managed to come even during the period of martial law), Stanley Parker of England, and Miro Mihovilovich of Yugoslavia.

Among the events in which our Tampa students participated were a national conference in 1969, and two subsequent international conferences, one in cooperation with UNESCO. Guest speakers and panelists in 1969 included Robert Hutchins, Arthur Schlesinger, and Robert Theobald.

In sum, other positions in other universities offered their own uniqueness for teaching the subject, but I look back on the last decade as most productive. Yet there had been contacts with the "real" world throughout forty years. I turn to some examples.

3
Consulting

It would seem that the streets and sights of Teheran, the huge Communist-built tower in Warsaw, the fountains of Lincoln Center in New York, and the thousands of Barbershoppers singing in their quartets and choruses throughout America would have little in common with the offices and classrooms of universities in Boston, Champaign-Urbana, Boulder, Tampa, and little Millbrook. To think so is to misunderstand the place of the contemporary university in the wider world.

In the small office, my student might want to know the directions he should take in his life. The shah had a similar question in Iran, as he and his superb national planners debated the mission of a post-graduate institution in the arts.

In the classroom when we talked of the place of economic conditions in the new "popular culture," we were on the same track as the board of the multimillion-dollar Lincoln Center in New York City, confronting the role of their vast enterprise in relation to the social levels of that city.

In our leisure classes, the uses of "free time" was a constant issue; yet the Communist bosses in Poland, after the strikes in Gdansk and the subsequent rise of Solidarity, had precisely the same questions to consider as part of their national policy—the needs and desires of their aroused population.

In the classroom, particularly in the School of Fine and Applied Arts of Boston University during 1957–1961, we often discussed the nature of popular and folk arts in the midst of a highly industrialized society. Exactly thirty years later, I was consulting for S.P.E.B.S.Q.S.A., whose thirty-six thousand men are beautifully fanatic and expert in their quartet and choral rendition of American songs of the 1860–1930 style.

Iran

While attending a conference in Budapest, a phone call came from Teheran: could I fit into my schedule before returning home a short visit to Iran? UNESCO, which had already funded a leisure and adult education program for Prague, was about to plan a similar program within the shah's Ministry of Culture.

Within a week I arrived at a Teheran hotel still under construction. Since I had heard that the Shah had announced his intention to bring his country up to the level of the great industrial nations, I noted that the workers busy on installing the hotel lobby enjoyed a break every ten minutes or so, to drink tea or engage in a wrestling match. Upon inquiring later who had built the imposing apartment houses on the edge of the city, I was told that German and Swedish construction teams had been imported.

In the next several days I met with about twenty members of the national planning team, men and women, all young, most trained in Europe and the United States. I met with the Minister of Culture and other high officials, but had no contact with the shah himself. Since the purpose of my first visit was to become acquainted with the planners and with several aspects of their cultural life, I visited a national school of music for children, run by the television network; I was told much about, but did not see, a project for training young producers, directors, and technicians in the motion picture program. Great pride was evident in a large building devoted to such crafts as the manufacture of musical instruments, highly advanced woodworking (desks, decorative panels, etc.) and weaving; masters in these areas were given lifetime stipends, and brought to this program to work with apprentices. Every room in every building had prominent pictures of the shah, or the shah and his wife. I was taken to a public park, also the result of the vast oil profits. On my own, I visited a large bazaar, had a Friday evening family meal with a well-to-do Jewish family, with whom I discussed the political situation for minorities very carefully, often with a shaking of someone's head instead of outright comment. I had met two young members of this family as I sat on a bench alongside a main thoroughfare one afternoon, amazed at the insane driving before my eyes.

The result of my visit was the decision that on future visits I would become involved in the planning and staffing of Farabee University.

My second visit, several months later, was entirely devoted to considerations for the proposed university, a special project of the shah's wife, who had allocated one hundred million toward the project (just a beginning, I was told).

Farabee was an important mathematician and philosopher of the twelfth century. In his name, the new university would be entirely devoted to postgraduate studies in all the arts, but deliberately representing both the ancient Persian traditions and the contemporary. Indeed, this balance of the old and the new was a basic principle of the shah's agenda for the rebuilding of his nation. Music would be included, although the tradition was not friendly toward music; and among the other arts would be poetry reading, even now an important aspect of Iranian culture. Three "tracks" or types of curriculum were to be presented to every student, with one adopted as the major purpose by the students from Asian nations, including the U.S.S.R.

The first track would cover creativity in each art, not unlike the curricula in major conservatories of the world. By the time I arrived on the scene, expert instructors in music had been engaged from Africa and Bulgaria. The second track would cover the administration of the arts, the use of public funds, the development of audiences, and national policies for facilities, presentations, and education in the arts. Again, this followed patterns that were established in such societies as the U.S.S.R., and to a far-less-developed degree even in the United States (programs at the University of Wisconsin's School of Business, for example).

The third track, which would have been my responsibility to conceptualize and implement, concerned the relation of the arts to the rest of the society. Among the elements of this part of the program would have been the nature of cultural or art statistics, the relations of art to economic and other policy areas, tax structure, and other matters that they in Iran had become familiar with in my various writings on the "sociology" of the arts. My role would have included some teaching on my part, especially in the larger theoretical aspects and the preparation of the third-track faculty.

By the time of my second visit, construction of the Farabee campus had already begun, about twenty-five kilometers from Teheran. One of my proposals was to explore relationships of new audiences to the arts and to leisure patterns, and this would include a world conference on leisure as part of the opening ceremonies for the university. Seminars had already been started on the second track, the preparation of managers and "commissars."

I submitted several planning memoranda in the following months. My view was that within the given political context, Farabee would be a remarkable experiment or demonstration, for nothing as comprehensive as this had ever been tried. Among the features that I liked, differing markedly from the American penchant for specialties, was that every Farabee student, although enrolled for a major in one of the three tracks, would be obligated to a core curriculum of the other two tracks.

Well, the shah was deposed and Farabee became a memory. In later months I sought to find out whether anything more might be continued under the new regime. Of course, I was certain that it would be dropped. I debated whether to correspond directly with my former colleagues and friends in Teheran, and decided against it. By then, all would either be jailed or destroyed. Even if not, correspondence with an American would not be helpful to their health. I had already confronted this situation with other colleagues living in the U.S.S.R. orbit. I wrote to Margaret Mead, the anthropologist whose daughter had been a student in Teheran; she herself had been on the advisory board of Farabee. I never heard from the mother, but the daughter, an academic person in the United States, replied that she had never heard from any of her friends and knew nothing about the fate of the project.

Poland

Long before Solidarity, the regime in Poland saw the need for economic reforms. Thus, following the strikes in the shipbuilding town of Gdansk in early 1970s, a decision was made to conduct a consumer study. In a most unusual step for a Communist society, social scientists of the Academy of Sciences were asked to determine the priorities among the Polish population for goods and services. To no one's surprise, the national study indicated clearly the demand for such items as TV sets and housing, but to everyone's surprise, one clear demand was for more *time*, free of the excessive waiting in queues at every store, in every government office, and in every medical clinic. Housewives, more than men, wanted more "free time."

The experiences we had in the stores and shops of Warsaw suggested the impatience with lines. In the leading hotel of that city, I went downstairs to the hotel bakery to buy some cookies. The first line, of course, was simply to select the cookies. However, the young lady at the end (I learned later) could not take my money because she had a high school degree, and could not lower her status. Thus the second long line was to pay and get a receipt. Back to the first line, I got my small bag of cookies with a receipt in hand. Now imagine if one were the woman of the house, without a refrigerator at home. She had to purchase small quantities of meats and vegetables, shoelaces, and pills—each in a different store, each with its own lines, each probably with the fortunate high school graduate.

To complicate the situation, the city fathers had created large, beautiful boulevards on the main shopping streets after much of the city had been destroyed by the Nazis. The many packages, the small refrigerators, the large expanses of streets to cross before catching the bus home—all this easily explained why women would welcome more time. Ironically, this was also a reason why women, more than men, were against an official decree for more free days: it would only mean more days to shop. They favored more time if it was accompanied by more availability of larger refrigerators, and (although the concept of American-like department stores was still ahead of them) they voiced a desire for general, rather than specialty, shops. Americans, whose malls go far beyond the general store, forget that a half century ago we told the store clerk what we wanted and waited for him or her to disappear—like the contemporary shoe salesman—and collect the items. From my observations, the Hungarians were the first Communist area to construct the well-stocked store in which the customer had choices of food available directly from the shelves.

Men as well as women had reservations about the value of added "free" Saturdays. This was the issue on which I was invited there as a consultant. Some had fear of boredom from too much time, others foresaw more crime. Ultimately, more free Saturdays were decreed, but upon coming to power, Solidarity brought that number to thirty, still a far cry from the weekly freedom that Americans enjoy, but a virtual revolution in the weekly schedule of urban, working Poles. My visit was largely spent with sociologists and others who were experienced in the study of leisure patterns and diary studies. Policy makers there had direct access to experts in their Academy of Sciences, who, in contrast with university scholars, were in fact a built-in staff for the government, commanded more pay than their academic parallels, but were limited on the projects they pursued. University faculty have less pay, but more prestige. In the course of our conversations I concluded that the Academy scholars in my field had on the whole better data than was available to Americans in contact with census data. Our categories of expenditures, for example, are cruder than that of the Poles.

As an American who takes every Saturday as a "given," there were amusing sides to the fear of more time, but as a consultant, in a foreign culture, one respects the values of others.

Lincoln Center for the Performing Arts

Lincoln Center was a resolution of two dreams, to clear a large slum area on the west side of the city, and to replace it with a center of the highest creative level. The plan was hatched on a bench of the state capitol by two powerful men, Governor Nelson Rockefeller and Robert Moses, the city planner. They were able to effect the proper legislation.

As plans for raising many millions of dollars moved along, contractual relationships were developed with the Metropolitan Opera and the Philharmonic. There were hundreds of committee meetings, thousands of phone conversations on the matter in the late 1950s and early 1960s; architectural studies moved along; debates went on among leading social and financial persons; arguments arose over such substantive issues as to whether the Juilliard School of Music should be one of the "constituents," since, as some argued, it was "only a school." Within Juilliard itself there was a difference as to whether under the new dispensation a dance curriculum should be included (a dance authority was sent on a mission to many countries to explore the matter).

One of the Lincoln Center Board members was George Stoddard, former president of the University of Illinois. One of his daughters and mine had been classmates at the University High School, a part of the university's school of education. I had been invited by the graduating class to deliver their commencement address, and had stuck my neck out in a paper that was very critical of Senator McCarthy. Stoddard was complimentary; when I moved to Boston University, he called one day, asking me to visit with him in an athletic club of New York. Since he had been ousted from the university through the machinations of political conservatives (the great football hero Red Grange had been elected to the Illinois Regents with the express purpose of firing Stoddard), I had publicly supported Stoddard. Now we were both on the East Coast. He had convinced the Lincoln Center Board that a portion of the funds raised should be reserved for some type of program in arts education. Would I be the consultant for the six to ten million dollars that would be set aside for this vague purpose? The fund could not be used for ongoing business of the opera, the symphony, or any other unit.

Soon thereafter, a meeting was called for my specific purposes in a famous restaurant. All the administrative heads except Rudolph Bing of the Met were there. A free-for-all discussion took place for potential uses of the fund. My responsibility was outlined—freedom to call upon any of the units and to explore the specifications for the unit now under my control, answerable only to Stoddard.

During the year, I took off from Boston about twice a week, called upon officials of all the groups; I also visited other agencies in New York, such as Young Audiences, the music and arts headquarters of the city school system, and individuals in the area whom I trusted. My position in the administrative structure of Lincoln Center turned out to be a delicate one, for although I was a stranger to the power structure among arts groups, everyone knew I might have an influence on the interest from many millions.

I reported to Dr. Stoddard every week, by phone or in person. I felt a hesitation among the Center groups in raising serious, "theoretical" issues, such as the differences between bringing the same child from the inner city several times to a symphony concert rather than bringing several children once. Such issues pertinent to building audiences had not bothered them before. I found also a lack of ongoing communications between either the Met or the Philharmonic with the school system, and a feeling among many that the entire project was based on arrogance and social status among some social groups. With more justification, in some quarters there was serious concern about bringing these great institutions into one center rather than decentralizing them in Manhattan. (This remains to this day an arguable issue among city planners and arts administrators.)

One day, through the efforts largely of Isaac Stern, the governor signed a bill allowing Carnegie to remain where it was rather than making way for a parking lot. By then the Philharmonic had already signed a contract for locating in Lincoln Center. Stoddard and the Governor immediately became concerned that Stokowski would create a major symphony to perform in Carnegie Hall, thus diminishing the fund-raising efforts of the older organization. I was asked to develop a special series of concerts by the Philharmonic and Leonard Bernstein to grab attention from the new orchestra. My immediate reaction was twofold: one, that a consultant is asked to explore a situation or to render an opinion, but is never told what to do; second, that their fear bordered on hysteria, for if Tokyo and London could support several major orchestras (four in the case of both), New York City could support more than one. I resigned on the spot, but was asked by Stoddard to carry out this last mission. Staying over several days, I met with administrators of the Philharmonic and worked out a series of special concerts for the next year; funds came from the program on which I had been working. That, in fact, was another major consideration, that contrary to all my recommendations, this was a unilateral allocation that would haunt further work on the plan.

The special concerts were given in time, and the allocation did haunt Stoddard; during that summer, he sent a telegram that reached me on a family trip in the west: what should be done, for now the Met was asking for a similar unilateral funding of a second company they had long wanted to highlight national winners of their competitions? I replied that he had no choice but to grant the request.

Also that fall, the Opera Studio came into being; I was called to New York by officers of the Met to help plan the new company. I engaged them (in part with funds I had set up the year before) for an appearance at Boston University, and thus ended my relationship for all time with Lincoln Center.

Among other conclusions from this experience, I realized that Lincoln Center, at least in its planning period, shared many of the same problems faced by smaller arts programs across the nation. About a decade earlier, I had created a program in Champaign-Urbana known as Community Arts, in which we had developed from scratch an orchestra, a theater group, a dance company, painters, and a string quartet. Instead of dealing with millions, we dealt with paltry hundreds and a few thousand dollars at best. But there, too, personalities became important matters, as well as the issue of centralization vis-à-vis decentralization and the allocation of the little funding that we managed. But everywhere in the country where I have been called upon to consult with the arts, a continuing issue has been that of setting clear goals, and that meant getting into "theoretical" matters that many of us seek to avoid in favor of quick answers.

Nevertheless, in New York certainly, it was a source of great satisfaction to have participated in a vast project, and to assume that a small input on my part may have helped launch this magnificent monument and facilitator to creative life. The New York fund was kept alive, and was for a number of years entrusted to the able direction of Mark Schubart.

Barbershoppers

Exactly a quarter of a century after the New York experience, I became exposed to a far more down-to-earth democratic activity for musical amateurs in communities spread across the United States and Canada. The Barbershoppers are those men and women who love to sing American popular tunes that prevailed in the period 1860 to 1930. With headquarters in Kenosha, Wisconsin, over thirty-thousand men in about eight hundred chapters worldwide are organized in S.P.E.B.S.Q.S.A., or the Society for the Preservation and Encouragement of Barber Shop Quartet Singing in America. There are two women's groups, closely related in purpose and singing style but autonomous in their structure.

Below, I reproduce a report I prepared for my colleagues in the *Leisure Information Quarterly*, at that time located in New York University, fall 1988, volume 15, number 1. The report is in the form of a research memo. The studies to which the last sentence refers took the shape of a volume of research papers prepared by a team of scholars.

> An ideal case study for an inquiry into leisure should meet several specifications: (a) It should lend itself to a study of motivations, both by quantitative data and less formal observations; (b) its participants should include a variety of geographical and cultural areas, including the international dimensions, (c) also permitting longitudinal timeframes; (d) participants should be willing to be studied, and open the investigation to documents or other types of records; (e) while the activity might indicate a variety of functions or purposes, one or a few should be emphasized by the group itself; and (f) the investigator should be close enough to the structure that its openness or resistance to social change from the outside as well as internal tensions should be observable.
>
> Such conditions do not often exist for students of leisure, in part because of the contemporary emphasis on numbers, in part because we have not gone after specific groups or organizations. Stebbins, in Calgary, has produced excellent analyses of general groups, such as amateur archaeologists, actors, and baseball players. The most massive study of many leisure activities on an international level—the *Uses of Time*, by Szalai and his associates—consists of time-budget data, together with accompanying discussions on a general, national level. There have now been two major studies of outdoor activities, the Outdoor Recreation Resources Review Commission (ORRRC) volumes that led to the establishment of the Department of Outdoor Recreation, and the recent report to the President's Commission on Americans Outdoors.
>
> *Dean Snyder,* emeritus historian of the society, a member of many years, who prepared an interpretative narration of the society's fifty-year history.

Max Brandt, an avid Barbershopper and ethnomusicologist from the University of Pittsburgh, who presented a historical view of "wood-shedding."

Robert Stebbins of the University of Calgary, authority on the concept of amateurism, who studied the process of becoming a member.

Phillip Bosserman, international authority on leisure, of Salisbury State University, who applied this concept to barbershopping.

J. Terry Gates, music educator from SUNY-Buffalo, who examined the concept of elitist art and popular culture in relation to this activity.

K. Peter Etzkorn, sociologist and musicologist from the University of Missouri, who explored the significance of making "live" music in an era of "media" music. Finally, I considered the future of S.P.E.B.S.Q.S.A. within categories of tradition and innovation.

The volume was published in 1993 by the Associated University Presses under the title *Barbershopping: Musical and Social Harmony.*

Observations

There is no one concept of a consultant, even within the field or discipline that Prof. Y. Dror of Israel calls "meta-policy," or the policy of policy. This is a theoretical discipline, relatively recent, designed to help decision-makers. The IRS has noted three conditions for determining tax policies for those who engage as consultants. They must be not instructed, they must be available to others as well, and they must have their own "business." The third of these is somewhat ridiculous in the face of the thousands of professors who are occasionally engaged, as in my case. The first two are reasonable.

Washington, D.C., especially in the area near the National Airport known as Crystal City, is occupied by lawyers and former government empoyees whose main function is to penetrate the huge bureaucracy. Those who consult for foreign governments are in the unique position of more freedom in defining basic policy for their clients with a propaganda mission, for they supposedly know much about America's "climate of opinion," among segments of the public here, or have even had a major hand in manipulating such national opinion. Kissinger might be a case in point.

Differing from the Crystal City crowd are many young people, with little idea of what goes into expertise in any field, but who are anxious to rush into "consulting" for profit. Permit one example. When I was still active in the leisure field, a national journal I had never heard of, *Private Enterprise,* ran an article about this "new" field. The Tampa program was mentioned, and in a few days, literally one hundred letters poured in from all parts of the country. Most writers wanted to know, by "return mail," how to become consultants on leisure. I replied in a form letter, laying out the complexity of the field and the many years of study and exposure needed to acquire some authority. One of my colleagues, the late psychologist John Neulinger of New York University, was also mentioned in the article. More pragmatic than I, in his reply John announced a series of seminars to brief them—for a price, of course.

Informal consulting occurs every time Aunt Jenny advises anyone who will listen to unsought advice—or to those whom she thinks need advice. Travel agents often become consultants, as do fortune-tellers, druggists, taxi drivers, or just friends. A serious consultant observes both functional and ethical principles, in addition to the knowledge that is needed by the client.

For example, as the first IRS specification notes correctly, a consultant is not "instructed," as I was in my final day with Lincoln Center. An assignment is outlined. He raises relevant questions, and as in the case of the Barbershop assignment, is given access to appropriate documents, records, personality profiles, history, inner conflict, or similar information. He, in turn, is pledged in principle to confidentiality. Soon after I moved to the University of South Florida, I contacted the administrators of Disneyland, then being planned for Orlando. After all, they are in the "leisure" business on a vast scale, and I proposed that—without cost to them—our leisure center become their consultant on a general level, or that they permit my students to live in the project in Orlando and study their clientele. Close contacts resulted, but in the end, the organization proved to be fearful that we would reveal or sell data about their operation. Disney has been known for its distrust of the academic mind, or for its monopoly on creative intelligence.

Another major principle of consulting is that always—always—there must be clarity on the purposes or goals being sought through the aid of an outsider. In the framework of Farabee University, my purpose, although open-ended, was clearly defined: to develop one "track" of the university curriculum according to their historical traditions and ambitions. How I went about it was my decision. In the case of Poland, about to expand the number of free Saturdays, my purpose was to translate the American experience; given the information and my interpretations of potential parallels, they would come to their own policy; in that situation, I avoided all recommendations. In the Lincoln Center case, I brought to them a theoretical framework for a unique situation in which the client was not entirely clear of its needs; my problem there was that the administrators, accustomed to short-range formula, wanted quick approaches rather than long-term issues.

The Barbershoppers specifically recognized the value of a sociologist-musician, even though he was not one of them, and grew up in a different artistic milieu; nevertheless, they knew that he was sympathetic, and experienced in working with people.

Unless the consultant understands his functions—his limitations as well as his freedoms—he runs the risk of being "used" by factions within the group for which he consults. A case in point was my experience with the hospitals of the Veterans Administration.

In the early 1950s, soon after my first book on leisure, I was engaged to visit a number of V.A. hospitals to consult with those units concerned with recreation, occupational therapy, and volunteer services. The major conflict—or issue—was the overlapping of functions, the confusion of roles, funds, and types of treatments for patients. Invitations came to me directly from a particular hospital head. My first visit was always with the head of the institution, who could paint the general internal situation. The chief of nursing was always a valuable source of inner currents. Internal conflicts raise red flags for outsiders. One technique is to locate the sources of power, attempt to see the situation objectively, and try to avoid traps that emerged from the inner heart, or bowels, of the hospital, and symbolic behaviors that can be both intriguing and exhausting. In addition to the three units that generally found it inherently difficult to cooperate, the traditional levels of power among physicians, psychiatrists, nurses, attendants, social workers and administrators are marks of a medical institution.

My contact with both general and psychiatric hospitals went on for several years. Let me jump to the incidents that led to my disassociation, for it reveals some of the issues and my type of enjoyment from the experience.

In a mental hospital, those who know most about the patients are the attendants, who are the least trained and least paid; in the process of treatment policies or evaluations, they have the least power. Next up the line were nurses, themselves subdivided and a delicate stimulus of conflicts among themselves. However, nurses can make recommendations, and pass on their observations to the psychiatrists; the latter, most trained and powerful, know least about any patient. On the top of the structure is the administrative chief, answering to the bureaucracy in Washington, and too often having to accept staff who are of advanced age, and "put out to pasture" in such institutions in isolated areas of a region. My part of this story concerns the nature of experiment and change.

In a lovely hospital near Chesapeake, I decided to advance a proposal that would elevate the role of consultant to that of therapist—a rash move. In one ward of thirty-six men, all schizoids, I proposed to take charge of the therapy for any six men they would pick. My program for them over an eighteen-month period would be to produce, as a team, a weekly newspaper for the institution, covering news and human feature items for all segments. Each of the other three groups of six would follow the traditional therapy programs, including drugs, hydrotherapy and shock. Afterwards we would compare the progress of each.

I had chosen the newspaper publication for good reasons: the opportunity for both individual and group action; the prospect of status-reversal when a patient-reporter has the authority to interview on all levels; the psychological phenomenon of seeing a blank page take on life with a substance of interest; the experience of the writing and editing; the applause and appreciation following the publication.

To my surprise, the proposal was accepted. None of my six men had more than high school background. None had done any substantial reporting or writing. I visited the group several times, for several days each, but followed their activity carefully by letter and phone calls. (That was the day before fax.) The newspapers came along, each more interesting than the last, and stirring much favorable comment from everyone. Before long, several patients from other parts of the hospital asked to join my half dozen pioneers. To shorten the tale, at the end of eighteen months—how that evaluation was done is another story of hospital structure—my boys had "progressed" medically about the same, no more, no less, than the others. (I should add that during this experimental period, my group was excused from all medical treatment.)

For a short period I returned, there and at other sites, to visits in which I merely asked pointed questions, such as why bed A had a Ph.D. and the bed next to it held a preliterate, and what use was being made of this juxtaposition; or why the program for all men scheduled a prize fight on Tuesday, a movie on Wednesday, a dance on Friday—and whether there was any logic or strategy in this progression? I might come across a situation in which I discovered several nurses who were amateur painters, but never had been asked to use their skills with patients; or why the lovely "Grey Ladies" who came to dance with the men were dressed up to their necks; or why the patient who had mastered the traditional rules of baseball could not communicate symbolically on the ward?

I was ready now for my undoing in a new proposal namely, that we inject several new "patients"—really, all psychologists borrowed from other hospitals—into a mental ward. No one of the resident staff would know beforehand of our conspiracy. Question: in each ward so tested, who would be the first to catch on—the attendants, nurses, or psychiatrists? I knew full well that the administration would never allow this threatening experiment. In similar classroom experiments, when students of various mental levels had been moved about, teachers were often fooled, and they taught students differently who were first identified by I.Q. My hypothesis for the hospital guaranteed its rejection: that the attendants would be the first to detect the ruse.

Thus ended my consulting for the V.A. The end was of my own doing, and fun besides.

4
Writing

FIRST, some observations about beginning as a writer, I need not repeat the characteristics of our family life—an immigrant Jewish culture in Milwaukee. Three sons, father a tailor, mother the dominant force, Socialist leanings, early violin lessons. A first feeling for words developed from four years of Latin in high school, from many letters I wrote to my cousin Jeanette in Sturgeon Bay, Wisconsin, and from wide reading as a boy. My tendency then was toward excessive verbiage. Writing was easy. Words flowed. Perhaps the first major check on uncontrolled outpouring came from debating experiences in college. Prof. Joe Cotton, a major influence on my life, trained us in public speaking, including the use of primary sources, quickness of thought, the organization of materials, and the careful use of words. We left the adversarial format and became a team of speakers who were expected to discuss all sides of public issues, not to win points over rival teams. We were sent out by the school to many audiences: other schools, civic clubs, women's clubs.

This was in the early 1930s. After graduation from the teacher's college in 1933—now a very large branch of the state university system—I created a research position for a federal program in adult education. Some dozens of well-known scholars, journalists, political figures, and authors were engaged, several each week. They were sent out by our office to the public with federal funds. My job was to devise evaluative studies. The level of "research" can be imagined by the composition of my "staff," all on welfare: a former funeral director, a former grocer, a retired diplomat with no professional background. However, we all agreed on one conclusion, that our statistical or interpretative observations sounded quite professional on paper, but that common sense has to be a constant ingredient of "science." For example, we attempted to correlate attendance with mass media attention to current issues. Informally, we discovered that in the depression, people more often came to the school or to the church to keep warm and save heating costs than because of interest in the topic.

A second employment opportunity came along that required considerable controlled writing. This, too, was a federal position. During the New Deal, it became apparent that one of the best distributive points for federal funds was the building industry. Further, homes built for the needy—like parks renovated under WPA—would outlast the welfare goals per se. However, a debate ensued as to the best location for public housing. One faction, led by Harold Ickes, argued for the rebuilding of slums; another group held that the ideal programs would be new towns along the model of Welwyn and Letchworth, both near London.

Both types of projects developed with planned communities scheduled for areas near Milwaukee, Washington, and Cleveland. I was chosen to head the research work for the Milwaukee community. The job included the gathering of considerable data from questionnaires we sent out to the several thousand applicants for the new homes, summarizing and interpreting for the planners in the Suburban Resettlement Administration. The report covered such matters as the recreational patterns of Polish families who would comprise the bulk of the village. A didactic, no-nonsense style of writing was essential, footnotes and all—a style I have never erased.

I recall some stabs at more expressive writing as a youth. At the age of about sixteen, with some historical sense already present, I decided to write out my "philosophy," deposit it in a safety deposit vault, to be unopened until the grand old age of fifty; I would write about beauty, and religion, and politics. I could not afford a bank box, and the weeks and years flowed by with no profound document. Either I had been overwhelmed by great men who had displayed their genius as youths, or it was time for daydreaming.

Thus, the early writings, except for letters to relatives, was related to my work, practical in purpose, but already subject to time frames.

Yet another major influence came from the experiences of writing throughout the seminars for the M.A. and Ph.D., especially for the dissertations on both levels. Here I must refer to the influence of five professors, William Bernard of the University of Colorado, William Albig, E. T. Hiller, Florian Znaniecki, and Robert Bierstedt—all of the University of Illinois.

Bernard got me into sociology as a "minor," with music as the major field. He saw the manuscript for *Music in the City* and offered to accept it as my dissertation in his field. His weekly seminar was my first graduate experience, and the most demanding of all to follow. Each week we were expected to have thoroughly digested a major classic in sociology, such as by Weber, Spencer, or Durkheim. In addition to an oral report, a paper was required. Rapidity in writing was necessary, in addition to clear thinking on social theory.

At Illinois, perhaps based on respect for my age and colleagueship as a young faculty member, I managed to get both degrees under the guidance of only three professors: Albig, Hiller, and Znaniecki. This proved to be a major political maneuver in campus terms, avoiding the danger of getting caught up in the internal intellectual struggles among the faculty as a whole. Each of the three had his style of thinking and teaching. Albig, a national authority in the field of public opinion, led his students toward concise thinking, with respect for empirical materials. Hiller, the pure theorist and a gentle soul, specialized in social role theory. Most influential was F. Z., under whom I wrote directly on the dissertation. So self-effacing was he that he could teach a seminar on "methods" and never refer to his book on the subject. About religion he knew very much, about music, almost nothing. Thus I had the advantage. True, he had been a poet and philosopher before his association with the great Chicago sociologist, W. I. Thomas.

The results was that F. Z. gave me almost total freedom in conceptualizing and developing my study of the social role of musicians in America. Upon retirement, he spent a year in Detroit.

As my studies moved along, especially by the time of the 1975 volume, my own emphasis moved from quantitative to humanistic concerns for personal and national values. This emphasis on larger issues, rather than dollars or hours, reopens such issues as the American Dream, a change in perceptions of social class or democratic equality. In 1948, Gunnar Myrdal noted the distinctiveness of leisure for Afro-Americans;[1] in 1950 David Riesman related leisure lifestyles to "inner" and "other" personalities;[2] in 1962 Joseph Pieper had called leisure the "basis of civilization;[3] in 1964 the Frenchman Jacques Ellul had spoken of the values inherent in technology, with leisure as one manifestation;[4] in 1962 Sebastian de Grazia wrote eloquently of leisure as an ideal in the Greek category of *paidia*.[5] These reinforced my own position, symbolized in my version of leisure as a Judaic "relocation" of heaven on earth.

Indeed, if my work is remembered at all in decades ahead, I want it to be from this broad point of view, both in philosophy and analysis.

As I look into the future, there is reason for caution, illustrated in this projection made in 1955 by Morris L. Ernst:

> ... close to one half of our people will, all through their adult lives, take courses by correspondence, or otherwise and effectively explore those aspects of life and the unknown which excite their curiosities. The new exciting leisure will establish prestige values of unorthodoxy ... millions of us will go abroad ... Our own people will learn at least three languages in childhood, as the Swiss do ... the cravings for narcotics and excessive alcohol will decline as people need fewer spurs for courage, and less forgetfulness ... our spiritual road map will carry the direction pointers: 1976—This way—Energy, Leisure, Full Rich Life.[6]

Yes, his target date was 1976, only two decades hence. More carefully, I see these developments, not for twenty-, perhaps in a fifty-year span. I see a growing consensus that the leisure "ethic" more than the work "ethic" will continue to shape our values and actions. This is evident even in contemporary Japan, where the large corporation is declining in its hold over employees. In the United States the Clinton economic package similarly wrestles for guarantees in health and pension provisions for protection against permanent pockets of technological unemployment that no politician dares speak about. Electronic applications in work will expand, but while the "leisure society" envisioned by Joffre Dumazedier may be far from general reality, we may be sure of more flexibilities, work-sharing, and a more creative infrastructure for recreational programs, both private and public. Inevitably, while serious studies of leisure will increase, the origin of these studies will, in all probability, expand into departments of philosophy, sociology, psychology, psychiatry, information theory, economics, history, and of course, the applied aspect of leisure theory—recreation. Educational institutions may be expected to experiment with leisure counseling from early grades upward. On the whole, many more explorations into leisure will attract scholars and policy makers. Both personal and public actions will demand it.

Indeed, for any scholar of leisure there are many self-doubts. Amidst the many issues that confront society—crime, drugs, international tensions, racial conflicts, national deficits—how does one justify a serious study of "play," "fun," "amusement," "games," or "recreation?" How does one explain the rise of an international program of research, attention of UNESCO and the Council of Europe, academic journals, world conferences, and the life-long commitment of a growing number of scholars?

During the six years of labor on my first book in this area, I had been struck by the paucity of contemporary materials. Aristotle had written on the subject, as had Joseph Pieper, the historian. Others in between had touched on it. The European scholarship of our time was as yet unknown to me in the 1950s. The "work ethic" had been ingrained in all of us, and in the first half of the century, "recreation" was thought of as a derivative factor. We spoke of free time as "left over" from work, and of recreation as "re-creating" ourselves for more work. During the first World War, recreation was found to be an important morale builder, and it was between the two great wars that the recreation profession emerged as a mature addition to the health community.

The transition of recreation from a derivative to a substantive status in the public mind came about in good part from studies of childhood by Piaget: childhood and play as legitimate, authentic phases of life. Time, too, need not be inauthentic.

In my view, a second source of change in the status of recreation came from labor unionism in Europe and America after the turn of the century. While shorter hours of work per day, full weekends, and vacations may have been peripheral negotiating points at first, they became increasingly central, beyond the rest needed primarily for subsequent work. Increased urbanization meant the release of older members of the family from household and farm chores, and thus came the new concept, "retirement," largely an invention of the twentieth century. This was the major factor in the creation and expectation of "bulk time," a noteworthy factor in a new perception of time as seen over the year and over the lifetime; this became a basic contribution to the "new leisure."

Somewhere along the line, with the emergence of substantive time as an end, a Greek Renaissance came into the picture, leisure with values of its own. . . "a state of being, a condition of men . . . a freedom from necessity," in the interpretation of Sebastian de Grazia. "The life of leisure leads to a greater sensitivity not to truth alone, but also to beauty, to the wonder of man and nature, to its contemplation and its creation in word and song, clay, color and stone . . . Leisure is an ideal."[7]

An example of this renaissance was the field of adult education. Courses for adults as an integral part of the school system—or, in the early days, "labor institutes"—were initiated by the formative industrial revolution to prepare workers to read directions and blueprints in manufacturing. Some industrial and political leaders correctly read the future, fearful that literacy in reading technical specifications could extend to the reading of political tracts. Indeed, at an early stage, especially in England, literacy as an end became manifest in cultural affairs, as in literature courses and theatrical activities. In the United States, only a few unions, notably in the clothing industry, followed this lead. (In the 1970s I sat in London with union officials as they made plans for a national symphony orchestra with union funds.)

When I entered the field in the late 1940s, leisure was primarily a study of activities; recreation departments were training centers for the techniques of organization and administration. They justified their programs with such platitudes as "the family that plays together stays together." It was no wonder that in the university pecking order, they occupied a low status, but have risen in late years as they turned to theory in their own field, to genuine research, and to related disciplines. Indeed, it was this search for integrations that changed the course of my life. Charles Brightbill and I came to the University of Illinois at about the same time. He was already a national figure in the recreation field from his leadership in WPA planning; I was there to obtain a doctorate in sociology, but soon became something of a father-confessor as I became a member of the faculty string quartet. Charlie's ambition was to expand the vision of his graduate students. When he approached the music chair to consider a special course designed for them, they turned to me as a flaky character familiar to both fields. My recommendation was to convene a state meeting of leaders in the recreation field to put their principles and philosophy on the line. In due time this occurred, and my own conviction was that a clear need existed for more sophisticated concepts and analysis.

In 1952, with the doctorate in hand, and engaged by both the music and the sociology departments, I created two courses, one in each department, with the same recreation students enrolled in both. For these purposes I wrote two textbooks, educating myself as well: a manual for recreational music (1953),[8] and *Leisure in America: a Social Anaylsis*.[9] (Working closely with three university departments at once is a story of its own.) The first of these volumes was useful, but inconsequential. The second, however, carved out a huge area of study that has served over the years since.

The volume attempts to place leisure into such large issues as the meaning of life itself, a Judaic relocation of Heaven on earth, the place of leisure in the universe of human values. This is already made explicit in the book's preface.[10]

> The problem of man's goals and his meanings in life has been with him as long as he has been able to objectify himself . . . Here, the new dimension stems from industrialization, and implicit in this are the ramifications of urbanization, mass education, mass culture, new transportation, and communication phenomena. . . . attitudes, on the one hand, of futility, uprootedness, malaise, conformity, quest for certainty, alienation, and other-directedness; on the other hand, of new adventure, creative possibilities for the broad masses, social-class fluidity, enlarged educational opportunities, longer life, and better health . . . The topic of leisure emerges in the middle of these varying interpretations and significant issues, for it deals essentially with the nature of the Good Life.

Again, the very last paragraph of the volume brings us to the broadest of perspectives:

> For leisure in America is not, *ipso facto*, a problem or a blessing; it is a phenomenon of abundance and material wealth. There is a tendency in some quarters to point the finger at leisure, to associate it with insignificance and decadence. But this is to think in past terms. Out of that leisure may arise humanitarian values to move us into the Hydrogen Age . . . in which thoughtful, responsible, and well-fed men will seek to assess themselves and to grow again . . .[11]

The three hundred pages in between those statements are devoted to drawing connections between leisure and culture, work, family, social class, subcultures, community, the state, and religion. Types and meaning of leisure are considered in another series of chapters: sociability, association, games and sports, art, movement (travel), and immobility (TV, reading, etc.) Finally, relationships are drawn to theories of social control, social roles, time structure and its modifications.

This was a rich content, perhaps too rich for one volume and a first attempt. But the six years devoted to the analysis was for me a period of intense learning, augmented by invitations to conferences, papers, and journal contributions.

It has been my experience that about three years are needed before a book is initially absorbed by its public—time for its discovery, for reviewers to publish, time for libraries and publics to respond. Often the author is disturbed by the "thunder of silence" that greets his books. But my book, unlike fiction, had a small but active profession behind it—recreation—and by the mid 1960s I was aware that a dent had been made. The profession, at that time, was uncomfortable in discussions of philosophy, history, or the social sciences. Yet these were precisely the volume's attributes that attracted European scholars and policy-makers.

I confess to some surprise then at the foreign response until I became aware at first hand of the situations in both the western and the Communist societies.

I recall sitting in the Bucharest office of Pavel Campaneu, in the national broadcasting offices of Romanian radio and television. He was in charge of keeping statistics on the popularity of types of programs. Among the twenty million population (far from one set for each family, social visits were common for this purpose) the most popular were sports, followed by pictures on space science and soap operas. Political discussions were low in rank, and in their regular meetings, political figures tried many ways of injecting party views into other types of programs. Ratings, of course, were not sought in terms of profits. But the point for persons like myself was the attempt at accurate readings of the public.

I discovered a high level of data keeping in Poland, Czechoslovakia, Hungary, and presumably in the Soviet Union (which I did not visit). Their primary purpose was, of course, to track the political interests of their populations; another was to enforce the special taxes imposed on owners of sets.

An advantage that all the Eastern European broadcasting and travel agencies enjoyed was the expertise of the various national "academies of science," "ministries," and university research scholars. Every unit of Communist government, not only transportation and communications, had access to various levels of research and consultation in exploring both immediate and long-range plans. For example, following the Gdansk strikes in Poland, it was to the National Academy of Science that the government turned for national sampling of what the population wanted; in itself this was a startling move for the regime. Academy scholars had the most prestige but modest incomes and high security on the job, as well as considerable freedom in choosing projects. Ministerial researchers were in-house staffs, much like in our own government. University scholars had to combine their investigations with teaching.

The Western nations, too, usually owned and controlled their communications and transportation, and were equally in need of dependable data and forecasting techniques. These needs alone put them into the thick of leisure theory. But their theory, as in the east, went beyond quantitative measures and responded to my own efforts in that regard.

The connection between the 1961 and the 1975 volumes was an adaptation of Max Weber's "ideal construct."[12] This was in opposition to the search for "definitions"—a search that seemed to me to be confining in its purpose at a time when the topic demanded flexibility. Constructs, as in Weber's classical study of capitalism and Protestantism, contained a number of elements that characterized the phenomenon even when not every element was essential. Thus, my construct for the nature of leisure, begun in 1960 and matured by 1973, read as follows:

> Leisure consists of relatively self-determined activity-experience that falls into one's economically free-time roles, that is seen as leisure by participants, that is psychologically pleasant in anticipation and recollection, that potentially covers the whole range of commitment and intensity, that contains characteristic norms and constraints, and that provides opportunities for recreation, personal growth, and service to others.[13]

The next essential step was to place the concept into the form of a model that could provide us with all essentials of a "theory" of leisure. My fifteen-year search concluded in a multidisciplinary visualization that is reproduced in chapter 5.

The entire 1975 volume, *Leisure: Theory and Policy*, is built on this model. One chapter constitutes a technical exercise or demonstration: given a change in the nature and perception of time (from "fragmentary" to "bulk") within each of the twenty elements, how might the other elements be effected?

The model, with its resulting sixty propositions, had been published as a pamphlet by the leisure institute in Prague before the book appeared. Thus several groups abroad had a chance to evaluate its usefulness in direct conversations with me. I recall especially my encounter with Jugoslavian sociologists in the Belgrade apartment of a colleague, Miro Mihavilovic; on the same trip I met with a graduate group in a sociology seminar in Lund, Sweden, led by that country's leading scholar in the field, Herald Swedner.

There is no need here to go into further details of the method. What is important were the findings, conclusions, insights, observations, hypotheses, even the recommendations. For national planners or administrators, all this ultimately enters into what Professor Y. Dror of the Hebrew University in Jerusalem calls "meta-policy," or planning for a plan. It is here that theory and application come together. This, too, is the basis for the kind of consulting discussed in the preceding chapter.

Over the past forty years in the field, my earliest impressions have been verified and deepened—that the leisure of a nation is a basic clue to its meanings and values. One immediate clue is found in the data of expenditures, available time and its uses, importance in the economy, space allocations and numbers of jobs involved. I recall the 1972 tables, showing that our consumer spending then for all forms of recreation came to more than our national defense. Now, with the 1990s well under way, the Academy of Leisure Scientists reports that fully a third of our national economy is bound up with leisure expenditures. For example, of the more than $450 billion we spend on all forms of transportation, in 1993, fully a third was recreational, nonwork related; if to this we add all expenditures in recreational housing, clothing, food, education, sports, and arts, leisure emerges as "the center of the economy."

Of course, a quantitative evaluation of leisure in economic terms or a psychological estimate in satisfactions depends on the types of motivations and actions that are included in that somewhat elusive term. Further, such a fundamental consideration as "hours of work" or of "time free of work" are undependable for historical comparisons, for the alternatives open to an "hour" of time in 1993 are far greater than a half century ago.

Nevertheless, the numerical, material expansion in our leisure remains impressive and is paralleled in other parts of the world.

5
Modeling

THESE writings—the twenty-seven books and several hundred articles—together with the multitude of reports and other odds and ends of institutional life over forty-three academic years, constitute a lifetime of scribbling. There were other efforts along the way that might have been books. I vaguely recall a tentative textbook on "social control" sometime in the 1960s. Even earlier, during my first professional post as an administrator of a federal program on adult education, I began a volume on the democratic process as seen through the town meeting. Even as late as 1991 I began a work to be called *Thrice a Great-Grandfather* addressed through my family to the new generations of the elderly.

But aside from the distractions of full-time teaching that paid my mortgages and groceries, those writings that did emerge represent some sort of balance between life of mind and family, or theory and reality; these are not exclusive terms, but between them there was the fact of two children to raise, errands to be run, papers to grade, and even—very important to me—practice on the violin, rehearsals, and concerts. More than once I have sought to articulate the differences among various kinds of creativity.

One clue to a record of scribbling over the decades, especially when several fields of study are the case, are some basic, integrative concepts or themes that lend stability and measure intellectual growth. In the present case, two types of conceptualization emerged to serve this stabilizing purpose: first, the "ideal construct," based on Max Weber, that began with an application to leisure but applied as a technique also to the arts and to gerontology. Second was the development of a comprehensive model that provided a route to the macrocosmic and the microscopic as they intersect.

What impact the construct and the model have had, or will have, I am not prepared to report or speculate. I find occasional references in the writings of colleagues, but certainly with no overwhelming adoption of either tool. As far as I know, the late

John Neulinger made the most explicit judgment in his *The Psychology of Leisure:*

> I want to return once more to the work of Kaplan, who has not only furnished us a definition of leisure but also has an elaborate theoretical model that attempts to integrate this concept into not only the personal and family context but also the group, societal, cultural, and even historical framework. Kaplan's model is complex, as it must be to be able to handle that multitude of variables that enter into the system. At the same time it is dynamic, allowing for the constant integration of the many components. Our primary intention here is to alert the reader to its existence and recommend the study of the original source. Perhaps it is reassuring to note that there is stability in all that flux. Just as Kaplan remains true to his 1960 definition in his 1975 version, so does he remain faithful to the kind of leisure theory he suggests . . . ultimately a theory of leisure can be little less than a theory of man and a theory of the emerging culture.[1]

The exposition of these major themes has led, of course, to lesser and more important insights. Indeed, the model became the basis of the entire 1975 volume. I find no need here to summarize the body of materials to be read there. Let me poke into a few random points that come to mind with no order or priority. I cannot, again, claim that the observations or conclusions have been seized upon by either colleagues or critics.

Aside from avoiding the simplicity of definitions, the value of approaching leisure—or education, religion, family, government, etc.—through a construct is that the overlappings and interactions between social institutions becomes apparent. For instance, leisure may include elements that are in common with religion, as in the use of symbols. Joseph Pieper pointed out long ago how the element of "play" can be seen in war, law, and religion. This advantage of the construct takes us immediately into the second major issue: the relationship of leisure to other institutions.

My tool for that was the creation of a model, proposed originally in the 1975 volume. Below I reproduce the construct and entire model, with explanatory comments:[2]

> Each of the foregoing methods in approaching leisure has its important place. The construct we seek as an ideal research tool should grow out of those presented above, yet move us closer to the institutional concept discussed earlier. The construct is to be used in the "ideal type" tradition established by Max Weber in his analysis of Protestantism, capitalism, or the Chinese literati. The construct is a *typical*, not an average, picture against which a real situation may be

assessed. *Leisure, we might say, consists of relatively self-determined activity-experience that falls into one's economically free-time roles, that is seen as leisure by participants, that is psychologically pleasant in anticipation and recollection, that potentially covers the whole range of commitment and intensity, that contains characteristic norms and constraints, and that provides opportunities for recreation, personal growth, and service to others.*

The first element of this conception is relative self-determination or voluntariness. There are degrees of freedom and varieties of self-deception: do I really want to cut the grass? am I attending the theatre because I want to go, or was the decision made by my wife? But even a psychological perception of freedom is valuable to the person.

Use of the term "activity-experience" implies an attempt to divorce leisure from the purely behavior element and to permit the possibility of inner, unobservable, or emotional results. Leisure as mere activity has, of course, long been a traditional assumption. The recreation profession, for instance, has often used the terms leisure and recreation interchangeably and, as in one of its authoritative manuals, deals completely from the activities approach, with a classification of arts and crafts, dance, drama, games-sports-athletics, hobbies, music, outdoor recreation, reading-writing-speaking, social recreation, special events, and voluntary services.

"Economically free time" immediately suggests that leisure is not necessarily the same as nonwork time, since one's "free time" is far more than his time for leisure. No one works 24 hours in the day. He sleeps, eats, washes, and engages in other biological or domestic functions related to keeping alive and functioning. It has been estimated, for example, that in a lifetime of 72 years, all of the hours spent in sleep generally total 22 years, those in work come to 10 years, and those of eating come to 6 years. Almost one half of the lifetime is still unaccounted for, and not even all of this would be called "leisure." De Grazia puts the difference clearly in the course of an introduction that sets the tone of his volume.

"Work (he notes) is the antonym of free time. But not of leisure. Leisure and free time live in two different worlds. We have got in the habit of thinking them the same. Anybody can have free time. Not everybody can have leisure. Free time is a realizable idea of democracy. Leisure is not fully realizable, and hence an ideal, not alone an idea. Free time refers to a special way of calculating a special kind of time. Leisure refers to a state of being, a condition of man, which few desire and fewer achieve.

"Disabusing leisure of free time," says de Grazia, is one of the principal purposes of his book, *Of Time, Work, and Leisure*. He goes even further, as we will see later, and argues that the amount of "free time" is less than we often assume. On that point, I will take issue, but on the separation of the terms we are in full agreement.

The next phrase of the definition, "pleasant expectation and recollection," raises a serious question as to whether the experience should be considered as leisure if these elements are not present. As a partial answer, a further distinction must be made between the general act and its substance and between form and content. One may, for example, read a book in his leisure; this is favorably anticipated by him, because *to read* is a "good thing." However, the book might be Hersey's *The Wall;* within the reading experience, therefore, one may find tragedy.

The psychological element of pleasure that precedes, pervades, and follows leisure refers, accordingly, to the choice of reading *as reading.* This becomes a crucial distinction when we turn later to a discussion of possibilities for deepening or obtaining values through leisure, because then the issue is precisely the same: can we attract the person to some experience for the formal aspect and then, by affecting the content of the experience, contribute to new personal growth?

By saying that leisure can cover "the whole range of commitment and intensity," we seek to destroy the myth and image of leisure as only relaxation, fun, amusement, or idleness. This is one of the pervasive myths that has colored the literature for decades. So that there can be no mistake of the intentions of the construct, three large groupings of content are included, "recreation, personal growth, and service to others."

The phrase on "characteristic norms and restraints" needs to be emphasized. It asserts that leisure—like religious, educational, familial, or other activity-experience—exists within a cultural context. "Cultural," of course, is used here in the social science sense. Indeed, a major specification of the conceptualization in the next section is that the components of leisure must be removable, and components of religion or other institutions must be put into their place. If this can be done, then the study of leisure has entered a mature stage, and a *theory* of leisure, not just a study of leisure minutiae, can proceed.

Furthermore, as I will note in a later chapter, the phrase "recreation, personal growth, and service to others" is related to an epistemological scheme to be outlined in relation to the meanings of leisure. The first will be paired roughly with the *assumptive* key to one's perception of the world, the second to the *aesthetic,* and the last to the *analytic.*

Another position in the formulation is the relationship to other disciplines that becomes explicit, and presents another reason for suggesting the broadest approach to the issues. If the statement is taken apart, some of its ties to special fields can be seen.

FORMULATION	DISCIPLINES AND ISSUES
1. "—relatively self-determined activity-experience"	Psychology-psychiatry-sociology-political science
	a. How judgments and decisions are made

                                                b. Power structure in families
                                                c. Bases of obligations to friends and peers
                                                d. External conditions that affect autonomy or freedom, and so on

2. "—economically free-time roles"

    Economics-sociology-history-law political science-industrial psychology
    a. Nature of "social roles"
    b. Nature of "work"
    c. Perceptions of time
    d. Psychology of wants and needs, and so on

3. "—seen as leisure by participants"

    Psychology, sociology, linguistics, information theory, and business-related disciplines, literature, aesthetics
    a. Cognitive and affective stimuli
    b. Behaviorist theories
    c. Differential perceptions, and so on

4. "—pleasant anticipation and recollection"

    Psychiatry, psychology, economics, human ecology, business, history
    a. Budget planning
    b. Dynamics of conversation
    c. Projected behavior, and so on

5. "—whole range of commitment and intensity"

    All social sciences, philosophy, theology, gerontology, arts
    a. Quest for self-identity
    b. Search for meanings
    c. Nature of responsibility
    d. Roles in retirement, and so on

Such an interdisciplinary approach can be applied to leisure as a social institution.

In substance, leisure differs from other institutions. In the method of its study, leisure is approachable in the same way as other institutions. In research terms, this provides handles or major classifications that are useful for reference, for anchoring our hypotheses, for classifications of data for bibliographical listings, or for coding data preparatory to computerization. Since scientific solutions when simply achieved have been called "beautiful," even by scientists, I have adopted the model of the string quartet—one of man's classical solu-

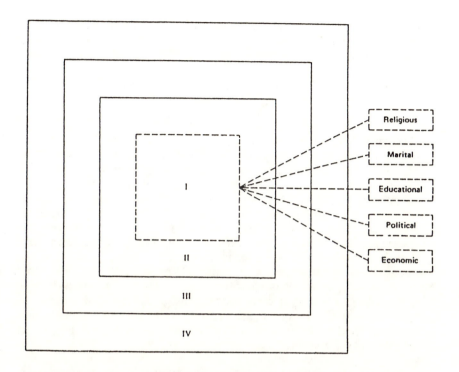

tions to the blend of individual and group—in a series of fourfold systems called institutions, clusters, cultures, and constructs. Into this mold, the "inner" square (i), the phenomenon being studied could be *any* institution, while II, III, and IV would remain as constants, applying to the central dynamic, whatever it might be.

The inner square, the institution, changes not only its basic identity but also its constituent parts.

There might be some difficulty among scholars in reaching a consensus of components for institution. I offer these as mere illustrations:

Religious: Deities, ethics, hierarchies, symbolisms.
Marital: Sex regulations, legal relationships, roles, life-styles.
Educational: Teaching, research, service, counselling.
Political: Legislation, administration, enforcement, symbol.
Economics: Production, distribution, consumption, ideology.
Leisure: Condition, selection, function, meaning.

Altogether, what we have above is the beginning of a visual model. Models are used often in the behavioral sciences, whether as constructions in words, mathematical symbols, physical objects, or pictures. Their main purpose is sufficient comprehensiveness and flexibility to suggest specific units, elements, or parts—but within a larger "system" that invites the drawing of *relationships*. A successful model is not a pretty, static thing but a dynamic construction that generates data, ideas, and even hypotheses. Bernard Phillips reminds us of its potentials and limitations.

"Like any device used in the context of discovery, models have their possibilities and their dangers. It is believed that the human mind learns best about the unknown by proceeding from the known, and the utility of scientific analogies or models lies in the fact that they dramatize the implications of the known. The use of models is standard practice in pedagogy: addition and subtraction, for example are often taught with the aid of concrete entities. . . . It is always possible to develop a model of a given phenomenon, for there is always some similarity between the system which constitutes the model and the system which constitutes the reality. The question the researcher must answer, however, is whether or not there is something further to be gained by setting up a model that goes beyond the apparent similarities with reality. Might such a model serve to suggest new ideas as to the nature or function of reality, ideas that might not otherwise be apparent?"

Phillips' question is met head on in Chapter 3, where 60 observations or propositions are extracted from the model as an exercise and as a basis for many pages of discussion throughout the volume. The model is intended as a tool, a sense of direction, a map of issues. In itself the model provides no answers. Its usefulness increases as it meets several specifications. It must (1) permit specific analysis of leisure activity-experience as well as of the total, institutional phenomena; (2) progress from simple (most measurable) to complex analysis; (3) include both time and space elements; (4) stimulate and simulate relationships between the model's component parts; (5) encourage both qualitative and quantitive investigations; (6) encompass as many disciplines as needed; and (7) move the theoretical inquiry toward bridges for policy formulation. Before proceeding to the model, two other questions can be raised.

1. What is the relationship of the *model* to the *conceptions* of leisure already given above?
2. Where does the model to be used as the core of this volume fall within the major methodological positions of the social sciences?

As to the first question, any definition or characterization is a mental construct that attempts to identify the subject being investigated; the model, however, seeks to explore possibilities for one or more theories. The model is a tool for potential exploration, to explain why and how certain things happen. Thus it makes little difference which conception of leisure is used as a basis for the study at a given moment; conditions such as health, income, or education must still be related to the community, to symbols of the culture, and so on. The nature of the propositions that emerge from the model will differ, depending on the conception of leisure that is the foundation of the entire study, and thus the differences between a humanistic or therapeutic concept of leisure enter prominently into the relationships established with factors such as social class. If the model is taken to be a "formal style" (distinct, for example, from a literary exposition), the nature of leisure as perceived by the participant, the scientist, or the society is the subjective "content." Obviously, propositions about content can be created without any model, but the model provides the overall system by which data exists within a totality instead of (as is often the case in social science) as isolated material.

The model finally provides a certain rhythm, order, and priority among the propositions—a rhythm that, as in the case of a musical theme, is not only found by the creator but, indeed, carries him along almost in a life of its own. Where the scientist ends and the artist takes over is not always easy to determine. In the present case, some of the propositions of Chapter 3 had been in my mind, perhaps somewhat hidden from consciousness; however, in what Abraham Kaplan calls its value for "deductive fertility," the model serves to "squeeze out of our data a great deal of content not otherwise available to us, or at least not easily available."

The relation of the model to traditions (therefore, to controversies) within social science brings us to the terms *empirical* and *rational-logical*. The first is a way of working with data that puts complete faith "in the senses, firm belief in the power of observation, willingness to be ruled by observable evidence, and belief that scientific conclusions should never get beyond the realm of extrapolation. . . ." In contrast, the rationalistic method holds that truth is derived by the mind, conceptualizations, constructs, and the use of logic.

The recent history of American sociology has been dominated by empiricism. The results were mixed, bringing both self-deception on the crucial matter of "objectivity" and more accuracy as a science. The long and often bitter debates between proponents of these positions need not detain us here.

I have long ago concluded, from reading critiques of my works and noting the references to my work by colleagues that what an author may think are his more important points can be ignored by others; conversely, the reader often seems to pick up on ideas or phrases that he himself thought were minor. The author, if he

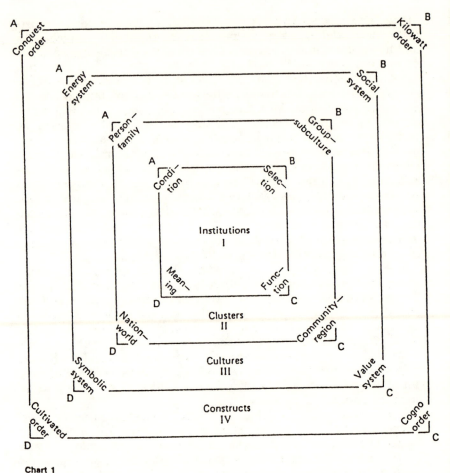

Chart 1

Conceptualization of leisure in society

is even-tempered and politic, seldom responds in public to such instances. Sometimes they are too blatant to ignore. A recent case of the latter followed a review of the arts book (1991) that appeared in the British *Journal of Aesthetics* (July, 1991). The matter is covered in my reply to the critic from the University of St. Andrews.

> . . . the reviewer notes his 'confusion on the diagrams, an integral aspect of the presentation, for 'nearly all lacked any useful purpose,' especially the Comprehensive Model for Arts Within Society. Most of the diagrams were inserted merely to help the reader to understand where he was at any given point in the total analysis. The "compre-

hensive" medel provided the skeleton for the entire analysis . . . No wonder the critic found the book "disappointing" for without understanding the model he missed entirely the writer's purpose, or indeed, the nature of a major tool in current social science, . . . A sensitive criticism should, therefore, be based on the judgment as to whether the present work has gained from the application of such a model. And conversely, whether the model's usefulness *vis a vis* the arts has contributed to other areas of concern. . . . An example of the critic's views on substantive matters is his observation on the importance of such topics as the relationship of the arts to economics and to technology; he claims that the volume fails even to acknowledge in passing the existence of such debates. I agree fully with the importance of these issues, and refer him respectfully, on the first, to pages 85–91, also to pages 21 on "issues for economists," to pages 86 and 91 on the "economic values of art," and to pages 85 on the "new economics and art." As to technology, the reader is invited to examine pages 162, 232, and a section of Chapter 13, titled "technology and the future."

6
Fiddling

The violin, as Yehudi Menuhin notes, was the soul of the eastern European *shtetl*.

> One must bear in mind that the Russian Jew of the village ghetto had, as well as the example of the village folk fiddler, that of the gypsy fiddler, whose melodies he also shared, to say nothing of the unique treasure of the traditional local heritage from the cantors and the Chassidic rabbis. It was the Jewish fiddler who always played the violin to express the joys and sorrows of the Russian villages; thus he had both played and listened to the Russian folksongs and those of the gypsies. This marvelous heritage suddenly dawned on me with a flash when I saw before me what I had never imagined in my wildest fantasies: a vast range of rustic, curiously divided, infinitely varied shapes in the Folk Museum in Moscow. For the Russian Jew, highly motivated, highly literate, and yet ever destined to start life anew, the violin was the passport, purse, and path to the summits of society. From the southern warm-water port of Odessa, that egress to the Mediterranean and the wider world, many of the best Russian violinists came . . . Indeed, there was barely a Jewish family that did not have its young, budding violinist . . . following the pogroms, Jews arrived at that time in Palestine with almost every child carrying a violin case.[1]

Humoresque was the story of a father's birthday gift for his son. In the music store, father suggests a trumpet; the son insists on a violin. In the magic of Hollywood, this talented boy is ready for his Carnegie Hall debut after a few reels of film. At this point in the silent film of 1923, as the young artist played the "Humoresque," the concertmaster of the pit orchestra stood up and played, bow for bow, note for note. I was fascinated, and went home to make a fiddle of cardboard, with threads for strings. Soon, Uncle Sam, himself a left-handed fiddler of sorts, came to our home with a real instrument, half-size, including a bow. Not long after that, the three Kaplan boys were sneaking through

6: FIDDLING

alleys with the small violin to their first lesson; Dad, the tailor, had made a blue velvet bag, from which the bow protruded. Thus, we avoided the sneers of the neighborhood boys . . .

Our first teacher was an old *klezmer* who made his living by visiting Jewish weddings and bar mitzvahs, often unannounced. At the appropriate moment in the ceremony he would contribute his kazatskes and pass the hat. His going rate for lesson was twenty-five cents. He would sit near the dining room table, hold the fiddle under his long beard, let go with a wild dance tune, smack his lips at this artistry, look around the room at mother and assorted relatives, and say to his students, "A-zay shpiel ich . . . nu, shpiel du" (This is how I play; now you play.)" This is called rote teaching by Suzuki and other master teachers of our day; for us it was a disaster, and lasted only a few weeks.

Mr. Zimbaroff was our next teacher. He was a violinist in a downtown pit orchestra. Mom paid one dollar each week for a package deal. This episode ended when Mr. Z., the father of seven, eloped with the theater pit pianist. About that time, the instrument had become mine by default: Sam, the oldest, made a unilateral decision that he could take no more. Frank was unwilling to practice. I was stuck.

Mr. Johnson was my next teacher. I recall only two remarkable things about that experience. One, he had his students come for sessions of string orchestra practice, and was way ahead of his time. Two, he was black. For that period in our social history, how he happened to teach the violin, probably to play it well, and gain a foothold in the white community would make a fascinating case study. Whatever the circumstances, he kept my interest until along came William Haydn.

Haydn was a mystery figure from another world. He took his students to homes of his friends, where half a dozen of us would play alone or in a group for his friends, of a higher social class whose homes were larger and fancier than any we had seen. He introduced us also to the real concert world. My first event was to hear the great Fritz Kreisler. I sat on the crowded stage, only a few yards behind the great man. My expectations were very high, but what impressed me the most was that, quite like myself, he produced some scratches now and then. This discovery encouraged me to go on with the violin. The family had a falling out with Haydn over the purchase of a violin, for which we had trouble keeping up payments.

That was the period, perhaps at fourteen, when I met Frank Glazer, who lived a few blocks away. I called him one day to ask if he would accompany me at a recital. We had no time to practice together; the first time we met was just a few minutes before we walked on the stage to play a Polish mazurka. I skipped a few measures somewhere along the way; without batting an eye, he stayed with me, and we finished together. This impressed me more than anything else. We became fast friends, and forty years later I became the academic dean at Bennett College, where he was pianist-in-residence. Meantime, he had become world famous as a concert artist, ending his career at Eastman.

One day, walking up the stairs of a violin repair shop in downtown Milwaukee, I heard some unusual fiddling of the Joachim cadenza to the Beethoven Concerto. I met a smallish, middle-aged man, husky, with a few hairs flying in all directions. This was Bruno Esbjorn, who had just come to town after the closing of the Busch Conservatory in Chicago. As we became friends in succeeding months, he taught me in exchange for the services I rendered as his "manager." This arrangement lasted for about five years, until I went to college. From him I learned how to approach the Bach literature for unaccompanied violin, the musical bible that still remains with me constantly. Although he played in the old tradition of the small vibrato and enormous technique—he had been a student and assistant to the great Sevcik—he knew the traditional repertoire.

Esbjorn was intensely vain. He knew six languages well. He had been the national Swedish chess champion, according to him. He lived memories of the glorious past, such as performing several concerti on one program with the Berlin Philharmonic, with Paganini etudes as encores—so he claimed. Now in Milwaukee before the days of Social Security, he was teaching chess on city playgrounds. His social thinking was ultra-conservative, Nazi-like. His violin technique was quite different from that of today's Sterns and Perlmans; he could play play gypsylike passages, as in the music of Sarasate, in a freedom that I have never since heard, yet his small, fast vibrato produced a flatness of tone that made everything seem out of tune. I had something of the same reaction when I heard Hubermann in his last American tour.

My last teacher was Horace Jones at the University of Colorado in Boulder. My two summers with him were to prepare a master's recital, comprised of a Bach solo sonata, a Mozart concerto, a showpiece by Wieniawski, and a composition of my own. Jones was a Welshman, whose voice was the model for the sound of his excellent string orchestra. His contribution to all of his students was largely in teaching them how to practice—slowly. One summer I served as his second violinist in the faculty string quartet. I still feel guilty about leaving the group shortly before our debut, when I received an urgent call to come to the University of Illinois. Jones badly wanted to divorce his wife when he fell in love with the pretty violist in the quartet. Not willing to take the initiative, he tried every ruse he could imagine to get his wife mad at him, including the practice of dull études on his violin at two A.M. Nothing worked, until the winter I left. He and the violist were both fillers with the Denver Symphony. As they returned from a concert one evening, a heavy snow descended, and they were stuck on the highway going home to Boulder. The next day, sure that they had made no attempt to get home, his wife left . . .

How does one summarize sixty-five years of making music—forty with the same Cerutti instrument? How many hundreds of concerts, dozens of recitals, thousands of rehearsal hours, alone and with others? There was the month that Stravinsky prepared a full concert of his works with the orchestra at the University of Illinois . . . playing for Ice Capades . . performing the Lalo Symphony Espagnole in 1941 with the Pueblo Civic Symphony . . . quartet sessions in Boston with the Polish-American virtuoso Roman Totenberg . . . Being part of Glenn Campbell's show orchestra . . . concerts for ten years in Alabama with the New Southern Trio . . . membership in the Florida Symphony under an arrogant, disagreeable, but capable conductor . . . solo recitals in Colorado . . . many evenings with Ernst Tarrasch, a Hitler refugee, getting "drunk" together far into the night with playing sonatas . . . six years as concertmaster with the Montgomery Symphony . . . weeks of forced inattention to the violin, then the agony of catching up . . . playing for the grandchildren . . . playing for Mother in exchange for her delicious *latkes* . . . playing Bloch and Achron for Barbara's appreciative Presbyterian church . . .

All this in the midst of a career, teaching, lecturing, writing, being a father and husband, reading, television, and travel. But then, sixty-five years is a long time.

All violinists will feel at home in these random recollections. There is nothing unique in my musical experience. I knew my limitations and abilities, and had better judgment than to consider a violinistic career. I could hold my own, even in the late Beethoven quartets, but the technique was undependable in the sense that at any time, university duties might interrupt the regular practice that is essential.

There was a crossing of interest—music and sociology—as I was often led to a consideration of the concepts amateur and professional. After all, many performances had brought some income, but for IRS or census purposes I was the professor, not the fiddler. I have long ago concluded that

(1) the amateur and the professional in the arts are not competitors, but close allies, and their fate is interwoven;
(2) in spite of current economic difficulties of professional artists, the amateur has never before had as many favorable conditions as now in the United States, and
(3) major credit for these favorable conditions now serving the amateur in art and music must go to the public school system.

Of course, it was some time before the country could afford musicians whose livelihood came entirely from music. Yet there was always a place for amateurs, especially for choir members. As Michael Mark notes,

> When the Pilgrims and the Puritans arrived in the new world in 1620 and 1630, they brought with them the sophisticated and refined music culture of England. Their music served an important purpose because of its use in worship. Life in the New World was difficult, however, and they had little time to maintain musical skills . . .[2]

Early education was practical, and music did not enter the public schools until the nineteenth century. The quality of church singing was low, stimulating a demand for music education in the schools. At first this instruction took the form of the "singing school," with itinerant teachers going from community to community. The Boston School Committee was persuaded in 1838 to add music to its regular curriculum. Chicago followed in 1841, Cincinnati a decade later. By then the first symphony orchestra had been created in New York (1842.) As John Mueller observed in his classic history of the symphony in America,[3] this delay in instrumental music-making on professional levels had been characterized by the absence of imperial courts or cultural centers like Vienna and Leipsic. "Musical instruments had to be imported in cargo space that was not always ample and certainly not cheap." Far more developed at that time were such arts as painting, sculpture and literature.

Yet, as I fiddled away on Kreutzer études and played with many groups, none of these historical or cultural considerations were paramount. I fiddled because I enjoyed making music alone and with friends. I enjoyed the process whereby an orchestra approaches a self-assigned task and ultimately brings it to fruition before an audience. Bach's solo sonatas and partitas became a thermometer of my current condition on the fingerboad. I enjoyed having an insight into the mechanics and aesthetics of great artists. I enjoyed an affinity with Heifetz in my younger years and Perlman in later years. A camaraderie was present with other fiddlers, anywhere and anytime; an understanding of fingerings in a particular passage of the Mendelssohn concerto or the common satisfaction in mastering a Schubert trio. I enjoyed the difference between re-creating a Beethoven score on the stage and listening to the same score played by the great Cleveland Symphony. There are subjective factors in each, and the historical continuity came alive when I was in a suburb of Vienna, in the very room that Beethoven composed his Third, and only a month later I was playing the same masterpiece with a fine orchestra in Montgomery, Alabama.

But objective connections of the fiddle to the world outside of the concert hall are relevant, as in a study of music within the broad leisure picture of a family, community, or nation. Making those connections is altogether another "cup of tea" than living them. The uniqueness of my situation was that I was living the subjective and objective at the same time, and yet found it possible to preserve both sanity and a sense of proportion. This sense of time, place, and purpose came to be well defined. Music has a craft and a technique; so does social science.

7
Ending

Public evaluation of important people, as on the obituary pages of the *New York Times*, may be necessary. For ordinary people what matters is the assessment we have made beforehand of ourselves in the winter of our lives, or that have been made by family, friends, and colleagues. Such evaluations move both backward and forward in time: *what has been, what is ahead?* What can be said of our accomplishments, and where do we stand subsequently in the judgments of time?

I do not recall having seen a serious attempt to summarize the various motivations or strategies of self-evaluations. The scholarship in such pursuits might try to assess motivations of persons about to commit suicide, for surely such an act has implicit judgments of one's past and future. Persons having marital difficulties surely have in mind some criteria of judgment, at least in the relationship of mates. Those who have been dismissed from a job, especially in midlife, must put to themselves the issue of career success and failure. One technique might be to confront persons with the "if" factor: have you had fantasies about choices you have had to make: where you might have lived, whom you might have married, the jobs you might have taken, the stocks you should have purchased. . . ?

The fact is that most of us go through life, day by day, year by year, and if we look back over the years and decades, it is in vignettes: the trip, the honeymoon, the birth of a child. Seldom do we examine the whole life, and even less often do any of us put that life into the perspective of the larger social milieu into which we happen to have been born.

For instance, here I am, with all of you in the same situation, only a few years before a new century. Given a long life, as in my case, I can look back a good part of the century, and consider those dramatic events that I can recall, or that have affected all of us. But what if it were 1897: would we likewise be pointing to a century of enormous social change? With good reason, indeed, we could. On a world level, French ideals had spread, starting with the Netherlands, Switzerland, and Italy. Napoleon had appeared in 1803. The Congress of Vienna took place. Romanticism replaced rococo art. It was the century of Rousseau, Byron, Hegel, and Beethoven. Clothing styles were freed from wigs and hoops. The Spanish colonies became independent. The idea of progress took hold. Darwin's *Origin of Species* appeared in 1859; Pasteur's germ theory came two years later; Freud was starting on his experiments. Socialist theories were being disseminated, climaxed by Karl Marx. The industrial revolution came, along with trade unionism and liberal legislation. Racism was given a false, but influential biological foundation in the writings of Gobineau; anti-Semitism flourished.

These changes, especially the industrial revolution and the coming of millions of immigrants, affected the United States deeply, even as the Civil War became our major political influence.

No one whose life was approaching its end with the close of the nineteenth century could escape those influences in the nature of the values he applied to an evaluation of himself.

Nor could the vast changes within either the nineteenth or the twentieth century have fully prepared one to assess what the coming decades might mean for his children and grandchildren. If it may be true that now there is a broad cynicism about the future, what might the retiree of 1899 have anticipated for his descendants? My hunch is that had an international survey on values and expectations been carried out then the general mood would have been of optimism. After all, millions of the generations of my parents had already migrated to America since the 1890s; many others were planning to do so.

Among all of us, the social factors that intrigue the social scientists and historians are relegated to the back of our minds at any time. What bothered the Irish migrant was the potato famine, what affected my parents were the pogroms officially carried out. What bothers us today is the crime picture, the lack of safety in our streets, the economic insecurity among masses of employees, the high costs of medical care, the need for both parents to work for family survival. It seems to be an ending of a century that is blanketed with doubts, suspicions, and worries. Half the population seems to sit up nights, calling several hundred talk show hosts, and complaining about everything from the president to the local baseball team.

Indeed, it is a sad time to approach my own ending. For none of us can escape from the twentieth century without some responsibility for the David Koreshes and the Rush Limbaughs, with their brand of fanaticism, destruction, and theatricalism. But simultaneously, to maintain our sanity without the help of drugs and gurus, another responsibility we owe to ourselves is to find within the total social scene those elements of creativity, humanity, and rationality that can still be found among our social institutions and communities. Indeed, such pockets can be found, not by reading the headlines or tuning into the talk shows, but seeking the unsung, the triumphant, the meaningful. My life has been fortunate in that regard: the academic life, the violin, the opportunity to see the world and expand my horizons, the enlargement of the greater family with grandchildren and great grandchildren, and the friendships of colleagues and neighbors.

The network of rationality and humanity has been enriched by public persons with honesty (a Truman and a Carter), with vision (a Stevenson and a Clinton), or with courage (a Thurgood Marshall and a Martin Luther King). Such heroes may not outweigh the Ross Perots and the Reagans in the public press, but they provide some hope for the world ahead.

Is there a beginning in death? Turning to my origins, Judaism is generally vague on the matter. The Torah hardly speaks of the afterlife *(Olan-has-be)*. Indeed, so obsessed is the Torah with the world that its priests were forbidden to come into contact with the dead (Leviticus 21:2). There was, of course, a conception of heaven and hell, and in the general scheme that Christianity imitated, heaven was the upper region of the universe, reserved for God and celestial beings. In more recent writings, Jewish thinkers referred to heaven as a spiritual state, not a place or region.

Given the certainty of death, Christianity's heaven was the reward for a virtuous life, a decision made upon death by the Divine Judge. In Judaism there were moral lessons to be learned from both heaven and hell, such as the state of cooperation among those in both; an example of this might be the relationship among those who, in every case, were without elbows, yet needed the help of others to eat. Early Christianity thought of heaven or paradise as a refreshed existence, with palm trees watered by the Four Rivers. (Water symbolism appears also in Mohammedism.) In sharp contrast, the Christian hell was viewed as a furnace, a dark cave for demons commanded by Lucifer.

The subject of death was enormously stimulated among Christians by the epidemic of the Black Death and the Hundred Years War. These leveled all ages, the rich and the poor, the laity and the clergy. The dervishes of death became popular depictions in the fifteenth century, thus providing a macabre spectacle that became familiar in the music of Saint Saëns. However, the dichotomy of paradise and hell derives from the East.

Among some primitive peoples there were (and perhaps still are) those who believe that after death the soul assumes a form that is related to animals. The animal may act as a guide to another world; there is the example of Cerberus, guarding the gates.

There were the elaborate death and funerary traditions of Egypt and Near East. We have in our museums seen the remarkable furnishings taken from such Pharaohs as Tutankhamen. Even for commoners there were judgments of the soul, made in vast halls, where the god Isiris sits with forty-two judges, each there to test a particular sin.

India offers a belief in the transmigration of souls, heading toward a great mountain around which are grouped the continents, anticipating the circles that were much later depicted by Dante in his *Divine Comedy*. Man's conduct determines where he will be reborn. In the hot hells will be found sinners who are burned and boiled as they embrace sinners of the opposite sex; in the cold hells, naked figures will be seen over frozen lakes. Heaven is represented rarely until late Vishnuism, when it is seen as a royal court.

One could move to Chinese and Japanese visions of death, None of these visions and practices should be ridiculed. In all these cultures there were "intelligent" men and women, fervent believers, supportive scriptures, and artistic symbolisms. Historical time does make an iota of difference. The Christian traditions that millions of Americans believe fall into this variety of explanations, neither true or less true, more sophisticated or less, more beautiful or less, more rational or less.

Any anthropology text could expand on this range of beliefs; thus I prefer not to go on, but to return to Judaism. Let me expand on earlier remarks, relying now on my son-in-law, Rabbi James Rudin, and Marcia. They wrote a moving book in 1986 about a friend of their's, another rabbi, who was gravely ill with leukemia, and now had to go through the soul-searching toward which he had always directed his flock. Since that book, Jim has been a member of a New York state advisory committee on medical ethics; he has had to wrestle with such matters as prolonging life by artificial means.

In their book, Jim and Marcia note that the traditional Jew emphasizes that finding God in this life is reward enough, "so promise of eternal life as a reward should not be necessary . . . Death is inevitable, and we must accept its reality. But we shouldn't dwell on it and let it detract from the value of *this* life. Ironically, or perhaps appropriately, the Kaddish, the Jewish prayer recited in memory of the dead, says nothing about death. Instead, it affirms life by praising and glorifying God and His creation . . . the highly organized mourning rituals are designed to channel our grief and return the bereaved to active life and a positive state of mind as soon as possible."[1]

There were other beliefs passed down in our family, but I cannot vouch for their historicity. One was that we should live virtuously every day, as though it might be our last. The prayer that night was given as if it were the last day. If in some cosmic balance sheet we had lived righteously, we could pass on some merits to a younger person who might need this inheritance. The basis of this myth was the status of an older person over that of youth. An example: when I would occasionally send a check to Mother, she always returned it with the comment that the old should help the young, not the reverse.

For my part, I draw upon Judaism for a basic social premise as a rational/theological concept of immortality. The history of persecutions and wanderings led to a strong emphasis on community. This meant, first, a focus on family; second, on education; third, honor to those who contribute to the whole of the community. The result of these beliefs has been a communal policy of social welfare in the form of hospitals, nursing homes, social work in general. In these regards—with Brandeis University as one example—the record of Jews in educational philanthropy is unquestioned.

Accordingly, I find it both rationally and traditionally satisfying to equate immortality with "good works." It is the unobserved deed that attests to sincerity.

These are my views, even as a nontraditional Jew. They hardly need elaboration.

The contribution that was made by my Mother and Father—together with other millions then—was to have made a long journey to the free soil of a new country. My journey in life has been of another sort, not of a higher level, but far different. I do not think of death, in spite of the opinion of younger people about their elders. When it comes, it will hopefully be in the night, an extension of peaceful sleep. There were small regrets along the way, far outweighed by the pleasures and small triumphs.

I regret that I left Boston, even as I enjoy the rural South.

7: ENDING

I regret that with many trips abroad, I was not more interested in varieties of food.

I regret that with trips to France and Italy, I did not master those beautiful languages.

I wish I knew more of our family history.

I regret that I do not know more about nature, especially flowers, birds, and the ways of the sea.

A more serious regret is that I have missed opportunities to relate my studies of leisure to public issues in a more active way than on paper. A special need existed for someone to take the lead in articulating, perhaps organizing, a movement to develop programs in creativity for older persons. In several writings I did outline the need for S and S Centers by which this generation could train itself for consulting assignments in communities, with appropriate preparation as "students" of community needs, structures, and processes. No agency or unity has, to my knowledge, picked up the idea and moved aggressively on it.

There has been a serious need for a journal about, by, and for the elderly, comparable in quality to *Harpers*, *Atlantic*, or *Commentary*. I am not a journalist, yet I had opportunities to be active in that direction.

Never have I felt the urge to act like a prophet of old, and yet, how much more I could have done to serve as a critic of the society during my period of "maturation," a society that today, with its $4 billion in debt, yet has the wherewithal to spend $5.6 billion for cookies, $8 billion for pornography, and $505 billion for hairspray.

The seventeen acres that Barbara and I live on was named Merry Oaks before our time here. On it we have our own two-acre lake, a pool, a garden, tennis court, barn, greenhouse, tool shed, and two smaller houses aside from our spacious residence; perhaps a hundred trees, many bushes, rose beds, and expanses of open land; and, of course, birds, squirrels, frogs, crickets, turtles, rabbits, mice, fire ants, and an occasional snake.

It is, indeed, a fine spot to finish out a life. The main house is five hundred yards off a highway leading north to Senoia, Fayetteville, Riverdale, and on to Atlanta. In Haralson, closest to us, superb sausage can be bought, and that goes well on a cool morning with grits. To the south are Alvaton, Gay, and Woodbury, before the road leads to FDR's Little White House. Along that route are the Callaway Gardens, among the most breathtaking in the nation.

We are aware of drug arrests (recently, sixty pushers in one haul), murders, and thefts. Among our losses to a burglar or two recently was a rototiller and a weed-eater. Several cars have careened off our road, and gone through our fence; one man died as he drove his car near us. An occasional dead deer is found on the road.

Thus, there is full life here, but for us Merry Oaks is primarily a peaceful retreat in which we can make music, read, relax, enjoy Sugar—our precious cocker—take afternoon swims, and peep into the world from the screen.

Merry Oaks is a perfect place to die, several miles from the family cemetery at Mt. Zion. Until coming here, I had preferred cremation, but instead I will enter eternity in the family plot that holds Barbara's relatives going back to the Revolutionary War. Those of us lying together there will never be violated by a real estate development. Further, with Merry Oaks as a natural gathering place for family funerals, her family and mine will finally meet one afternoon, and names will become people. It will be a good afternoon.

Finally, speaking to my three great-grandchildren, I am not sure that your world will have become more harmonious by AD 2082, when the two youngest will have reached eighty-two. By then you will probably have found, as I did, that your 40s, 50s, and 60s will have spilled into each other. And strangely, *your* great-grandchildren will find it difficult to understand or to believe that you will not feel older in your winter. The world will have changed in many ways, and one of your children may be born on a space station, if Isaac Asimov was right. At least, you will have available to you, in this document, something that I wish I had had—some commentary on his time by an unknown great-grandfather.

Part 2
Vision

Introduction

It is easy enough, on paper, to envision a world free of war, crime, disease, poverty, alienation, marital discord, and governmental chicanery. Honesty among lawyers, no punk rock, no Madonna. Utopia. Candide . . .

But life is not lived on paper, even though, as Daniel Bell noted, "Men have always been attracted by the mystical lure of the *chiloi*, the Greek word for a thousand, from which we get our religious term *chiliasm*, the belief in a coming life free from imperfections of human existence."[1]

The realities are inescapable, even to those of us with the most optimism, the most faithful readers of literary utopias, or those, like myself, who contemplate the lives of our great-grandchildren. Isaac Asimov, the late science fiction writer, suggested that one of our descendants, not too far down the road, may be born on a space station. Asimov, a former colleague at Boston University, was in the tradition we had already begun with Armstrong's walk on the moon. The daily science accounts had convinced the sociologist-journalist, Max Lerner, of the need to replace the terms pessimist and optimist with the term "possibilist."

The mood of the possibilist is the acceptance as normal those gadgets, processes, and services that only a few decades ago would have been laughed at by informed men of science.

The possibilist on the grandest of scales, like Alvin Toffler in *The Third Wave*, is not necessarily timid. I am drawn more to the wave analogy than to the absolute gloom of Oswald Spengler in the loss of national "soul."

Toffler's challenge reminds one of the prophets of Biblical days, as he booms out his message:

> A new civilization is emerging in our times, and blind men everywhere are trying to suppress it . . ; as profound as that of the First Wave of change established ten thousand years ago by the invention of agriculture, or the earthshaking Second Wave of change touched off by the industrial revolution. . . Some speak of the looming Space

Age, Information Age, Electronic Era, or Global Village . . . technotronic age, post-industrial society.[2]

Yet I draw short of his judgment that "we are engaged in building a remarkable new civilization from the ground up." Both the first and second waves provided an enormously strong foundation of custom. As the futurist Bertrand de Jouvenal has noted, "social order has always been regarded as a Common Good, whose preservation was essential." In more homely terms, Daniel Bell foresees that:

> the year 2000 will be more like the United States in the year 1967 than different. The basic framework of day-to-day life has been shaped in the last fifty years by the ways of the automobile, the airplane, the telephone and the television have brought people together and increased the networks and interaction among them.[3]

It is therefore presumptuous for one like myself, well into the eighth decade of life, to play the optimist to affirm the innate "goodness" of man, and to pass on to his great-grandchildren the assurance that we will muddle through the new miracles ahead in communications, leisures, flights to the moon, TV on our wrists, pictures on every telephone, or rationality in all quarters.

The possibilist in me, which is an academic ploy or futuristic safety net, assumes the posture of hope, in part built on the tradition of demography, "in the short," "in the long run," and "in between."

Often, these attempts were too short-run by highly paid CEOs. The failure of the Edsel is a case in point, and the ongoing mentality of the TV industry contributes to a lack of vision and courage.

About midcentury, a more scientific posture began to take shape in both university and think-tank environments. "Futurology" became popular among many in need of more systematic guidance in academic and research groups. By the early 1970s one could read about such techniques as the "assumption-related," the "process-related," the "output-related," the "system-related," the "use-related" and such developments as causality, morphological analysis, and other in-house terms. The 1960s alone saw the publication of futurological writings by Baade, Baier, Boulding, Clarke, de Jouvenal, Drucker, Eurich, Ewald, Flechteim, Fuller, Gordon, Helmer, Jungk, Kahn, McHale, McLuhan, Marek, Michael, Peccei, Polak, Theobald, and Woldtenholem. Alvin Toffler's popular book *Future Shock* came out in 1970.

Of those named, Helmer was the expert in approaching other

experts to gather their individual, and ultimately, their collective insights into the future. It is known as the Delphi approach. After a round of opinions is gathered on a particular set of issues, summaries are presented to each participant for a sharpening or modification of his own projections. I have myself participated in one such panel on the matter of anticipated consumption of alcohol within the leisure context.

It is interesting now—thirty years after Helmer's work with this technique—to see how successful he was with the Delphi method. Among his "certain" projections that have stood the test of time: world population has reached five billion; we are largely a credit economy; we employ many teaching technologies; and there is a wide range of personally-affecting drugs. Among Helmer's "not quite certain" projections that proved feasible: "Highly intelligent machines will exist that will act as effective collaborators of scientists and engineers."

Yet the same scientist also expected, by the turn of the century, a permanent colony on the moon, control of the weather, ocean mining, and farming on a large scale, and automated highway transportation.

Arthur C. Clarke, the eminent science fiction writer, wrote his *Profiles of the Future* in 1963, taking delight in how other futurists had missed the mark. He quoted the eminent American astronomer, Roger Newcomb:

> The demonstration that no possible combination of known substances, known forms of machinery and known forms of force can be united in a practical machine by which man shall fly long distances through the air, seems to the writer as complete as it is possible for the demonstration of any physical fact to be.[4]

In a happier mood, Clarke reports on Friar Roger, who wrote in the thirteenth century,

> Instruments may be made by which the largest ships, with only one man guiding them, will be carried with greater velocity than if they were full of sailors. Chariots may be constructed that will move with incredible speed without the help of animals . . . as also machines which will enable man to walk at the bottom of the seas.[5]

The good friar anticipated Leonardo da Vinci by several centuries.

Even this cursory glance at projections is enough to avoid making a fool of myself in the current complexity of change. My approach will be simple, as I search for agents of change in terms of their respective power or influence, and from them, seek visions that reach out to no more than possibilities.

I begin with the assertion, self-evident, that each of us, and each of our institutions is at once a guardian of the past and a guide to the future. Every school curriculum, for instance, passes on the civilization while also serving implicitly as a miniature statement of the world that is likely to confront its students. We are all subject to an enormous constellation of signals, symbols, and "significant others," and these, altogether, serve as originator and propellant into the future. They can roughly be classified as individualistic and institutionalized; with an effort that I do not propose to undertake, they could be put into categories of greater and lesser influence.

An overall label, prophet, can be placed on this array of influences and persons; even my mother was a cultural prophetess of sorts: "When you grow up, don't lie or you will be unhappy with yourself." No Jeremiah, this simple Lithuanian immigrant; but in her own way she preserved the values she knew in the Old World and a guide in the New.

8
Roles: Prophets, Activists, Scientists

PROPHETS—those who tell the rest of us how to live—arise from a scold of ancient times, a grandmother of today, a preacher next Sunday, a teacher in the classroom, a politician being interviewed. We have amateur and professional prophets. In the aggregate they all concentrate on *values.* They know right from wrong. They comprise the most powerful factor in a determination of the future, and at the same time, so obvious and penetrating that they are the most difficult "variable" in any systematic attempt to look ahead. Futurologists readily admit this Achilles' heel in their projections, this manifestation of values that are subject to unpredictable change. One example is the attitude of young women toward having babies; abortion is clearly open to fashions of thought.

Some prophets are more effective than others, hold more symbolic influence, and have a more distinguishable audience. To the teenager, for example, one's peers are a powerful cadre of prophets, more than ministers, parents, or teachers. In parts of the community, role models—prophets, of course, may be a gang leader, a drug pusher, or the friendly grocer on the corner. Nevertheless, the institutionalized guardians of our values have been parents, teachers, relatives, and ministers. They are associated by ceremonies, writings, and national legends. A classic collection of values in one community is the list uncovered in *Middletown* and *Middletown in Transition.* The creed of the Boy Scouts provides an indication of values, and more basically, the Bill of Rights.

A favorite preoccupation of cultural historians is to record either the violation of such codes in practice or the gradual change that takes place, if not in the mouthing, the practice, or observance of such creeds. Among those institutionalized prophets who emphasize the past are those known as "strict constructionists" on the U.S. Supreme Court. Among the prophets who , even institutionalized, are more likely to point to the future in respect to values are the so-called liberals of the congress—the Kennedys as distinct from the Hatches.

A second source for discerning clues to tomorrow's social landscape is the young community of *Scientists*. I say "young" for I am told that about 90 percent of all "scientists" who have ever lived in history are still alive. Of course, the definition of science is a critical factor. In recent months I have re-read parts of George Sarton's great *History of Science*,[2] chapters from the five volume *History of Technology*,[3] edited by Charles Singer, and *The Creators* by Daniel Boorstin.[4] The experience is breathtaking, to grasp the immense creativity in such areas as mathematics, astronomy, medicine, and the various fields of construction.

Yet the progress of science is more than a matter of individual minds, but rather, of the general tenor of the society. As George Sarton put the matter in the Preface to his great *History:*

> Science never developed in a social vacuum, and in the case of each individual is never developed in a psychological vacuum. Every man of science was a man of his time and place, of his family and people, of his group and church; he was always obliged to fight his own passions and prepossessions as well as to assail the superstitions that clustered around him and to choke out the novelties. It is just as foolish to deny the existence of those superstitions as it is to ignore contagious diseases . . . the growth of science implies at every step the fight against errors and prejudices; the discoveries are largely individual, but the fight is always collective.

Today, even in Manhattan or Silicon Valley, Americans enjoy their superstitions, some that are medieval indeed, but the collective values of our time support novelty and experimentation, both in industry and in universities. In this sense our scientists thrive, not fighting the academies and the clergy, but encouraged and sought after. There can be no doubt that in such a society, more miracles will continue to advance in the lives of my six grandchildren and three great-grandchildren. Asimov was probably right on births on the space station in the next generation or two.

The major sources for the look and the life of tomorrow are already imbedded in the gadgetry, the transportation, the military, and the communications of the present. Jacques Ellul has argued well that this is a reality that has become our dominant value, technology as both the means and the ends of social change.[5]

A realistic view of our times makes it clear that the relative influence of the activitists has little to do with the rationality or even with the momentum of social values. Rather, we must look to the relationship of values in part—sometimes in tragic part—

to the profits and benefits of business, agriculture, education, the medical community, the insurance industry, veteran's groups, and so on. In recent years, for example the National Rifle Association has successfully blocked the activists for gun control. Yet, with growing concerns by the public, on 5 May 1994, the House passed by two votes a ban on assault weapons. The future of this issue, among others, will absorb the influence of an older population, urban-rural relations, and the nature of leisure patterns. Changing values are the Achilles' heel of futurology.

My point, however, is that all three of our types will provide clues for the shape of tomorrow:

. . . from the scientists, clues to the processes of existence.
. . . from the prophets, clues to the possibilities.
. . . from the activists, clues to the dynamics of social change.

I venture now to several projections, safe in the knowledge that a half century from now there will be no critique of them by a contemporary Arthur C. Clarke.

A revolution is presently occuring that will be in full swing in several decades. I refer to *globality* or *globalization*. Although it is an awkward term, it avoids the political or geopolitical connotations of the term "internationalism." Every supermarket is already stocked with products from many parts of the world. The "made in America" or "made in Japan" automobile is no more a reality. Our homes are equipped with foreign objects and gadgets from TVs to watches. Our stock market, our banking system, our major corporations are all inevitably woven into patterns of global finances and political structures. Tourism took almost forty-five million Americans to foreign areas in 1991 and brought about the same number of visitors to our shores. From television we can now watch people in wars and genocidal tragedies from Africa, Somaliland, Bosnia, Sarajevo.

The United States was surely tied to events abroad since its beginnings, but never as intimately as today. Further ties will reach ever more deeply into such particular areas as education, investments, military theory, and recreation. From 1970 to 1991 the number of our telephone calls to other countries rose from twenty-three million annually to well over a billion. Unfortunately, diseases such as AIDS have no respect for political boundaries, and will lead to global public health networks far beyond those of today. As to education, both as to students and faculty, exchange between cultural areas may be expected to expand dramatically, supplementing the electronic developments in classroom facilities.

Paradoxically, *globality* will be balanced by an expanded sense and reality of *community*. The second emanates from the ongoing desire among us to find security in the environment close to us. In leisure, as I noted in a volume of 1975, "mobility" in leisure is generally balanced by the need for "immobility." The simultaneous love of television and cars by us meets this duality—leaving home and staying home. The late sociologist Paul Lazarsfeld and I prepared a joint paper for a congressional survey, and found[6] that even within the immobile act of watching TV, we often obtain information and encouragement for such outdoor activities as fishing, hunting, horseback riding, and traveling.

A second projection from a study of prophets can center around the polarity of spirituality and humanism. Both are fed by the condition of social complexity that defies simple explanation. Surely there can be no doubt about the growing alternatives in any aspect of life, including the religious. If, along the lines already envisioned by Carl Sagan, communications were to develop with the inhabitants of another planet, Christianity will be stood on its head, and variations of the "new age" spirituality could become mainstream. Even if not, I find it plausible to foresee serious conflicts between denominations within Christianity and a worldwide stress with the growing Moslem population.

As to the first, mainline churches and evangelical groups may come into a sharper competition for members and influence. There are in the United States alone about three thousand cults, many of them claiming to be based on religious convictions. These may grow, in spite of active efforts to reveal their methods of mind control and financial gains of the leadership.

On the other hand, the more honest movement of the new-age spirituality, illustrated by the books of Shirley McLaine, embraces an enticing set of mystical, Eastern-based "truths" exist in a pseudopsychological setting, dramatic symbols, dramatic incidents, and fashionable manner of expression. In the decades ahead of us, this blend of medievalism and modernity will produce more literature and groupings to serve those in quest of certitude and mysticism.

A more serious trend is the alliance of some churches with far-right political groups. Jerry Falwell and Pat Robertson have thus enlarged their roles of minsters of the faith to advocates of ideology. These roles, confusing but powerful in their union—though contrary to the principles of our founding as a nation—may trip over themselves, but not before successes in actual campaigning for offices of power and in legislation. Fortunately, subtlety or subterfuge is not characteristic of such groups, for as one leader confided to Rabbi James Rudin of the American Jewish Committee, his group seeks control of the "court room, the school room, the library reading room, the legislative room, and the bedroom." As the rabbi correctly notes, "much of our public and personal living takes place in these five rooms."[7] Occupants of these rooms such as women are not without their own power and strategic talent to dampen the Falwells and the Robertsons.

The development of science, in both its pure and applied aspect, has given rise to major ethical issues. Perhaps the most discussed issues have been the nature and meaning of life itself, in its very beginnings and in its end. This has plagued the abortion debate in the first case and the "dignity of dying" in the second. Assuming the eventual control over the sex of the child, the desirable proportion of males to females has intrigued ethicists.

A more recent issue, following upon the memory factor of computers, is the possibility of extensive information about all of us that has traditionally been a "private" matter. In view of LePlay's selection of the family budget as the key clue to an understanding, not only of the family, but of the society, his thesis would have been verified a thousand times over. The extent of such information about each of us was noted in a report to the *Atlanta Journal and Constitution* for 5 June 1994 which speaks of the one-page sheet of data kept on file by credit bureaus ... "a more concise and orderly record of your finances than you have at home."

> It lists all your credit accounts, old and new, and your payment history, your mortgage, your spouse's name, places you used to live and where you work, court records about you, and the names of all the people or companies that have taken a glance at your page. Atlanta-based Equifax and the nation's other credit bureaus make updates every month to 2 billion credit-card accounts. And 2.1 million times every day—550 million times a year—they sell your files or someone else's to a business trying to make a decision about whether to hire you, sell you an insurance policy or grant you a credit card or loan.

There are, of course, both legal and ethical rights that the public reserves about the individual: where one dumps his garbage, whether one molests children, the addition to our property for tax purposes, the licensing of dogs and cars, the inspection of food we buy. Thus we take for granted the innumerable and flexible lines between public and private. However, the United States Senate in May 1994 overwhelmingly approved an updating of the Fair Credit Reporting Act, with the House to follow. The business lobby is strong; the Atlanta company, Equifax, noted above, is a Fortune 500 company with twelve thousand employees worldwide. The financial industry as a whole remains one of the most powerful lobbies in Washington.

The possibilities and practices of compiling data of even greater consequence touches on the military, governmental operations, and business itself.

My point, in looking ahead several decades, is that the new infrastructure of communications will intensify the processes of confusing, crossing, eventually destroying the lines from private to public. These prospects, and the parallel attempts at control through legislation are not pleasant to think about, but deeply important to the freedoms and controls of a democratic society. As to the new power of the growing bulk of Americans who own, and to a smaller extent, use their home computers and begin to pry into the electronic lives of others, Neanderthal persons who are computer idiots like myself have less to fear, but we will soon die out. The coming world will have no place for those like us, especially in the workplace, in education, and sad to say, even in many forms of recreation.

One reason for errors and difficulties in the field of futurology is that in its formative stages it has been empirical—mostly economical sources—rather than a combination of quantitative and humanistic or qualitative factors. As to sources of data and their shortcomings, we note this compilation of expenditures for recreation, as summarized by the U.S. Bureau of Economic Analysis, the national income and product accounts of the United States, Volume 2, 1959–88:

Yet other data, from the Department of Commerce, reports that about 60 percent of all car travel can be attributed to pleasure or recreation, as in vacations. For 1991 alone, 60 percent of gas and oil (117 billion) and 60 percent of repairs (95 billion), total 212 billion. These additions come to 84 percent of the official total that was supposedly spent on all recreation. If, in addition, we were to add another 60 percent of expenditures for motel costs during pleasure trips, we might arrive at a doubling of the "official" 1991 expenditure. Then add to this the extra cost of highway construction. . .

And yet, the social scientist plays a highly important role as he

No. 398. Personal Consumption Expenditures for Recreation in Constant (1987) Dollars: 1970 to 1991

[In billions of dollars, except percent. Represents market value of purchases of goods and services by individuals and nonprofit institutions]

TYPE OF PRODUCT OR SERVICE	1970	1980	1985	1986	1987	1988	1989	1990	1991
Total recreation expenditures	91.3	149.1	195.5	208.4	223.7	240.0	250.9	257.3	258.7
Percent of total personal consumption [1]	5.0	6.1	6.8	7.0	7.3	7.6	7.8	7.9	8.0
Books and maps	10.5	10.2	11.4	11.7	13.0	14.1	14.7	15.2	15.4
Magazines, newspapers, and sheet music	13.2	18.4	17.9	18.0	18.8	19.9	20.3	21.2	20.3
Nondurable toys and sport supplies	9.5	17.4	22.3	23.6	25.5	26.2	27.5	28.1	28.4
Wheel goods, sports and photographic equipment [2]	10.3	20.2	24.4	26.3	28.3	28.9	29.0	27.7	26.4
Video and audio products, computer equipment, and musical instruments	8.8	17.6	29.7	35.4	39.0	45.5	49.2	53.2	56.2
Radio and television repair	2.7	3.5	3.3	3.2	3.3	3.4	3.4	3.4	3.5
Flowers, seeds, and potted plants	4.0	5.9	7.0	7.6	8.5	9.2	9.7	10.0	9.3
Admissions to specified spectator amusements	8.2	9.9	10.2	10.1	10.2	10.5	10.6	11.0	10.4
Motion picture theaters	4.2	3.8	3.6	3.6	3.5	3.4	3.4	3.2	2.9
Legitimate theaters and opera, and entertainments of nonprofit institutions [3]	1.3	2.7	2.9	3.0	3.2	3.4	3.5	4.1	3.7
Spectator sports [4]	2.8	3.4	3.7	3.6	3.5	3.7	3.7	3.7	3.8
Clubs and fraternal organizations except insurance [5]	3.8	4.0	6.3	6.6	7.0	7.2	7.4	7.7	7.6
Commercial participant amusements [6]	6.3	12.5	16.1	16.4	17.3	18.5	19.0	19.3	19.0
Pari-mutuel net receipts	2.8	3.6	3.2	3.2	3.3	3.2	3.1	3.2	3.4
Other [7]	11.3	25.8	43.5	46.3	49.3	53.4	57.1	57.3	59.0

[1] See table 699. [2] Includes boats and pleasure aircraft. [3] Except athletic. [4] Consists of admissions to professional and amateur athletic events and to racetracks, including horse, dog, and auto. [5] Consists of dues and fees excluding insurance premiums. [6] Consists of billiard parlors; bowling alleys; dancing, riding, shooting, skating, and swimming places; amusement devices and parks; golf courses; sightseeing buses and guides; private flying operations; casino gambling and other commercial participant amusements. [7] Consists of net receipts of lotteries and expenditures for purchases of pets and pet care services, cable TV, film processing, photographic studios, sporting and recreation camps, video cassette rentals, and recreational services, not elsewhere classified.

Source: U.S. Bureau of Economic Analysis, *The National Income and Product Accounts of the United States: Volume 2, 1959-88*, and *Survey of Current Business*, July issues.

explores the future through a study of trends, mores, and fashions (as in demography, or in such family practices as abortion, divorce, and single parenthood).

APPLICATION TO WORK-LEISURE

Two dynamic aspects of work can be noted. The intriguing fact is that these trends have entered into the purview of social scientists, prophets, and activists. These trends also enter the discussions of post-industrial and Third Wave writers (Bell and Toffler) and more moderately a *flexibility* within the work framework, as in hourly arrangements, the allocation of work tasks, retirement by stages, release from work assignments for community volunteers, pension plans, as well as vacation and sabbatical practices.

More extreme is the projection—some would call it the ideology—of the *end of work*, recently formulated by Jeremy Rifkin in his book by that name.

The second trend is the duality of the workplace itself as a material setting for transactions or manufactures, but also a social community or "second home."

The analysis of work in both these aspects as a social institution centered on such facts as the entrance of women in the workforce (largely for labor needs during WWII), the demise of family farming, the contradiction of the assembly line, automation, the democratization of processes (largely stemming from Scandinavia) cooperative ownership or management with employees, pension legislation, federal safety measures, and (starting in Central and Western Europe), flexibility in hourly and yearly work time, paid vacations (a national commitment in France), labor unionism, the growing professionalism among middle-management, personnel research, workplace therapy and recreation; and even the agitation by liberal-minded stockholders for social investments. These includes issues of direct interest to our roles.

Within this wide range of issues, a middle ideology has emerged, in part through the recent studies and activities of leisure—students as they enter the applied area of recreation. This position, held by the present writer, is that the "heavenly" goal for the faithful workers is being replaced by the "leisure ethic" and the lessening of work commitments in favor of earthly personal and family rhythms. A larger literature, expanding from the initiative of sociology, provides evidence for this generalization, especially from studies of satisfactions in work and from studies of early retirement, even from the choices of occupations by young adults in the universities and the community.

As we may expect, the ideology of leisure has moved into a serious concern with creative activity as a value and guide, going beyond the familiar levels of relaxation, travel, games, and hobbies. The elderly will perhaps be most affected and influential through their own prophets and activists. Adult education, both terminal and long-range in seriousness, will grow in its range and depth. A recent collection of serious essays on barbershopping—an association of men and women who seek to preserve a unique style of American singing—is one significant illustration of creativity in music. Other examples can be found in theater, plastic and graphic arts, crafts and poetry. In part stimulated by the motion picture *Schindler's List*, there has developed a literature from Holocaust victims that may in turn encourage historical, family portraits by older Americans, such as the Irish, who have diverse memories.

Most ideologists or scholars in the leisure camp are moderates when it comes to projections on the "end" of work. An example of a mild effort was attempted through a modest publication started by David Macarov, retired professor of social work (The

Hebrew University) and the late psychologist John Neulinger (New York University).

A significant contribution has been made by Jeremy Rifkin, an economist, in *The End of Work*. He concludes that:

> On the eve of the third millenium, civilization finds itself straddling two very different worlds, one utopian and full of promise, the other distopian and rife with perils. At issue is the very concept of work itself. How does humanity begin to prepare for a future in which most formal work will have passed from human beings to machines? Our political institutions, social covenants, and economic relationships are based on human beings selling their labor as a commodity in the open marketplace. Now that the commodity value of that labor is becoming increasingly unimportant in the production and distribution of goods and services, new approaches to providing income and purchasing power will need to be implemented. Alternatives to formal work will have to be devised to engage the energies and talents of future generations. In the period of transition to a new order, the hundreds of millions of workers affected by the re-engineering of the global economy will have to be counseled and cared for. Their plight will require immediate and sustained attention if we are to avoid social conflict on a global scale.[8]

Rifkin provides a wealth of data to support his thesis that "the triumph of technology appears more a bitter curse, a requiem for those who will be made redundant by the new economy and the breathtaking advances in automation that are eliminating so many human beings from the economic process.[9] He notes that already eight hundred million persons in the world are unemployed or unemployable.[10] The Third Industrial Revolution is substituting software for workers, while raising the productive capacity of America, Europe, and Asia. "Re-engineering" can reduce or eliminate between 1 and 2.5 million workers in the United States as the workerless factory becomes the goal.[11] Peter Drucker estimates that there will be a drop from 33 percent of U.S. workers engaged in manufacturing in the 1950s to less than 12 percent in the next decade,[12] calling this disappearance of labor the "unfinished business of capitalist society."[13]

Rifkin derides the familiar theory of "trickle down" benefits to the masses of workers in the form of cheaper goods, greater purchasing power, and more jobs.[14]

The one hundred million computers presently in use throughout the world, says Rifkin, will become more than one billion in a few years—computers more advanced, of course, than the present generation in respect to "intelligence."[15]

Special attention is paid in the volume to the situation of African-Americans and of farmers. He ends with proposals for the shorter work week, increased volunteerism to fill the enlarged portions of leisure, public works programs, and other steps for the "independent sector." The future, concludes this economist, must center in "human relationships, or feelings of intimacy, on companionship, fraternal bonds, and stewardship—qualities not easily reducible to or replaceable by machines. This end of work could spell a death sentence for civilization as we have come to know it; could also signal a beginning of a great social transformation, a rebirth of the human spirit."

Among the many predictions at the end of 1995 found in the *Futurist, a Journal of Forecasts, Trends and Ideas*, published by the World Future Society (reproduced in the *Atlanta Journal* and *Constitution* of 1 January 1996), little is said about the "end of work." A more moderate projection is provided: "The concept of the job is fading from the working landscape. In the future, workers will possess a variety of skills and responsibilities, rather than being confined to the parameters of a traditional job description. . ." This conforms to my stance on the matter. There will be no close to the challenges of the prophets or the activists, or to the tasks that will continue to confront the social scientists.

Thus the roles will increasingly intersect, and if we were to examine other issues, such as politics, or domestic/international commerce, their interaction would differ. The challenge offered by this essay is to distinguish the roles more carefully than I have done and to interrelate them more realistically. One clue to method can come from the interviews in the various books by Studs Terkel. Good anecdotal reporting is essential, and eventually, systematic case studies must come into play.

Everywhere, this development has been both campus-bound in Europe and America, but also in good part it is made possible by the free academic as he wanders to the society.

Alas, I will not live long enough to witness the directions predicted for the Third Industrial Revolution. As a "possibilist" I rely on the changing nature of human values; as a Dewey-ite, I rely on the intelligence of the coming generations. As one who has spent a career on the theory of leisure as both a set of actions and a source of values, I recognize more than even before that I and my colleagues worldwide have been engaged in thinking through one of the major solutions offered by Rifkin. His analysis confirms my deep-seated conviction that we have just begun to explore the possibilities of the workless segments of the present and future generations.

Finally, there is another development that should pose an ongoing challenge to the free academic: *social conflict* in an increasing complex society. A university commencement address I gave in 1994 began as follows:

> If Charles Dickens were here today addressing the graduates, he might begin by quoting—in the present tense—from the first paragraph of his *Tale of Two Cities:*
>
> It is the best of times, it is the worst of times. It is the age of wisdom, it is the age of foolishness, it is the epoch of belief, it is the epoch of incredulity, it is the season of Light, it is the winter of despair, we have everything before us, we have nothing before us, we are all going direct to Heaven, we are all going direct the other way. . .
>
> Indeed, what a dramatic time to graduate. The prospect for jobs is increasing, to be sure, yet it is a time of many doubts and much cynicism. . . We distrust the medical profession, the large corporations, the mass media, all politicians, and police. Children sue their parents. The corridors of elementary schools house policemen. . . A sports hero is accused of murders and is idolized by many, including a nun. Talk shows delight in dirt. Guns and drugs are for sale everywhere. My generation of elders is afraid to be on the streets.

The reality may be even worse. Many of these suspicions will pass in the decades, almost as fashions. The one that may not is the growing duality/polarity between haves and have-nots, the technology literate and illiterate, the young and old, those in power and the dispossessed, the blacks and whites. One example, illustrated in the Oklahoma City bombing, is the militia movement, terrorism against the symbols of society. Perhaps most important is the matter of two Americas, that of the African-American and the white Americans.

For a period, especially with the leadership of President Johnson and the moral message of Martin Luther King, it seemed that that course of events would continue to be constructive. And certainly, a middle class among the blacks became more evident; they occupied a sizable number of public offices on national, state, and local levels. But the inner city remained, summer riots led to the Kerner Report, many blacks chose to resent Jews, and several events of great interest to the TV public, produced or reflected the "two nations." One was the Rodney King beating in Los Angeles. A second was the acquittal of O. J. Simpson. As of this writing, it is early to project the consequences of the trial but it has been made clear, especially to the white community, that the duality goes beyond the Rev. Louis Farrakhan and the "million-man" march to Washington of October 1995. As for O. J., the editor-in-chief of the *U.S. News and World Report*, Mortimer B. Zuckerman, wrote on 16 October 1995:

> It is easy to understand why blacks are suspicious of the system. It is perplexing and dismaying to find the level of feeling so intense even in 1995 that many African-Americans can make a martyr out of a man who has no history in the civil rights struggle and who is a proven wife beater. It must surely be that for many blacks, the trial was not about O.J. Simpson but about reparation. He was merely incidental. A convenient symbol for paying back whites for the injustices suffered by blacks in a criminal justice system controlled by whites. The roots of the verdict, in this construct, hark back not to the blood trail left by the trails in the Jim Crow South, when white juries took little more than a heartbeat to acquit white defendants for the slaying of blacks—like Emmett Till—knowing that the whites were guilty.

Fortunately, many social scientists come from within minority groups, including Jews and blacks, and it is to that part of the campus that we may look for the dialogues and studies, even for formulations of public policy and community action. Perhaps the reconciliation of the technological and the humanistic can provide the fundamental task in the years ahead to the free academic.

9
Flexibilities: Lifestyle, Time and Place, Work

FLEXIBILITY OF LIFESTYLE

FLEXIBILITIES in lifestyle that *we* identify will be a mark of the decades ahead.

The older person—indeed, the middle-aged as well—can decide, and display in action, how old he or she wishes to be. Going back even more, I have often noted publicly, following four decades of teaching, that too many university students commit intellectual suicide as sophomores in the fraternity environment.

The flexible lifestyle is becoming a common pattern. The ideal of uniformity, expressed in the philosophy of assimilation, gave way to free-floating values. Contrary to the fears that Jacques Ellul expressed about the dominance of technology over every aspect of our lives, the position may be taken that technology has freed us, removing the obstacles of distance and time, bringing us into closer contact with strangers, with vast stores of knowledge and unusual experiences. As is often the case in social analysis, the polarity also presents itself that the lowest and highest denominators of entertainment and communications are also affected by technology—the pornography and violence on the same home screen that brings us Shakespeare and the Met.

For such creators as painters, sculptors, choreographers, musicians, architects, and writers, enormous advances have been made in areas of memory (for the dance), visual reality (for the architect), and experiments in sound (for the composer). Few writers, such as myself, still use pen and paper.

Looking ahead, the significant flexibility will be not only in the patterns of family (single-parenthood, for example) or education (bringing the lectures and laboratory demonstrations into classrooms from great authorities of the world), but across the life span. The European Community now speaks of my generation as the Third Age. It is a term that I find preferable to senior citizen. But it is possible that elements of the First and Second Ages will intermingle with the Third. Fundamentally, the course of biology dictates the sequence of childhood, adulthood, and mature age. Yet, new possibilities emerge for a change in the relative expectations for each. More older people, even "retired," are finding paid work for part of the week, and not alone for economic reasons. Some years ago the California senate considered a bill that, in part to alleviate unemployment, would permit several persons to be in the same job—job-sharing—and retirees were prominently mentioned in the testimony.

At one time, during my active period as consultant to agencies and countries abroad, an arm of the United Nations considered my proposal that an "hour bank" be studied, whereby a young person could be granted several thousand hours to travel, study—and soon—with full pay, and "work out" these hours in later years. The international labor union failed to take seriously this proposal, as I fully expected, nor did the American labor movement understand the idea at that time. (However, a guaranteed lifetime employment moves in that direction, if it includes generous sabbatical periods.)

One can foresee a pattern in which the person, with adequate financial support, does not live a sequential life of childhood, education, work, and retirement, but a life in which elements of youth (education) are naturally pursued in one's forties and fifties, just as the mature adult has always enjoyed childhood play all his life. A natural consequence of this is the mingling of several generations, in the classroom, in the park, in the community center, in the library and concert hall. On the matter of understandings, a cartoon recently showed an adult buying a theater ticket. He is told that he must be accompanied by a child because the picture requires considerable technical knowledge.

The discerning reader will put the question, finally, does the refocusing of work, or the restructing of time and place, or the greater flexibility of lifestyle, say anything to the ultimate issue of the *quality* of the leisure that is ahead of us, and constantly expanding in its importance and alternatives? The futurist is finally forced to admit that his instruments of projection can hardly encompass the changes in values. Ultimately, the future involves changing attitudes, intellectual fashions, new social patterns. The larger expanse of leisure is neither "higher" or "lower" in its potential. I recall the afternoon that we all heard the New York Philharmonic play a concert over the radio, celebrating its century of life as an organization. I said to myself that the orchestra that afternoon reached more audience than in all its one hundred years in the concert halls of New York City and elsewhere. The distribution of knowledge and the arts is a remarkable fact. Yet, evening after evening as I listen to the TV news channel of Atlanta bring the news, about all I hear is murder, rape, robbery, and more murder. All the rest that goes on in that interesting and vital community is ignored. Who makes those decisions? Who wants that emphasis? What is in the minds of the commercial sponsors? Distribution is merely a device, a tool, at the mercy of persons in power, the tastes and demands of consumers who speak up, and in the largest sense, to what some call the "spirit of the age," the "climate of opinion," or the "state of the culture." Some scholars, like Pitirim Sorokin, the eminent sociologist of Harvard, injected such terms as "sensate" and "ideational" into the discussion.

The "possibilist" position is the only possible position to take in the light of the three origins of the future.

1. One origin of the future is the *cultural momentum*. Even that is a matter of interpretation, not easily measurable, not always a consensus among historians, sociologists, or others. But large directions are discernable and indisputable, such as a growing technology, major demographic directions, and the like.
2. A second origin of the future is the *cultural conflict* that already exists today among those interests, motivations, and centers of power which have a stake in the future. The mass media is one, the corporate economic structure is another, the politics of ethnicity are a third, the current effort of the Christian coalition to invade education and government is another.
3. A third set of origins for the future is the *cultural breakthrough*, as in the possible revolutions in the life sciences, unpredictable directions in values, lifestyles, or social and political structures.

Each of these, and the interplay between them, can take us far beyond the scope of my present discussion, and yet it is in the light of such comprehensive thinking that a particularistic theme like leisure must ultimately be considered.

Thus personal safety and simple (humble) wisdom leave no other alternative than the stance of possibilism. Since my great-grandchildren, Rocky, Sara, and Michael, will see the unfolding of much of the twenty-first century, I designate them as my informants, whether to my space station or cosmic sphere far above or far below. Either eternity is a possibility.

THE RESTRUCTURING OF TIME AND PLACE

A remarkable fact of the present century has been our timidity in the use of time... The industrial system uses time as if we are still in the agricultural age, dominated by light and dark, night time and day time. Millions of workers descend on such cities as New York, emerging like rat packs from tunnels and roads because daylight has arrived, or will soon. Yet everyone has had good artificial light for decades; nightwork is looked down upon as somehow lower in prestige—a time for cleaning forces in the offices, at-risk waitresses and clerks in food stores or restaurants. The fact is that once inside, employees during the day are often unaware of rain or sun, warmth or cold.

The refocusing of work, discussed above, will force a rethinking of time and place. Alvin Toffler, in his *The Third Wave*, speaks at length of the needlessness of vast armies of employees following the sun, and equally important, "going" to a job that can as well be done at home.[1]

Even using work spaces in the city, especially for process and transactions that require the interplay of workers, another industrial superstition has been that there is something deified about the hours of eight to five. As in the case of TV programs in our homes before the VCR, we have as a mass of workers been unable to recognize a basic psychological and emotional fact—*that people work best when they want to work, and when these wants spring from the nature and family composition or personal taste.* Some of us are early-"morning" people; some of us are not awake until midmorning. All of us have moods when we would rather be at our favorite fishing hole than in an office cubicle. The working mother may want to be with her child on the first day of school. One's birthday may bring a pining for a short vacation. We are told by insiders at the auto plants not to buy a car produced on Monday or Friday, given the moods of men and women just before and just after the weekend. When I taught at a university in Florida, among the first observations I made was that it really was a four-day institution, with a minimum of courses on Fridays, especially in the afternoons.

Already, especially in central Europe, labor unions and managers have recognized those individual differences in temperament and in personal conditions, and instituted flexible work plans. Of course, many American companies have also done this, but the bulk of work scheduling goes on as in the past.

9: FLEXIBILITIES: LIFESTYLE, TIME AND PLACE, WORK 119

I feel safe in projecting a major change, with a resulting decline in boredom, accidents, and personal anxieties. Even farmers, as I have heard in meetings of cooperatives, can adjust their hours to achieve better lives. One such meeting I attended in the 1970s was on a cooperative in Bulgaria, where the term "post-industrial" was to be heard. Long overdue is a conference of leaders in New York City on the coordination of time to even out the ingress and egress of daily traffic; indeed, a national conference on the matter would be useful.

On the personal level, although we are responsible for ourselves, we also remain prisoners of the past. We recognize the need to "get away," but few of us dare to do so. I purchased a home in Champaign from a fireman who did; he decided to drive down the coast of Florida, find a desirable spot to fish, then find a job there that give would him the hours he wanted.

As early as the 1970s, U.S. Steel provided a sabbatical of thirteen weeks of paid free time for every five years of faithful work. But perhaps the most dramatic movement toward personal restructuring of time has been the move toward early retirement. This urge has coincided with the needs of many corporations to adjust their workforce. Both psychological and economic issues are thus being attacked.

So impressive is the benefit of retirement—if finances permit—especially with increased longevity and reasonable good health, *that the elderly segment of Americans are fast replacing the middle-aged as the role model of the successful man or woman.* Before the proportion of older persons levels out shortly after the first quarter of the twenty-first century, the elderly may discover their creative powers as they have already discovered their political power.

Well before the social gerontologists began using the terms "new-old" and "old-old," my elderly peers were well aware of the distinction. There were those of us who were, and still are, content to survive, follow the obituary columns, and await calls from our grandchildren. There were, and we are in growing numbers, those for whom survival is not enough. We are politicking, traveling, reading, painting pictures, and satisfying a wanderlust-mental need in Elderhostel classes. Some observers of this group of elderly, like Dr. Robert Butler (former head of the National Institutes for Aging) and Jacqueline Sunderland (former head of the artistic wing of the National Council for Aging) have been active on creative levels with the elderly for a very long time. Some, like the energetic Betty Friedan, while a pioneer in awakening the women of America, are now making rediscoveries of latent and active creativity among us, in her 1993 volume, *The Fountain of Age.*

I dare to submit the projection and vision that one day several major groups will discover us, and turn fresh attention to us as role models for creativity and wisdom. One is the segment of the mass media, especially the TV industry, whose inattention to my generation is not only naive but stupid, even in light of its own profit standards. The second is education, where studies and programs geared toward the nurturing of creativity remains fixed on children. A third is the community of the arts, which has assumed that the retired elderly in nursing homes form "kitchen bands" when they are not watching TV or sleeping. In painting classes that do exist for us, too many red barns are being pictured.

The Refocusing of Work

As my generation grew to maturity in the first half of the century, our thinking about the future came from the usual sources: a wide array of journalistic commentators, historians, novelists, science fiction, writers, economists, and other scientists. Demographers were widely respected. The Jean Dixons of the popular press were widely read. Walter Cronkite narrated an elaborate series of television projections called the "21st Century." Secretly, the military had to formulate its armament and research needs on insights into emerging international conditions. More immediately, and openly, Social Security administrators had to rely on the demographers for the directions of population growth.

All of education, implicitly, assumed the shape of the future in the curricula laid out for both general purposes of students, from K upward to the professional schools. And American industry and commerce, in spite of their ideological opposition to planning for governmental purposes, were themselves constantly looking ahead, whether they were making cars or building houses, calculating insurance rates, or financing the production of baby carriages.

Often, these attempts to look ahead were too short-range by highly paid CEOs. The failure of the Edsel is a case in point, and the ongoing thirteen-week mentality of the TV industry contributes to a lack of vision and courage.

It is my observation that a serious split has been occurring between various elements in work. This became evident several decades ago when careful studies of the American workers indicated a declining satisfaction in work. The general explanation then was the increasing "depersonalization" in work processes, especially as electronic processes invaded the environment, but beginning with the assembly line and the Taylorized attitude of managers toward workers, and ultimately the presence of robotics, computer controls, and anti-union attitudes.

My view is that the decline of the two-pronged model of work in the past was also due to the shortsightedness of corporate managers, for whom profit in the short run was the essence of success. On the other hand, the worker began to bring to his workplace a new set of needs and attitudes from his family life, his golf course, his stamp collection, and his longer weekend. He developed a sharper memory for his life away from work.

This refocusing away from work—*while at work*—was further influenced by the new teaching from the total of pseudopsychological influence of wives, relatives, therapists, and TV documentaries—to preserve family life, to avoid overemphasis on work, to spend more time with the children. One manifestation of these influences is the increasing pattern of changing careers in midlife.

These, it seems to me, are all interrelated, and contain the essence of leisure life tomorrow.

It has long been apparent that the concept *work* is divisible into two aspects: the first consists of actions, locations, materials, and the ultimate products. Increasingly, a second aspect has attracted the attention of personnel staffs, psychologists, family counselors, counselors on stress, and workers themselves, that is, the attitudes, emotional commitments, workplace friendships, work satisfactions or frustrations, pride, and personal judgments of success or failure. Most recently the factor of dependence on the powers above one in his work, including pension and retirement policies, has risen to the fore. Thus, the job or the work has its objective and its subjective elements, the productive and the humanistic.

These two elements have, together, marked the fact and the nature of work, and more important, the fact and nature of life. This twofold meaning of work has run through the industrialization of the past century. Its most obvious example is in farming, not as a way of making a living but as a way of life. The military provides another clear example of this merging. But even in the factory, the corporate office, and the commercial environment we see this duality. It provides in all these settings the model of manhood and successful living. At the expense of family life, the corporation rewards those who accept fully this pattern, even to the point of the kind of car one drives, the clothes he wears, and the willingness to relocate one's family.

Of course, what I am saying now is that *the sphere of leisure has invaded the sphere of work*. Put roughly, Homo Ludens (Man the Player), begins to replace Homo Faber (Man the Maker). Increasingly, work is the conscious means, and a full life is the conscious end. In 1967, Joffre Dumazedier named a book *Toward a Society of Leisure?*[2] This does not signify a diminution of work at all. It does signify a replacement of values that is made possible by the modernization of work, the distance of managers, and the total absence of investors in the lives of workers. The crowning irony of this development is that even the ending of a work career, capped by a dependable pension plan, is too often marked by outright deception or gross mismanagement.

I see no reason to doubt that this trend will continue. Here and there are spots in the industrial picture where such steps as flexible work schedules and profit sharing provide bright spots, and again ironically, some of these instances are in plants in the U.S. taken over or created by Japanese money. This trend has brought about the restructuring of time and space.

Part 3
Realization

Introduction

By "realization" I mean the fulfillment of contact between the campus and the world. At one time it might have been possible to discern a dual kind of communication, that in which a person is primary, and one in which the channels consist of publications, reports, articles, books, and so on. Such simplicity must now be avoided, given the wide use of computerization. There is no need here to track down the full significance of the present information flow as a bridge among institutions and sources of knowledge.

Professor-scientists who teach or carry on research will still write their books and articles, with materials available to them beyond the wildest dreams of their parallels in former history. This access to worldwide sources will not eliminate the functions of the academic person as *person;* indeed, his role will be increased, since he embodies the necessary integrative skills.

For the following section I have selected six pieces to illustrate several types of realizations by the author. Three are general in character, dealing with leisure and theory policy, leisure and ethics, and generational differences among scholars of leisure. Three are addressed to specific groups and issues: the professional of music education, a cultural agency within Puerto Rico, and the Knesset of Israel. Before each of the essays the reader will find information on the situation that led to the report.

Of course, the primary mission of such a volume as this is that it should be concerned with the impact of the free academic, first, on the institution and tradition that is represented as well as on those who are reached. Some institutions, like MIT, rely on outside relationships for some of their funding so that they may attract major scholars, provide research equipment, or bring in graduate students with potential. In addition, graduate students are often directly associated with their professors in the research project. This part of the inquiry is relatively simple, although issues of ethics may enter the picture.

Far more elusive is the question of the impact of the free academic upon the general society. The reality is highly complex, in view especially now of the computer revolution. The world is becoming a village, as has been often noted, and the village is now a presence in the information world. As far as I know, a systematic analysis has not been made of the complexities, and I am doubtful that definite, measurable analysis will be possible without a highly sophisticated model for the flow of information in multiple directions and on many levels. I speak for the situation now, not for a decade from now. Indeed, the vision expressed above for emerging flexibilities in the use of time and space may prove to be rudimentary; already flexibility in work is old hat in Europe.

The pace at which these complexities are resolved will depend in part on the politics toward the free academic taken by administrators of educational institutions, the deans of colleges, the heads of departments, and directors of research. I ask the question of myself: where in such a position of responsibility or guidance, and given the presence—actual or potential—of free spirits, what policies should guide me? The familiar trinity may still hold: to create knowledge, transmit knowledge, and to serve through knowledge. Underlying this trinity is, again, the principle of freedom for my faculties, my trust in them, and my dedication to the tradition of scholarly integrity.

As to the free academic, I have been in that role, and can set forth several convictions for my colleagues in this position.

1. Do not abuse academic freedom, violating the principle with arrogance or other forms of excess.
2. Do not hide behind the partial reality or the myth of "objectivity" to provide a shield for noncommitment.
3. Do not count on students as a shield or battalion for support from the outside, especially in light of their dependence on you.
4. Seek to avoid popular fashions or current sound bites of your field.
5. Avoid, as far as institutional policy permits, the pressure to publish before you are ready.
6. Be consciously aware that parts of the society, often among those in dominance, look down upon the academic person as "impractical," "theoretical," "liberal," "soft," etc.
7. Just as the industrialist these days, if he is progressive, provides a situation in which the workers can contribute ideas for development, so can students be given such opportunities; this is especially true where the students are increasingly of older ages than formerly, extending even to "senior citizens" as students.
8. The free academic has visions and he/she develops new thinking, but maintains a high regard for traditions and intellectual history.

Plato in philosophy, Maimonides in theological thought, and Max Weber in sociology, remain great sources of thought, and will remain so in spite of New Age fashions or advances, just as Beethoven will be Beethoven a century from now.

9. The free academic exists inherently in an environment that brings to the campus a microcosm of major human interest; it is his privilege and adventure to reach into those interests that may relate to the studies at hand, with an equality of respect for the many "truths" that are found there—truths that include kinds of evidence (as in the arts) that go beyond the empirical.

10. Finally, the free academic is a scholar with joy and pride in the life of the mind as well as in the welfare of the community and world. His success is a measure of how well he balances these hopes.

10
Leisure and the General Process of Theory/Policy

IN 1974 I met in Warsaw with the Minister of Work, Wages, and Social Affairs on leisure progress within the Communist framework. Less than a year later I was invited by a Prague affiliate of UNESCO, the European Center for Leisure and Education, to prepare a statement on leisure theory from a policy perspective. I decided to utilize the Polish experience. The paper serves here as one realization for the free academic in the international range.

The report appeared in the Czech publication, *Society and Leisure*, May 1975.

The growth of social science should not imply a singular solution to problems of "theory" and "policy," to thought-application, talk-action, or similar references and pairings. Debate and consciousness of some continuum from the realm of discourse to that of decision, action, or implementation are implicit with all social organization since the beginning of humanity, and they have always taken place in families, tribes, work groups, and the infinite variety of social structures. Ancient civilizations and rulers dealt with these dichotomies when they called upon sages for advice or carried on debates among themselves before undertaking wars. An objectification of political processes reached a high level with Aristotle and—within his own framework of moral goals—Machiavelli.

Certainly, one of the consequences of the enormous sums invested by governments and foundations in "pure" research since World War II was a mood of reckoning about the results of such expenditures. In the United States, for example, President Lyndon Johnson's request for a social accounting led to special conferences among "hard-core" physical scientists, reheating the familiar issues regarding their roles and responsibilities. The social sciences are less capable of demonstrating their usefulness, with such notable exceptions as the theorists investigating public opinion and the market research pollsters working for politicians and businesses.

If, as has been said, a remarkable characteristic of our time in history is "the invention of invention," then perhaps the combination of the social sciences with policy formulation has created the *evaluation of evaluation*. What social scientists attempt to do is to test the goals and assumptions that are integral to policy by a conceptualization of the whole process that moves from "problem" to "policy." In the most general terms—and hardly ever in the simple succession to be noted here—the continuum that penetrates all policy (in a tribal meeting or in a parliament) embraces these phases:

1. A feeling arises that something needs attention; that a "problem" exists; as for "crime," for instance, sociologists or the FBI produces *data*. The data confirm that something needs to be done.
2. The data, gossip, or perception is interpreted vis-à-vis some *perspective*, ideology, norm, standard, or philosophy; facts never "speak for themselves," but always fit into some prior or imposed construct of the nonproblematic condition.
3. Based on the recognition of the "problem"—i.e., the gap between what is and what should be—a *decision* is made by the king, sheriff, university regents, Congress, or Mother; the "policy" can, therefore, range from a decision to spank to the establishment of a new tax.
4. *Implementation* may follow or it may *not* as when the U.S. Congress does not appropriate essential funds to realize the decision it has reached. However, usually the spanking does crystallize after Mother's decision, or the jail term does follow a judge's sentencing.
5. *Evaluation*—sometimes—is formally made; informal evaluation is practically *always* made following any decision to act either on a personal level or on a national scale: (1) "I'm glad I took the new job"; (2) "The new law to save our town from pollution is succeeding."

The student of social or personal policy is interested in more than a spelling out of such items in the continuum. At least three issues confront her/him. First, she/he is concerned with the dynamics within each of these five components; for example, what are the origins of the philosophy? Second, how are the bridges established between the various elements of the process: the relevant roles, rules, traditions, bureaucratic barriers, communications, or levels of information? Third, what are the interrelationships of the various policies to the whole, i.e., of policies about crime, education, tax structure, energy controls, etc., to the national values of the United States in the mid-1970s?

Studies of leisure now proceeding in many parts of the world illustrate the points above. Since World War II, there has been a pronounced interest in this subject in all industrial nations—indeed, among so-called underdeveloped nations as well. They have all seen the impact of technology on changes in work structures, the aspiration for more time free from work, the increase in the number of cars, the enormous growth in uses of the mass media, the trends toward earlier retirement, and the larger expenditures for recreation. The past fifteen years have, therefore, witnessed a growth in research in universities, government offices, and such private quarters as marketing agencies and manufacturers of recreational equipment; also many conferences—regional, national, and international—have been held.

The *data* are clear: productivity increases under industrialization, earlier retirement, and longer vacations. *Philosophy* in the use of these data is highly unclear, perhaps involving the substitution of what Havighurst and others call the "leisure ethic" for the work attitudes that hang on from the past. *Policy* is similarly unclear as to how labor unions should negotiate vis-à-vis flexitime and the spread of work hours; educational policy has almost ignored the relevant data, and thus does not know how to develop appropriate attitudes. *Implementation* is cloudy, as the leaders of adult education, gerontology, and recreation still seek new programs for their clients and better curricula for their students. *Evaluation* is the most unclear of all as we seek to weigh "happiness" in general, "adjustment" for the retiree, or "equity" for those disemployed by cybernation.

As to the clarification of bridges from one of these to the other, Dr. Claudine Attias-Donfut of Paris and I went through an example of the difficulty. As coeditors of a special issue of *Society and Leisure* on the subject of leisure and the elderly (the "third age," to use the favorite European term), we decided to invite papers on current or recent research on the issue of "bridges." The directive to our authors is reproduced in the published issue; addressing ourselves to gerontologists, we noted that:

> The profession has its own theoreticians, but it is primarily a complex of persons and agencies who are responsible for governmental programs, nursing homes, and a variety of other "real" situations. Those who create policy or administer programs are not unaware of

theoretical studies on aging or on leisure; like policy or program makers in all fields, they rely heavily on experience, common sense, or intuition; aided (often spasmodically) by the professional journals, which they may (or may not) read, and the conferences which they may (or may not) attend. Their need for the help of scientists of leisure is real, with the rapidity of changes they confront.[1]

As an aid to the formulation of principles, we reproduced the generalizations of the American sociologist James Coleman.[2] Further to assist the authors, we postulated a total of eleven specific questions under the supposition either (a) that the scientific study was commissioned or suggested by a policy or administrative agency, or (b) that the scientific study was concerned and executed largely or entirely by the group of leisure scholars.

Although the resulting papers from various countries were valuable for their content, little if anything was addressed to the subject—*bridges* from theory to policy! Of course, much the same might have happened had we dealt with any other subject; yet the leisure field—especially as it relates to the elderly—offers a relatively direct opportunity for applications because of the number of applied areas that are affected by changes to an increasingly nonwork or lesser-work lifestyle.

Finally, leisure studies inherently integrate a range of issues that cut across and move into the micro- , macro- , and mid-range issues, as I have sought to demonstrate in my model. While these statements have not exhausted the theoretical issues of theory/policy, they do set the stage for later generalizations based on the current Polish experience.

In November 1974, I had the privilege of meeting for ten days in Poland with various teams of researchers and individual scholars whose major areas of interest lie in studies of leisure.[3] Aside from formal meetings with groups of teams, I spent many hours in informal conversations or social gatherings (which in Polish history—whether in homes or cafes—have long played an important role in molding opinion among intellectuals).

Poland's recent world importance and economic expansion are first noted: In 1970 it produced almost 40 percent of Europe's sulphur, almost 15 percent of its hard coal, and almost 5 percent of its seagoing ships. In 1974 exports increased 20 percent over those in 1973, with a 40 percent growth in exports to nonsocialist nations. The 1973–1974 industrial development equalled that of the total previous five-year period. Suffering from the energy crisis less than many other countries, Poland's sales of domestic products in the first quarter of 1974 exceeded by almost 12 percent those of the same period of the year before. Building, for instance, went up in comparable periods by over 20 percent. The total income of the Polish population during the year rose about 17 percent.[4]

Following the well-known revolt among shipbuilders, this expansion in consumer goods was in part a reaction to new political policies. For our purpose, it is to be noted that a planned economy must place a high value on accurate data about its own resources, needs and social trends—a point often ignored by western public opinion. Questions arise: What resources are put into the data-gathering process (as in the purchase of computers or the training of programmers)? What policy decisions are made for the use of such data (within the political "conflicts and compromises" to which Rokkan refers)?[5]

Thus, a special interest may be found in a statement by Edward Gierek, the First Secretary of the Polish United Workers Party's Central Committee. Noting that 1973 was the year of Polish science, Gierek said, "We must work out and introduce in practice an effective programme of a harmonious combination of scientific research efforts with a long-range development programme of the economy." On the same occasion, Jan Szydlak, PUWP Secretary, noted in more specific terms:

> Viewed against this background, the standing of the system of social sciences grows in importance as a base for theoretical research, helping to shape party strategy, which gives concrete shape to upbringing programmes and adds substance to our party argumentation. The programme outlined by the VI Congress and the overall shape of the policy practiced by our party established a propitious climate for general development of the social sciences. As a result, we noted significant progress in drawing social sciences increasingly into the practical service of society.[6]

The opportunity presented itself to explore high-level intentions more directly in Warsaw during two hours that I spent with Minister of Work, Wages, and Social Affairs Bralczyski. He was flanked by two staff members (one responsible for new investments for outdoor recreation, the other concerned with wage and hour policies); also present was Dr. Edmund Wnuk'-Lipinski, who headed a research team responsible to the minister.[7]

This ministry was only established in 1972. Although political policies relating to work and nonwork time had been established previously, the recent recognition of "new weapons"—i.e., new

10: LEISURE AND THE GENERAL PROCESS OF THEORY/POLICY

policies as well as data and research—resulted in the establishment of a "social fund" to help give direction to leisure enterprises, such as social centers. An example of another "tool" is the establishment of central libraries throughout the country designed to provide newspapers, journals, and books on an international level. Electronic data resources are being established, with the cooperation of ILO, to keep abreast of world scientific materials and research.

The Minister listed three obstacles in these efforts:

a. Social consciousness: society is not accustomed to extended leisure periods or its uses;
b. Governmental structure: older established agencies that are related to such issues are hard to change, such as the Ministries of Culture and of Trade (his office was therefore established as a coordinating agency);
c. Funds: other needs (pensions, housing, etc.) are also pressing for attention, incomes are low, and fee structures for recreational services must be limited, while simultaneously the level of life goes up.

All of these difficulties will decline in the future, but the Minister says that "convincing proposals" are needed both to arrive at political decisions and to achieve public support and "pressures."

The opportunity could not be ignored to raise questions about political processes with the Minister, bearing in mind a relevant comment made by Mr. Gierek in the speech quoted above:

> In accordance with our practice to date, we shall so organize state work and political life as to make every party member and every citizen, every worker, farmer and intellectual able to take part in the shaping of developmental concepts of Poland. Only in this manner will the collective wisdom of the nation be embodied in our development programme.

My question, therefore, was: Is there a realistic opportunity for policy pressures to develop from within the society, eventually affecting decisions at the top?

As to the use of the democratic process, the minister's reply emphasized that ideas and pressures already come from below; further, "by creating facilities we create needs, but this takes time." The research, by Dr. Wnuk'-Lipinski and others, is intent on finding what the population wants and what it needs, as well as how it acts. Organized groups constitute an important influence. "Social consciousness is determined by the social reality." Poland, he noted, does more social research than the other socialist societies.

An interesting thought was suggested by these replies, reinforced as they were by the heavy demand for social research (verified in close conversations with the researchers themselves)—that perhaps the research community, through this invitation to sound out the nation, is actually engaged in a cautious preliminary step toward a conscious democratic influence. If, indeed, the sociological studies show that the public wants more consumer goods, this would not in itself imply a criticism of the socialist system. What about *time*, a new demand also in the West, as evident in the labor negotiations of the past few decades? If Polish workers seemed overly anxious for more hours away from work, a serious issue might arise for socialist philosophy. One of the questions I put to the minister was whether there is not a "natural antagonism" between the traditional socialist ideological emphasis on work and the very recent interest in leisure? His reply was that there is no theory of leisure under socialism, that "connections" now have to be made. The image of the socialist citizen, he observed, is "active." Leisure can be seen in this light as an enrichment of the whole person, the "new person." Again, he returned to the tool of social research, because under socialism "recommendations based on data can be implemented." Indeed, based on just such studies, Polish workers have had, since 1975, their number of "free Saturdays" increased from six to twelve per year! What the population is doing with this new increment of time has become the immediate object of considerable research.

I must confess that this research "problem" of the new Saturdays for leisure struck me at first as somewhat extraneous. Yet, the American, typically used to fifty-two such Saturdays, is, after all, asking a similar question vis-à-vis the additional Friday in the growing four-day work pattern! Nor can the outsider remark that "there is no problem"—no matter how many free days are opened up to nonwork preoccupations—if there are sufficient alternatives for activity or participation, on the assumption that every person will somehow adapt. For now there are other questions: What is the relation of adaptation of free-time use to knowledge of opportunities, to one's "personality," to one's circle of acquaintances, to the nature of one's work habits and values? Those social scientists already admitted into the parlors of policy perhaps do well to maximize the risks of rapid change at the same time that they uncover and articulate the growth of new consumer demands and of emerging lifestyles. A real issue for "active" or "concrete" sociology is that it remains useful for policymakers only as long as it strikes an operational balance between data and debate. Apparently the acknowledged lack of leisure "theory" in Poland has not yet produced a conviction among the social scientists there that more time is, ipso facto, desirable.

Here, then, is the dilemma in the theory/policy continuum that seems to emerge from the current Polish experience:

The given situation for social scientists in Poland:

1. The political leadership is actively looking for new social directions.
2. The ministers in charge of administration and policy formulation are encouraged to draw on researchers.
3. The researchers in the leisure field are invited—indeed, expected—to contribute:
   a. to cultural policy directions,
   b. to knowledge of what the population does in its leisure and what it wants to do,
   c. to analysis of new work experiments such as flexitime.

The dilemma for social scientists in Poland:

1. The sudden demand (only since 1970) to come up with both general theory and specialized data.
2. The problem of developing a leisure theory:
   a. which is in accord with socialist theory,
   b. which is related to the mainstream of western social science,
   c. which is both action-oriented and "pure,"
   d. which is microcosmic, middle-range, and macrocosmic, and all at once,
   e. which is multidisciplinary.

3. The problem of so studying the Polish population that the results reveal what the present leisure practices or "needs" are and how potential patterns will develop without prior models for the public to observe.

In facing this series of situations and dilemmas, the institutionalization of Polish social science provides some clues to possible outcomes. Broadly seen, the Polish Academy of Science contains teams in the various disciplines that are relatively free to select research problems; and each of the ministries has related institutes, with scholars whose teams work on more immediate issues for the ministry, obtaining less scholarly prestige but higher salaries. If the theorists in the academy may be presumed to be conceptualizing in the sense of developing directions as well as in defining research, then Joffre Dumazedier's model for leisure policy is strikingly met. In his latest volume, *Sociology of Leisure*,[8] the eminent French scholar lists the following rules as essential for action in the leisure field: the research worker, the cultural expert, the administrator, and the politician. As to the first, Dumazedier advocates an "active sociology," so that the researcher not only lets the subjects of the inquiry "in on the feedback of his inquiry, he associates them to all its phases. He thus contributes to the progress of rationality in the thought process of men of action." The author speaks of the "cultural expert" role—the person who "is best qualified to propose the values a cultural policy should promote, with regard to creation, dissemination or the participation of the public." We may assume that in such an institutional arrangement as the Polish scholarship enjoys, members of the academy may properly assume the "cultural expert" role, largely because they are permitted to define their function. Indeed, Dr. Anna Olszewska, leader of leisure research in the academy, is presently preparing a book-length position paper in which she deals explicitly with values and national goals; further, she is secretary of a national task force headed by Dr. Jan Sczcepanski which has been given the assignment of defining Poland's "changes in culture, consumption, leisure, and system of values." The outsider may safely assume, therefore, that academy and institute scholars can be working on similar research problems; the real distinction lies in the "cultural" breath of the former, their explicit concern with goals, and the tendency for relating to other disciplines which a value orientation necessitates. Those Polish scholars who are affiliated with institutes, on the other hand, are deeply involved in more traditional research tasks that tie them closely to empirical studies in other countries.

The roles of *administrator* and *politician* are self-evident in the Polish situation. In western society, these roles are less distinct; we are inclined to think of the politician as the first of these two steps, with the administrator as the implementor. In the Polish structure, the post-1970 caution of political action arises from the greater heed of internal pressures, which may run contrary to national political policy vis-à-vis other socialist nations, particularly the U.S.S.R.

Another characteristic of Polish sociology is the nature of administrative leadership. Thus, the head of the Institute for Philosophy and Sociology, Dr. Jan Sczcepanski, is a scholar of world standing. In his other roles as assistant director of the academy and as an elected member of the Polish parliament, Dr. Sczcepanski's views on the place of social science scholarship in formulating national policy are singularly relevant.

The basic concern of all theorists and researchers is whether their studies and recommendations will be read, studied, and seriously considered by top officials. Americans still have a vivid memory of national commissions appointed by presidents—on pornography, civil rights, crime, national goals, etc.—and ignored. Sczcepanski, on the other hand, chaired a national commission to revise the educational system; the commission's work was completed in 1973; its findings were considered and debated in 1974; its proposals were implemented in 1975. Leisure scholars are presently participating in a new national task force on consumption patterns and lifestyles. The previous experience bears out the earlier statements by Edward Gierek; the sense of participation by social scientists in the current effort can be imagined. Sczcepanski is acutely conscious of the search for scientific objectivity and the necessity for a conceptualization of the research role vis-à-vis implementation. This does not imply a rigid organizational separation; indeed, there are academic scholars on the nation's planning commission.

To generalize on the Polish case study, no one has yet developed a classification of "problems" or "issues" that relate to leisure. Perhaps the time has not arrived. Overt issues can be specified, such as the uses of time, expenditures, or planning of public facilities. More covert or underlying issues are definable: new aspirations for discretionary time, relationships of "free time" to the restructuring of work or to such institutions as family and education. In Poland, the concern over the doubling of free Saturdays appears to the outsider as a *long-range* issue; the allocation of national investments is surely a *long-range matter. To these dichotomies we might add a third, the relation of leisure policy to the humanistic* and the *technological.* Iran may be used as an illustration of the last.

Even before the recent upheavals by which the oil-producing and exporting countries (OPEC) have become the dominant concentration of world capital, Iran had concluded that its cultural problem was to strike a balance between the model of western life and the preservation of its Islamic art and tradition. The plan to achieve this, announced by the shah, is noted:

> The discussions and debates which led to the delineation of the principal aspects of Iran's cultural policy became the occasion of a new cultural awareness among the participants. On the one hand, this self-awareness was coupled with return to the past, and on the other, with a rejection of unpleasant manifestations of Western cultural influence. The growing influence of Western culture in Iran, the reception of this, the search for a suitable antidote to it, and the preservation of the nation's identity, were questions which formed the core of these discussions. . . . The cultural policy of Iran chose the path of balance in this situation by making its goal the preservation of Iran's culture and its alignment with the conditions of the present.[9]

Leisure in the contemporary world moves ideally in both directions—toward the maintenance and understanding of nature and the handicrafts as well as toward the unabashed use of electronic and transportation facilities.

On another level, especially in nations younger than Iran, and where the many cultural and leisure facilities are developed as part of the profit-making economy, it is often the public segment that stresses the old (as in the preservation of parks) and the private sector that pushes the new (as in the mass media).

Poland's experience highlights the importance of political ideology as one crucial issue for leisure policy. In American terms one might refer to the issue as *commercial vs. public:* Presumably, the commercially oriented leisure (which comprises about 80 percent of recreational activity in the United States) represents the private interest and the public-oriented leisure represents the collective interest. In a thoroughly socialist society, there is little or no "commercial" entity for providing leisure goods or services; there is, of course, private discrimination in the selection and use of available resources. Organized effort is conceivable by action groups to enlarge the private domain, with little or no success at the development of privately owned profit-making services. A capitalist society such as the United States has not reached the relative balance of private/public to be found in the mixed economies of Scandinavia or in the variety of systems of west central Europe, but the direction of leisure facilities seems to be increasingly toward more public ownership and control of facilities. In the United States the Amtrak railroad system is a combined federal and private corporation; our 707 commercial television stations are somewhat balanced by the public stations; our national, state, county, and local park acreage far outweighs the total of commercial parks, resorts, and amusement areas.

The Polish report—referring to the public statements of its

post-1970 leadership—suggests a greater reliance on attitudes and wishes of the public as to what the government should provide. This is a far step, of course, from democratic control, for we may assume that the public demand will not be allowed to exceed the basic political limits or structure, although the analysis of Poland above suggests that current research bodies are in an unusual position to discover and report all demands that may deviate from past practices.

These observations suggest that although planners of leisure function within the traditions of their social and political systems, these systems are in the process of significant modification, with the leisure phenomenon as an increasing tool and manifestation of change. Expenditures for commercial recreation may be expected to decline in the next few years as living costs (including gas and oil) go up. Simultaneously, however, interest in nonwork patterns will paradoxically grow—as in the socialist, work-oriented societies—so that national planners in all societies must look to other indices than expenditures for an understanding of the emerging leisure milieu. The work ethic is doomed as machines are applied to carry out the dirty and tiring and repetitive tasks; socialist or capitalist ideology will not stand in the way.

This implies a shift of the problem from *culture* as such to the more inclusive concept of *leisure culture;* what this conceptual enlargement does is to combine *process and content*. If science and art can live side by side—and, indeed, serve each other—then leisure becomes a pivotal or integrative force between culture and technology. One is, in fact, led to the conclusion that this issue will dominate all others with regard to national leisure planning. In such areas as the United States, the current realization resulting from the energy crisis is that we have overlived, overspent, overlit, and overfed; the necessity for living within our means coincides with the appeal led by youth in the late 1960s for Reich's Consciousness III—i.e., for a return to simple things and to humanistic values as a reaction to overcomplexity and impersonalization.

All industrialized countries have already experienced this confrontation to some degree. It is on smaller issues—uses of time, retirement policies, etc.—that various nations will differ, depending on their traditions or degrees of technology, and their work/nonwork structure. My view is that the success of our emerging theory construction about leisure will depend on how clearly we can see connections between these secondary issues and the major area for which Iran has provided a sharper illustration than Poland.

The Polish case makes clear the reliance of leisure planning on theoretical conceptualization and knowledge. On the level of *national* planning, the European nations as a whole are ahead of the United States. In the democratic societies, the nonprofit, professional organizations are more developed and effective in applying pressure on their respective governmental bodies. In the United States, for example, the National Recreation and Park Association (at least until it discontinued its research branch) could be expected to possess an unequalled body of data as a basis for its recommendations to its members and to governmental agencies.

It may seem that the capitalist society possesses a larger array of agencies that help the public to make decisions on the uses of leisure, especially the manufacturers of equipment. For there is no doubt that such equipment not only *responds* to the desires of its consumers, but also serves as "tastemaker." However, in Poland, as in the other socialist societies, there are agencies that do not exist in nonsocialist nations. For example, labor unions assume responsibility for providing vacation services for their employees at low cost.

Research on decision making is needed from scholars in leisure. Attention is called to the current research on decision making within the family—including decisions about leisure behavior—by the seven-nation team under Dumazedier and Bosserman.

Researchers in Poland are presently dealing with traditional sociological issues: how persons are using their time, perceptions of their needs, trends in work structure, and the like.

An inventory or testing of services delivered enters such studies indirectly, as in a comparison of satisfactions derived from houses of culture (community centers), television, movies, the use of cars for vacations, and so on. It would be possible, in the context of any society, to draw up lists of typical activities—travel, adult education, sports, arts, socializing, etc.—and to note the major agencies that make such experiences possible—schools, churches, unions, clubs, public or private travel facilities. A host of issues then arises with respect to comparative costs, controls over client or user, regulations over services, and trends in types of service—to list just a few.

The concern over the doubling of free Saturdays in Poland suggests that the implementation of national work policies has direct impact on leisure prospects. In this case, the conjunction of two

10: LEISURE AND THE GENERAL PROCESS OF THEORY/POLICY 141

twenty-four-hour periods, forming the "weekend" that is familiar in other countries, is far more than twenty-four plus twenty-four; the "bulk" time opens opportunities far different than a mere doubling of free time. The Congress of the United States has decreed the change of five national holidays so that these become part of a three-day weekend; these fifteen days comprise a distinctive illustration of bulk time.

Thus, the implementation of leisure policy involves legislation or impact on time segments as well as agents of information and service. For instance, in Poland there is a special national fund which makes money available to poor families to be used exclusively for vacations. A longer-range form of implementation consists of the education of school children or adults in the use of time, as in visits to museums; in the United States considerable activity of this type goes on, as in centers for the elderly.

There can be few abstract principles to guide leisure policymakers along these lines. Only in the most general way—and pointing to both eastern and western cultures—can we suggest such principles as the provision for a wide range of tastes or the adequate dispensing of information about alternatives. But the view will be heard that these are principles of a different order than must concern the body of research. However, the Polish example has already set apart those abstract researchers of the academy from those responsible to administrative bodies. The latter translate the research into programs; in a reasonable period, the success or failure of the decisions will cast an evaluative light on the early research findings. If 1975–76 is a crucial period for Polish researchers in leisure, 1980–81 may be such a time of early evaluation; among Polish commissions is one committed to forecasting/planning for 2000 A.D. By the latter date, leisure scholars there, if successful in their general analyses, will have firmly entrenched themselves and led the way for all other socialist societies. The tests of their theories will come through pragmatic applications, not through mere acceptance of theory by other theorists.

Implementation is the means through which goals may be realized. The remarks of Dumazedier are appropriate for bridges to other areas of public policy as well as to the field of his own expertise, leisure:

> ... the relationship between thinking about objectives and thinking about means is renewed ... has always existed in common sense decision-making, but it has not become more rigorous. To the same objective correspond several possible choices of means. ... Studies

are required to formulate *all possible interventions* in a given field and a given period, and to foresee the likeliest result of each given occurrence. . . . Should priority be given to equipment or to the men who operate it? Should there be more public or more private institutions? And what should the ratio be?. . . . Even the problem of nationalization or socialization can now be put in terms of the social or cultural output of the given organization, in connection with development criteria.[10]

The most difficult type of evaluation is that which is the most important—i.e., evaluation of the progress toward the realization of cultural goals. The difficulty arises from (a) the problem of formulating such objectives as "personal growth" in measurable ways that do not obfuscate what are inherently nonmeasurable elements; and (b) the problem of devising the measurement techniques, even with a clearly articulated ("researchable") design. If the decision is made to use criteria other than those that are measurable, a gain is made by involving canons of proof from such fields as philosophy; a loss is expectable from the variety of perspectives and the familiar inability or refusal of different disciplines to talk to each other.

Polish statements of broad objectives are understandably couched in Marxist terms. There is no substantial disagreement from the various socialist sources. An important Czech study states that leisure should be linked with "the transformation of work" and that leisure policy should stimulate subjective wants that are "in harmony with the development of the individual and therefore of the society, too."[11] In Hungary, changes in cultural life call for "more conscious and more purposeful social action" combining empirical study and "social thinking." Such countries—much as they may speak, as did the minister in Warsaw, of the importance of establishing "new connections" between work and leisure—are perhaps not yet ready to consider leisure itself as a positive cultural entity which carries possibilities of human development separate from work, nurturing human values and providing a basis for genuine creativity. The latter view—leisure as a base for cultural development—is even more difficult to evaluate by any criteria of success. At least the therapeutic view of leisure is somewhat measurable in the success of its antithesis—work.

The ultimate assessment of leisure in any society is a part of larger evaluations of the given culture. Data on use, as in most countries, are now available for such items as time in watching

10: LEISURE AND THE GENERAL PROCESS OF THEORY/POLICY 143

television, the amount of reading, club life, and so on. As isolated bits they are revealing, and more so (as in the Szalai study) when many countries are compared. But ultimately the usefulness of such data must be considered in relation to a nation's own traditions and goals.

A major issue has emerged in all industrialized parts of the world, and in the form of a warning among the less-developed nations: recognition of the stages at which technology becomes counterproductive. Jacques Ellul, Lewis Mumford, and Radovan Richta (and the report of the Czech Academy of Science) have articulated the warning in the broadest levels; environmentalists have been the most conscious of the issue. The concern goes beyond the balance between cultural traditions and technology which was noted in the statement earlier from Iran; in its present form, the question is whether humanism, whether interpersonal relationships, whether "quality" rather than quantity of life can remain inviolate, or whether (as Ellul argues) technology has a momentum of its own that stultifies leisure and all other human expressions. Poland has already reached the point of confrontation, at least in such intellectual centers as Warsaw and Cracow. But the outsider suspects that at this point it remains more on the intellectual level than in places like New York or Tokyo, where pollution of the air and the glut of population have deep impact on attitudes. Leisure serves public policy in such settings as the pivot between the "social structure" and the "cultural life." It is the confrontation of these levels, says Daniel Bell, that will mark the ultimate issue of the post-industrial society.[12]

11

Leisure and Ethics: Connections and Judgments

In mid-April 1989, a Leisure and Ethics Symposium was held at Boston University, cosponsored by the American Association for Leisure, the American Alliance for Health, Physical Education, Recreation and Dance, and the Boston University Program on Leisure. Dr. Gerald Fain of Boston University served as initiator and chairman of the sessions that attracted papers from thirty scholars. It was for me a pleasant return to an important institution and city after a quarter of a century, when I had been at its College of Fine and Applied Arts—literally a block from the site of the symposium.

Ethical considerations are often dominant in the relation of the two parties of our concern. As a free agent who is an outsider to the agency he is serving temporarily, the consultant may be in a vulnerable position of not being sure of the real purposes for which he is engaged. This was a feeling especially within communist institutions, but one that I also felt within VA hospitals of the United States. It is a situation that often occurs when there is an overlapping of functions, and the consultant is called in by the representatives of one profession or the other.

This essay is reproduced with the kind permission of the American Alliance for Health, Physical Education, Recreation, and Dance of Reston, Virginia, and Dr. Gerald Fain, Director, Leisure Studies Program, Boston University.

This historic conference provides a climax to a quarter century of significant studies of leisure. That is a short time for systematic beginnings to a new contemporary issue. The term itself goes back to Greek times, as the political scientist, Sebastian de Grazia, reminds us in a philosophical work.[1] A historian of medieval Europe, Johann Huizinga, provided the classical commentary on "play."[2] Among the shrewdest insights on leisure in relation to

11: LEISURE AND ETHICS: CONNECTIONS AND JUDGMENTS   145

work, aside from our own Stanley Parker,[3] are those of a recently retired professor of social work at The Hebrew University of Jerusalem, David Macarov.[4]

Observations on leisure have come from other historians, explorers, missionaries, anthropologists, and archeologists.

Projections have entered analysis and public policy as leisure values injected themselves into labor-management negotiations, into national socialist planning, into the industrial transformation of Japan, and more recently, into Third World thinking.

Judgments have entered our field under the guise of policy making, the process of grant-gaming, and the responses of publics to our programs.

Earlier approaches by both academics and decision-makers emphasized the available data. Our studies in America began at a midpoint in this century, at the time when the social sciences were developing a virtuosity in quantitative techniques, enhanced enormously since then by technological gadgetry. It was a simplistic but a natural step to base our studies on such manageable items as expenditures in time and money, with a passing glance at more difficult issues such as objectives, goals, or meanings.

In that elementary phase, still with us in many ways, ethics hardly entered the discussion. It was simpler to tabulate the answers given by Delta passengers to the questions we prepared for them, and ethics arose only if we sold the replies to American or United Airlines.

Yet the more successful we became (as in the massive material gathered for the recent President's Commission on Americans Outdoors), and the closer we came to an influence on legislators or administrators, the greater became the need to attach qualitative judgments to our quantitative data. The public was constantly engaged in its implicit judgment as it used—or did not use—our areas of play, our community centers, parks, concert halls, museums, or even the streets; it was helped or hindered by the authors of blue laws, by parents, by peer groups, by critics of the popular culture. The larger application or impositions of "user fees" will force closer judgments by the public.

Questions of values and judgments do not make sociologists comfortable. We squirm in their presence. They take us farther from the idols of the hard sciences, which are more adept at avoiding "soft" answers. Values are foreign to the Bunsen burner or chemical symbols on the laboratory wall. Coming from the field of music, I had always been comfortable with truths other than those espoused by my more positivistic colleagues in sociology and their neighbors in the silent parts of academia. I was less allergic than were they to such heretics as C. Wright Mills, Pitirim Sorokin, and Howard Becker.[5] Even in such a great department as Illinois, it was possible to obtain the doctorate in 1952 without even one course in statistics, before Apple, software, and Fortran were heard of. If philosophical considerations entered our consciousness, as it did among the early plowmen in the field, it was soon uprooted by the seeds from Silicon Valley. Max Weber's sermon of an earlier epoch on science as a vocation[6] was resurrected by the new generation, not entirely aware of his less-than-quantitative "ideal construct," which Florian Znaniecki endowed on his students,[7] together with such other pre-Fortranites as Simmel.

I smell a new direction among our children and grandchildren in the academic corridors. They will be more willing to reread the giants. They are all virtuosi in the use of gadgets, but may be more inclined with the passing years to hold them at arm's length. It may be related to the ending of a century, to dramatic social and symbolic changes, perhaps even to an older public that is increasingly critical of confusing accuracy with significance. This new scholarship, I predict, will be less likely to worship numbers-oriented hypotheses in the face of more humble propositions as the following:

1. Leisure, either as a social phenomenon or as a base for public policy, cannot be understood except with ethical considerations.
2. This is fundamental because even the analysis of leisure, and certainly its structure and organization, is naive—indeed impossible—without implicit or explicit concern with goals, objectives, purposes.
3. These goals or purposes are external to leisure actions or interests per se, originating in the larger concerns of the society; therefore leisure is inherently tied up with both the nature and sources of values in general and ethical systems in particular.
4. The term "ethics," from either a scientific or a philosophical view, needs to be broken down into types or thematic systems, and applied specifically to the nature of leisure as a form of social control, social conduct, or symbolic action.
5. Similarly, leisure is also too broad a term for loose reference to ethics, and must be broken down into its major approaches or subsystems.

As a caveat in even suggesting the huge task implied in this approach, especially the last two propositions, I note that an ad-

11: LEISURE AND ETHICS: CONNECTIONS AND JUDGMENTS

vantage of a long lifetime is a freedom from both institutional and disciplinary parameters. Now long retired, there are no deans to fear nor jobs to seek. Hence one may, with impunity and even a happy irresponsibility, venture where scholars and fools, sometimes mutually replaceable, might fear to tread.

Hence, to save us three lifetimes and endless footnotes, I shall complete the task in three short sections of this paper. With ethical systems now delineated by a miracle, another three sections will guarantee sainthood through another trinity of approaches to leisure. In only a few more pages of Ruskie-ite imagination calculated to enrage this august scientific community, connections will finally be drawn between the double trio. Then, God bless us all, the conference can proceed with blessed stability. I recall, during my years of happy residence in Boston, the story of three Beacon Hill dowagers who passed on about the same time and confronted St. Peter. With the graciousness that is accorded proper Bostonians, he invited them to pass down the cosmic corridors and decide for themselves where they will spend eternity. They saw a neon sign, HELL, and knew this was meant for New Yorkers. Then came a mellower, hand-painted sign, HEAVEN; here, of course, they belonged. But just before turning in, they spotted a *Webster's Dictionary* on an antique stand at the entrance to a corridor marked LECTURES ON HEAVEN AND HELL. Let us go with them on this path that they took; surely, both destinations can be encompassed on the journeys to either ethics or leisure. . . .

Three views of ethics will be considered: ethics as *morality*, *power*, and *rationality*.

I

Morality

There is, first, a conception that equates ethics with morality, with the good and the bad. We speak of ethics among physicians in the hospital, lawyers in the courtroom, or priests in the confessional. There can be foul-ups, such as the sociologist who went to jail for carrying a hidden taping device with him into jury duty, or the national scandal as another sociologist and a psychologist carried hidden tape recorders throughout Italy as they confessed to a variety of sexual transgressions to find out what various types of priests would say.[8] With this conception of ethics we assume, according to our cultural traditions, those transcending principles of good and bad behavior with roots in theology, law, custom, or the maxims of motherhood, manners, and manhood. Children are taught such principles in school, often through legends, folktales, nationalistic songs, holy writings, proverbs, salutes, culture heroes, and role models. One George is remembered not only for his career as our first President, but also through a cherry-tree tale; a later George will some day also be judged on his career as our forty-first President, but also for a highly unethical, voodoo television campaign that brought him into office.

All societies, regardless of degree of development or ideology and economic structure, must have rules of conduct, teachings on right and wrong, even if mouthed only on holidays. All segments of behavior, including the use of discretionary time, are imbued implicitly with the resolutions of such mores and morals.

Power

Morality is the first basis for ethics. Power is the second. Its core is not the "good" or the "bad," but based on active or passive relationships between persons. Thus, Martin Buber spoke of the "I" and "thou" relationship.[9] Germans equate the closeness of persons with their use of "du" and "sie." Confucianism emphasizes in its philosophy the interaction of roles: the governed and the governor, the parent and child, the teacher and student.[10] Sociologists speak of majorities and minorities, not numerically per se, but in anticipated behavior. The ethical principle here refers to the dignity of those with the least power. Dignity for the weaker was elevated to an international level in the human rights agreement of the United Nations, brought about largely through Eleanor Roosevelt. Christianity has its Golden Rule, expressed by all major beliefs and humanism, all relying on the common good, or the moral imperative. Leisure absorbs this principle.

Rationality

A third form of ethics, based on rationality, was advanced by the American philosopher E. Jordan of Butler University. Ethics, he wrote, is concerned

> with the relation of knowledge to control, and this relation rests on the nature of man and of the world in which he lives . . . But its primary purpose is not to understand the relations as they are given

in fact but as they are possible between man and the world, for it is this region of possible relations that imparts the action its ethical character.[11]

In other words, when a society does not make use of the knowledge that exists for moving toward desirable objectives, an unethical relationship exists between scientists or those whom Florian Znaniecki called "men of knowledge"[12] and the policy-makers. In this sense, the responsibility of those with knowledge is to produce accurate and relevant information and to make this available in understandable form to others. Men and women of knowledge, especially of the academy, are guardians of rationality.

II

Next, I propose three approaches to the study of leisure: leisure as *theory*, as *action*, and as *symbol*.

Theory

The first responsibility of the leisure theorist—no matter what disciplines are involved—is the delineation of leisure among such other interests or institutions as science, religion, education, law, family, or government and economy. This major task may call upon political science, sociology, theology, history, philosophy, demography, geography, anthropology, psychology, psychiatry, or combinations of these and other disciplines. That sociologists were among the pioneers in serious studies of leisure may be historically true, but the case can also be made that until Spencer and Comte, sociology itself was born as a hybrid.

While social science theory draws upon or even rests upon such other hybrids as logic, symbolism, and empiricism, the theorists' role—not so much in the academy as in the halls of government and in the community—is to prepare tools for the actions of others: legislators, educators, parents, counselors, prison wardens, recreation leaders, the general public, and private persons. This ethical responsibility, implicit in the theorists' historic function, assumes and demands a respect for truthfulness, completeness, innovation as well as stability, and—within the traditions of the theorist's discipline—a certain objectivity. The Greek origins of ethics is *ethos*, or *character*.

Character, in reference to scholarship, means that integrity is not for sale, that cultural ethnocentricity is avoided as far as possible (especially since leisure studies are increasingly international) and that in leisure there is a respect for all tastes and a simultaneous respect for accumulated wisdom and moral principle. Scholarship, in our field perhaps more than others, must avoid such academic drugs as wasteful grants, or the temptations of current academic fashions.

Actions

The second approach to leisure is through actions, that is, a consideration of its unlimited activities and experiences. The theorist cannot avoid categories, and we all follow Dumazedier's list of the intellectual, social, physical, and aesthetic.[13] My 1975 book seeks to move away from this tradition, dealing instead with categories of purposes and dynamics, such as rest-restlessness or mobility-immobility.[14] Recreation leaders are primarily interested in specific typologies as guides in determining training for leadership, essential equipment, appropriate spaces and times, and the self-selection by publics.

However, we must not narrow the group of recreation leaders to those who are profoundly trained in universities, belong to NRPA or WLRA, or attend conferences. Among those who are taste-makers for leisure activities are sports promoters, magazine editors, drug pushers, distributors of pornographic materials, owners of legitimate bookstores, employees of the local press, gun distributors, astrologers, and travel agents. Collectively, they design the facilities that the rest of us use; they influence what we see, hear, and do the thousands of hours we devote annually to our private, so-called "free" periods, where we spend our evenings, weekends, and vacations; even with whom, how long, at what cost, and in what sequence. These makers and shakers collectively augment, supplement, and undoubtedly surpass in power and influence the more angelic souls who play for us in the Boston Symphony, organize children's games on playgrounds, and dispense library cards. As leisure activities grow in scope, those who influence the nation's leisure will not have followed our Bostonians to those lectures on heaven and hell. Ethical considerations will be at a minimum.

Symbol

The third approach to leisure is through the commitment by the public itself to symbols, especially to the so-called "leisure ethic." By this we imply that leisure as a whole has become a major value, both a means and an end. The end is seen in various ways: as a personal reward for prior hard work; as one's right to rest, or play; as an inherent part of the rhythm of life; or, in the socialist agenda, as time to be devoted to study and serve an ideology.

But by the "leisure ethic" we also imply a triumph of the human will and of the industrial enterprise over work itself, based originally on survival needs and embellished later as symbolism for heavenly reward. Currently, the Japanese government is advocating more leisure for its masses, as an economic national measure; thus Japan moves toward a major social, symbolic transformation. Our transformation accompanied the rise of our industrial and economic power, an integral part of the emergence of social values; Japan, already highly developed, seeks to use leisure as a break, a control, a policy means. Among us, leisure as end has caught up with its function as means. Scholars of leisure will have the task in the next fifty years of comparing these cultures, and perhaps modifying Max Weber's work in the course of this cross-cultural study.

Within our own Western cultural frame, I have a very personal reading of the leisure ethic: a theological, at least a spiritual three-act drama: Judaism in the first act set the issues, inventing through the Sabbath what Abraham Heschel has called the "architecture of time."[15] Christianity found these issues of time, lifestyle, and rewards central to its maturity in the later centuries as capitalism and industry evolved, and relied on heavenly stimulation to confront the oppression of the have-nots by the haves. Now came, in our lifetime, a humanism that seeks to combine the earthly orientation of Judaism and the heavenly rewards of Christianity. The day may come when some theorist expounds on leisure itself as a new religion. This newborn Georg Simmel of tomorrow will perhaps note the various archetypes of leisure actions—sports, arts, etc.—as quite comparable to denominations, each subsuming types of values, attracting types of minds, requiring types of sacrifices and commitments. Already we are aware that the arts, as a leisure form, serves to link the present with past generations, as does sports. The new physics, when it matures from the present infant stage, is already speaking of a "wormhole theory," in which a "time traveler" might theoretically be able to change events of the past as an application of Einstein's theory of relativity. Already the minds of each of us are historically and laterally compartmentalized, so that our politics may be ancient, our musical tastes baroque, our attitudes about love romantic, and our worship of the gods, primitive. In our work processes as we sit before a computer terminal, we may be entirely postindustrial, yet we think, pray, speak, eat, read, and dress in a multitude of time levels. What the religions do, including the anticipated religion of leisure, is provide some thread of continuity; as a Jew, I find a remarkable paradox in the adaptability and usefulness of that tradition as it served through persecutions and Diaspora, a fact that was celebrated in 1992 in the five hundredth observance of the Spanish Inquisition, and now finds itself as one unique guardian of leisure in a moment of triumph for mankind. That is the ultimate significance of the leisure ethic: a celebration, a triumph over labor, a universal and democratic reaching for self-actualization on a grand scale.

III

The introduction to this paper had promised that following the exposition of ethical approaches, and similarly a threefold view of approaches to leisure, connections would be drawn between these trinities. As the skeleton for these linkages, I offer the following hypotheses, or for the more humble among us, three propositions.

   a) *That those among us who are primarily theorists are responsible for the ethics that Jordan talked about: the rational use of available knowledge.*
   b) *That those among us who are primarily the policy makers, that is, those who administer or lead leisure-recreation activities, are responsible for the ethics centering on power relationships.*
   c) *That of those among the total population who speak of the leisure ethic there is responsibility for the general consideration of ethics centering on morality as a general postulate.*

Leisure theorists and the ethics of rationality

On the whole, it is my judgment that theorists of leisure have performed this ethical responsibility effectively. Any policy maker who looks into this field for such purposes as recreation programming will by now find a wealth of data amid careful observations. For example, a quarter century ago, the federal legislation concerned with the purchases of lands for national parks launched a massive collection of twenty-two reports for the Outdoor Recreation Resources Review Commission, the ORRRC;[16] this led President Kennedy to establish a Department of Outdoor Recreation. Only last year, President Reagan was handed recommendations and a massive anthology of working papers in the President's Commission on American Outdoors.[17] On leisure in general there have been numerous reports by private and public agencies, including Harris polls, books and innumerable articles and monographs by individual scholars, and bibliographies and studies by the research committee of the International Sociological Association and by the World Leisure and Recreation Association.

The ethical aspect of these many surveys and tabulations is probably on a par, no better and no worse, than in other social science areas. I am as guilty in the shortcomings of our field as anyone, as unethical as anyone—if that is the judgment—in missing obvious leads and closing my eyes to obvious materials. For example, with others I have often noted the reduction in the number of hours we work now in comparison with the year 1900. Almost no attention has been paid to a more significant number, that is, the expansion in the hour's potential during the intervening decades;[18] such comparisons do exist for the value of "real" money in purchasing power. Even worse, we have no quantitative or qualitative comparisons of the meanings of a day in potential time, a weekend, and now with many retirees, of a year or a decade of so-called free time. I had at one period opened these issues with Buckminster Fuller when he was carrying on his ingenious inventories of resources, but I did not push him far enough. Perhaps my problem was one of omission and mental laziness, more than ethics. But I turn to a more serious omission in scholarship that touches directly on the ethics of knowledge in E. Jordan's insights.

Since its publication in 1972 a massive volume has been prominent on my shelf, *The Use of Time,* a study of time budgets in twelve nations.[19] Its editor, the late Alezander Szalai of Hungary, and his brilliant team came up with 525 pages of text and 300 pages of tables, based on about 30,000 interviews. Over ninety basic leisure activities were named by men and women over the age of eighteen in urban and suburban areas. It is a triumph of international cooperation. Yet as I was preparing a paper for the WLRA conference last May in Lake Louise, my thinking turned to some destructive aspects of leisure. Returning to the Szalai volume, I noted that all the activities listed by the subjects, or perhaps elicited in the interviews about a specific twenty-four-hour period were positive, such as radio, TV, conversation, attendance at cultural events, participation in sports, and so on. Obviously, what was obtained from television or from a book may have been negative in value, but we generally accept reading per se as good. Strangely, not a single mention was made explicitly of gang activity aimed toward fun through violence, no mention of drugs or alcohol, or of sex whose objective was less than procreation. The word sex came up only in connection with divisions in the workplace. Yet in some nations, especially socialist ones, alcoholism is openly noted as a major social problem. In this comprehensive study these negative aspects would almost certainly come up for empirical investigation. Why did they not? Were these simply omissions of fact, or do they in some way suggest an unwillingness or hesitation for middle-class scholars to accept leisure as anything but a good? Objectivity is an ethical as well as a scientific matter. The unethical, cacophonous notes creep in when objectivity and social values become confused. Anyone who imagines that social science departments are necessarily the rational guardians of objective knowledge is not experienced in such processes as the games played for promotion, for obtaining grants, or even with interdepartmental and cross-departmental politics. But I gladly leave this aspect of scholarly life after forty-three years in it to look at our second proposition.

Leisure policy makers and power

These real people, both the leaders-organizers and the public-clients, are in hospitals, workplaces, prisons, parks, concert halls, community centers, nursing homes, schools, campsites, gambling halls, movie houses, sports arenas, taverns, drug gatherings, bridge tournaments, chess matches, alleyways, alongside rivers or lakes, and on the mountains. They are in every home.

Some of the directors, leaders, planners, or promotors of this mélange of leisure pursuits and settings are trained for their jobs, and if they think of themselves and are considered by others as "professional persons," are aware of ethical codes; they come to conferences of their peers; they have come out of institutions of higher learning and have supposedly been exposed to principles or human relationships; they have been observed in practical situations before getting their degrees or certificates.

However, the great bulk of leaders or policy makers in so-called leisure, recreational, or cultural settings have little or no training or intellectual and moral perspectives; their indoctrination is in arranging trips for tourists, managing a movie house, or selling

11: LEISURE AND ETHICS: CONNECTIONS AND JUDGMENTS   155

sports equipment. Ethical perspectives may be vaguely present in the recesses of their minds, and not at all in those of the corporation executives who touch on such services. An example is in order.

The planners of the 1981 White House Conference on Aging subcontracted with the U.S. Department of Labor for a study of the desirable specifications for the position of recreation director in a nursing home, even though only 5 percent of our elderly live in private or public nursing homes. The issue was, what is the need for professional leadership in such situations, and how is the need being presently filled? The data became clear: that administrators in such institutions were most often ignoring the recreation profession or the guidelines laid down by gerontologists, and simply pulling in so-called recreation leaders off the street, with little or no training, at minimum wages. Those of us called in for consultation by the department agreed that much of the fault lies at the door of the recreation profession for its lack of political savvy in obtaining licensing legislation, familiar in such work as cosmetologists and barbers.[20]

Permit an example of successful political action, theoretical planning, and the close cooperation of several professions. Those who joined in their efforts to transform a 4.7-mile strip of desolated and crime-ridden land of South Boston into a fifty-five-acre park included recreationists, landscape architects, social workers, engineers, hortoculturists, social workers, and engineers. According to a report in the *New York Times* of last 13th October teenagers now bicycle along paths planted with trees and bushes, young men shoot baskets beside the rolling lawn of a church, and children play in a nearby sandlot.

Somehow, having known this desolated area when I lived in Boston, this transformation to me is an ethical as well as a social, physical affirmation of vision; it was surely based upon a creative, constructive relationship of power on both political and professional levels, turned to the good of the powerless residents of the inner city. Perhaps the central issue that penetrates the second proposition—the profession and the public centers on social class, race, and ethnic differences. Philosophically, as noted earlier, Martin Buber conceptualized the broad dichotomy as the "I-thou." Politically, we are in UNESCO territory of the difference between the democratization of culture and cultural democracy. In vernacular terms, to what extent should leisure activities be funded and transmitted from the standards and values of this profession; to what extent is there the fundamental respect for indigenous values of the segments being served? This is an issue that concerns public educators as well. One example is the hot dispute over bilingual education. This vast array of actions that we call leisure or recreation includes the full range of elitism and mass or popular culture, from the viewpoints of de Tocqueville to William Morris.

In practical terms, this ethical issue came to a climax in the United States when we left the assimilationist values that my immigrant parents embraced at the turn of the century and moved into a pluralistic "black is beautiful" value structure of recent times. As to the relevance of leisure and recreation, I remind you that soon after the 1948 desegregation ruling by the Supreme Court, public recreation was singled out for a parallel decision.

The more direct implication of ethics to many of you in the profession arises from tighter public funding and the consequent movement of trained persons to the private sector such as theme parks and company-controlled programs. I am employed, say, by IBM or 3M, both known for their advanced employees recreation programs. I ask for a sizeable sum to hire a top recreation person, but the company is cutting budgets; I am asked to find a recent graduate; what balance do I come to, short of leaving the job? At what personal risk shall I insist that the corporation should install safer equipment? Other fields face similar issues, as in the Atlanta *Constitution*, when an innovative editor resigned when he was chastised internally for investigative reports on the differences in bank loan policies for blacks and for whites of that city. Ronald Riggins, in the *Journal of Physical Education, Recreation and Dance*, had advice of sorts to his profession. "Our task," he wrote, "is to balance the need to address economic exigency with a renewed commitment to the significant service mission to which our profession is called."[21] I sought to find this "balance" on one occasion when I sent a larger budget for one of my projects; But before appealing to the dean I had offers for two other positions in hand.

Still without a satisfactory answer to the issue of professional security vis-à-vis ethics, I turn to the third proposition. It reads, "That among the total population who speak of leisure there is a responsibility for the general consideration of ethics centering on morality as a general postulate."

Leisure publics and morality

This, of course, is the most nebulous and important of the three propositions. It speaks to cultural values, to all segments of the population. While leisure theorists number a few hundred, recreation administrators and leaders number several thousand; the consumers or participants of leisure are every one of us.

The key phrase widely used to cover the collective desire for control over our own time is the "leisure ethic," as opposed to another popular phrase, the "work ethic." Both are vague terms, denoting leisure for work as ends, purposes, major objectives. We have no catchy word about the leisure fanatic to match "workaholic": yet there have always been and still are those whose lifestyle has focused on play; perhaps this has been implicit historically in the category of the "upper class," who have proverbially found others to work for them. John Galbraith has observed that to the rich the work ethic is for the poor. Bernard Shaw thought of the worker walking and the nobleman riding in his distinction of English classes as the "equestrians" and the "pedestrians." If they could express themselves thus, the milk horse and the polo horse could have their say.

Yet the dichotomy of work and leisure has, since the Industrial Revolution, become too complex, psychologically and productively, for such simplicity. The bosses too often are the workaholics; the workers are guaranteed paid vacations and retirement benefits by the government. France, long ago, had a month paid vacation for everyone by law. In much of socialist society, the guilds or labor associations maintain their own facilities, such as those I have enjoyed on Lake Beleton in Hungary. Japan, just now, is officially encouraging new attitudes toward leisure as an economic policy. The Third World has begun to pay attention to this matter in face of its larger proportion of elderly and the formation of ideologies about work as they modernize.

In the industrial societies, moral attitudes toward work and leisure passed through several stages: free time as a *reward*, then as a *right*, finally as a *resolution* or *realization*. To trace this progression would take a review of labor history, religious history, the story of the middle classes, the struggle for equality of women, the emergence of industrial psychology, the fashions of therapy and psychiatry, and the gradual but difficult enlightenment of capital and industrial managers. My feeling is that while this attitude toward leisure as a right, reward, or realization will continue, no matter how many hours we work, the next stage will turn to leisure as a means of adjustments in the economy aimed at special needs and populations. I have in mind the latest concern for women in America, based on the so-called "momma's track." To assure their equal rights—which of course they still do not have in much of our management areas—it is now suggested that women fall into two categories, those with or without concerns for family needs. The answer has been known throughout Europe for some decades, but as our experience vis-à-vis the Japanese has amply illustrated, American businessmen are sometimes strangely bereft of common sense in relation to their employees; they have yet to master a fundamental fact, that people work best when they want to work, and the principle of flexible work schedules has not yet penetrated here, as it has in central Europe. This principle, if applied to the entire work force wherever feasible, takes women off the hook, and enlarges life's possibilities for men as well.

But I and others have made several dollars from the stupidity of even America's largest corporations, feeding them information that we were teaching in introductory courses of sociology. Among such information is the simple fact that leisure and work attitudes and values are related, that 3M and IBM and Philips are not visionary but practical when they take an interest in the full life of their employees. American industry will match its competition only if it takes new directions, not only with the Japanese and their effective constellation of capital-management-workers-government, but also the European Common Market. Among the new directions must be more than the ethics that have been exposed in recent years, ethics of greed, ethics of nonconcern with the human aspects that often accompany mergers; or ethics that include enormous waste and chicanery in military contracts. American ethics for business must move into a concern for the honesty that the Iacoccas hear about on Sunday morning in their suburban pews, but more, for the concern with the total cultural, educational, and family life of their workers. The work of O'Toole's task force on the dissatisfactions in the workplace are as important to America's industrial future as the next handbook on the next computerized system for their productive network.[22]

Without this social and ethical transformation among those who control our lives economically, there is some nebulousness in talking about the ethics of leisure and life for the millions whose lives are at the mercy of the economic forces. That we are the masters of our souls, the captains of our ships, has long been a poetic sentiment worthy of romantic trash in the drugstore literature or in soap operas. Yet whatever freedoms the average person has, aside from those that can be obtained through the ballot box, through unionization, or through direct action as in civil rights struggles, will come in good part from the uses that

11: LEISURE AND ETHICS: CONNECTIONS AND JUDGMENTS

Americans will make of the leisure facilities and experiences. That is where the personal and the social come together. That is where there are greater opportunities for choice than in the work areas of life.

I plead that this conference not get bogged down from the beginning in a concentration entirely on the individual as the actor. Yet, the conference will be right to recognize that it is in private action that most of us have some voice, if at the same time it is more than isolated in its consequences, even in its conception. We will be right to ask the questions, how do I choose the uses of my freedoms, how do I apply my skills, what commitments do I make? What satisfactions do I expect or desire as I fiddle, or travel, or watch, or hear, or paint, or drink, or read, or walk, or catch butterflies, or write a poem, or flirt, or drug myself, or simply sit? Each has meanings, each falls into or violates some ethical concepts that lie dormant in the back of my mind.

The study of this ethical presence in a field of human activity that has seemed to be free of responsibility is perhaps the next major stage in our leisure studies. It will be a far more difficult stage than the gathering of data, the creation of tables and models. Finally, it will take us out of the dominant purview of one discipline, and even of social science alone. Philosophy, even ideology, will again resume their rightful place in future discussions of leisure, taking us full circle to the *paidia* of the Greeks, and the "architecture of time" that came from the Judaic perception of the cosmos and life.

12
Apostles of Accuracy, Exploration, Significance

This volume would not be complete without a recognition of the many differences among "free" academics. While reference has been made to the many interests within any university, a major distinction is that of the academic levels known as instructor, assistant professor, associate and full professors. These terms represent more than an internal pecking order, and may enter into the power politics as well as salaries, responsibilities, and tenure. There are also special "chairs" named after benefactors, as well as "distinguished" professorships. Age enters the levels as well as accomplishments, reputation, awards, or length of service.

This paper was prepared for a special issue of *Loisir et Société*, Université du Quebec. This is the official journal of a Research Commission on Leisure, an integral part of the International Socialogical Association, Autumn 1992. It is reproduced with the kind permission of the journal *Loisir et Société/Society and Society* and its editor, Dr. Max D'Amours.

Age is invariably a major factor in the analysis of activities or trends in leisure. Without the inclusion of age divisions it is practically impossible to explore differences in tastes among the mass media publics, sports participants, or enthusiasts in the arts. The age factor was vital in the study of the twelve nations conducted by A. Szalai and his associates.[1] The Ford Foundation survey of arts audiences in twenty-two cities of the U.S.A. made much of age[2] and three years later, a special study of elderly Americans by a group from the University of Wisconsin concentrated on the elderly generation in respect to their interests, and equally interesting, the attitudes of administrators in the arts toward older persons.[3] One can be sure that the marketing and research agencies employed by the television industry are increasingly aware of the older population, although American policy-makers in the production or financial centers of the east and the west coast continue to display their imbedded faith in audiences of children, youth, and young adults.

Given this necessity for respecting the age factor among actual or potential publics and participants, leisure scholars might look unto themselves, asking the question: assuming the need for a "sociology of sociology" as a general axiom, how is leisure theory affected by the age factor *among scholars?* Is there a generation gap, now that our field is old enough to include "First," "Second," and "Third" Ages of scholars and administrators? Can these generations be identified by the training that they have received, the kinds of issues they tend to explore, indeed, by their conceptions of "leisure"?

"First," "second," and "third age" as a tool of analysis, is of course, too bland for a trigenerational approach. This is evident in the convenient term, Third Age, for older persons in Europe, yet it is a better term than the American references to Senior Citizens or Golden Agers. The habit among scientific observers has been to use terms that describe behavior patterns or states of mind. Among them is C. G. Jung's introvert and extrovert, E. Kretschmer's schizo-thymic and cytothymic, V. Pareto's rentieri and speculatori, W. I. Thomas's philistine, bohemian and creative, or David Riesman's inner and other.

For our purpose, an age-oriented categorization is required that also relates to mind and behavior, but in some sense of emergence or sequence. As far back as 1840 we find this homely observation by a Parisian, Ben Levi, writing in the *Archives Israelites:*

> The Grandfather believes, the father doubts and the son denies. The Grandfather prays in Hebrew, the father reads the prayer in French, and the son does not pray at all. The Grandfather observes all festivals, the father only observes Yom Kippur, the son does not observe any. The Grandfather is still a Jew, the father has become an Israelite, and the son is simply a deist . . . unless he is an atheist, a Fourierist, or a Saint-Simonist.

A century and a third later, the English scholars Rhona and Robert Rapoport apply a contemporary phrase, the "family life cycle" to the phenomenon of generational differences. In the discussion that follows, I will use their terms, "young adulthood," "establishment," and "old age."[4] These are constructs in the sense that Max Weber developed the term, i.e., we should not expect a precise fit for individuals within categories. Further, a contemporary observer of generations is well advised to note that all age categories before WWII need to be reconsidered with the growing activism of older persons ("new-old") and simultaneously, the growing sophistication of younger persons ("mature-young?")

Young Adulthood

While parameters of young adulthood are flexible, the Rapoports have in mind those persons from the end of school into the first few months of marriage. They regard an "identification with social institutions" as the major drive of this age group; young people—often "tentatively and experimentally"—build new commitments, intimacy, and a sense of identity. Important contributing factors are social class and family.[5]

With some differences from English patterns, this stage in American life is similarly the transition from graduate studies in the university to early professional life for our new colleagues. In this career, they might start in a municipality (as in public parks and recreation systems), in therapeutic situations (hospitals, nursing homes), or in industry.

Graduate education is still fresh in their minds. Attendance at state and regional conferences becomes important. Already the university had introduced them to forms of professional gamesmanship, institutional bureaucracy, and (largely from other young colleagues) useful attitudes and strategies for career development. Strong loyalties to their former faculties remain, including memories of intrafaculty conflicts that often had emerged from varying attitudes towards values and from commitment to differing types of "science" and "evidence."

Young adults in our field will mostly move from the university to careers in recreation, that is, to an applied facet or expression of leisure theory. Few departments such as psychology, sociology, economics, or philosophy turn out young scholars in special studies of leisure. More even than with leisure theory, recreation students become closely acquainted with computer techniques, for no up-to-date recreation "system" can function without machines for record keeping, annual reports, budget analysis, analyses of "costs-benefits," and so on. Political boards and commissions are more responsive to data that emanates from machines than from theories that come from the mind.

When the young generation does, indeed, start to theorize, its first efforts are the attempt to define leisure. I have seen many

12: APOSTLES OF ACCURACY, EXPLORATION, SIGNIFICANCE

such attempts, sometimes ending up in little boxes to distinguish leisure from work, or to come to the "content" of leisure or its "outcomes," and even these are fed into machines. A facade of hard science is thereby erected. The mystique of science is sought. Certainly, easier publication is assured for the *Apostles of Accuracy.*

Apostles of Accuracy

However, it would be a misconception to limit the output of these apostles to statistics or to quantitative data alone. Their current contribution is wider and merits our close attention. I take as one example the research of a young Korean scholar, presently at the University of Georgia in Athens.

Youngkill Lee is heading toward a career in therapeutic recreation, but his doctoral degree (University of Oregon) and his postdoctoral research addresses the question: "What is the experience like when people are engaging in leisure?"[6] Rather than relying on memory, or even on the diary method used in the Szalai comparative studies, Lee seeks to avoid the "subtle, often idiosyncratic and sometimes even contradictory dimensions of immediate experience." His method, therefore, is to have his subjects carry a tape recorder and to describe their leisure experiences during the episode or immediately thereafter, based on some open-ended questions.

> In this study, a total of nine categories of leisure experiences naturally emerged from the verbatim transcription. They include: 1) social bonding, 2) escaping/getting away, 3) communion with nature, 4) physical stimulation, 5) intellectual cultivation, 6) creative expression, 7) introspection, 8) relaxation, and 9) fun/enjoyment. In some cases, sub-categories were also identified to recognize distinctive but related dimensions [. . .] subjects also reported negative experiences during their own definition of leisure events which included the characteristics of: disappointment, frustration, nervousness, apprehension, worry, and exhaustion.[7]

Going far back into the tradition of "phenomenology," this promising social scientist brings together these subjective narrations or self-evaluations with an attempt to "capture the real or actual time content of leisure behavior." Indeed, such an apostle of accuracy is well on the path to mature explorations, especially if in the coming decades he can apply his insights and methods to the several cultures of his own Korean-American experience.

THE ESTABLISHMENT PHASE

A sign of movement toward the second of Rapoports' category of the adult cycle is a greater courage, a bold perspective of leisure, a willingness to accept other canons of the truth than numbers.

The establishment phase (middle-age, mature adulthood) brings the leisure scholar to larger dimensions of life. By then we have not just the typical experiences of life between the approximate ages of twenty-five to fifty-five, but a passing from "rehearsals" to "explorations," in which one plays with "ideas, relationships, and activities." Now has come the time for "more enduring commitments."[8]

Leisure in the minds of mid-age researchers has risen above the concept of play and games. Writing a poem now enters the purview of study, as well as observing fishermen or baseball players. The "costs" of leisure, so convenient in the numbers game, takes on a new reality when the subject has deliberately moved to a rural area for the delight of living on a lake or by the forest; the costs of this change never enter statistical tables. Other considerations, unthought before, confuse the numbers game, such as the hours of both work and non-work; the nominally simple total of the latter reminds a matter of astronomy in the Department of Labor while the potential content of hours has ballooned enormously in potential movement. Hours are now related to giving birth and being with family, to air travel vis-à-vis the Chevrolet. An hour is not a static entity.

Let us call this generation the *Apostles of Exploration*. Its major discovery is the nature and meaning of time in the new age. These explorations move in several contexts: time is perceived differently in work and in leisure, in various types of actions, and among differing age groups. Thus the "society of leisure" of which Dumazedier wrote[9] is perceptually distinct from the context of the "work ethic" of which the Japanese are presently boasting vis-à-vis the Americans. One perception is grounded in an ethic of survival and responsibility, the other rests on pleasant expectation and freedom. Yet the common element is a physical or astronomical property. A general thesis may be forwarded, that for those in work that is repetitive, time perception slows down the physical; among younger persons in fascinating pursuits, time goes

12: APOSTLES OF ACCURACY, EXPLORATION, SIGNIFICANCE

"faster," it "flies." In distasteful experiences, such as being a night security watchman, one is inclined to go without a watch to avoid reminder of the boredom. This juxtposition of physical and mental time awaits serious study among several fields, including the recreational and psychiatric. De Grazia's simple comment can remain a classic statement of the dilemma for mental health as well as for the Apostles of Accuracy.[10]

> Thus, by using a strictly quantitative assembly-line conception of time—time as a moving belt of equal units—one ignores the significance of much activity. A moment of awe in religion or ecstasy in love or orgasm in intercourse, a decisive blow to an enemy, relief in a sneeze, or death in a fall is treated as equal to a moment of riding on a bus or shoveling coal or eating beans.

Franz Werfel observes the age disparities in poetry:[11]

> The nursling sleeps the night and day right through
> Time is to him as meadow-grass it were.
> Youth's sleep tips up the scales by adding to
> The waking hours which endlessly recur.
> The man, who futile problems must pursue
> Consumes eight hours in sleep, though he demur
> The aged rise betimes, refreshed anew
> By curtailed slumber rendered livelier.
> The westward slope of life has this relief:
> God lengthens time, as time becomes more brief.

Yet the research into these perceptions may be "futile" as new technologies in technology, such as "virtual reality" in computerization, leads to ever new psychic possibilities.

As an illustration of such psychic possibilities by an explorative, mature scholar, I choose my favorite contribution to *A Literature Review,* a collection of studies by seventy-five scholars preparatory to the recommendations of the President's Commission on Americans Outdoors. Holmes Rolston III comments in an unusually penetrating way on the leisure experience of being in nature:[12]

> Aesthetic experience indoors is the experience of art—a painting, a statue, a symphony, Chippendale furniture. One appreciates artistry. Art objects have their frames, their pedestals; symphonies and plays are on stage and fine furniture is placed with interior design. Outside, everything is different . . .Nothing is framed; nothing is on stage; nothing is designed. The participant is in the midst of it all, surrounded by plain or forest, or standing high on the edge of the can-

yon. Even when observing the mountain on the skyline, the scene runs right up to our feet. Persons are challenged to do their own framing, to select what dimensions of the scene to admire, how to respond to organic forms of geomorphic processes, to wind and water, smell and sound. Americans outdoors are not an audience, not beholders of a programmed performance. They go outside to see what thrills, expected or unexpected, spontaneous nature can arouse.

What a standard Rolston has set for similarly sensitive analyses of other leisure prototypes!

Old Persons

Finally, we come to "old" persons in the leisure field, the old scholars. Some rough relationships may be drawn from the role of elder to that of prophet. To be eighty in our time is to have lived through such remarkable social and technological changes as to have earned the right to opinions on the emerging or even the desirable future. (Young people are not necessarily qualified to lead us into the future, for they are generally uninformed about the past.) Translated into the needs of our field, the older scholar can come to grips not only with his own conceptualizations of leisure, but the full range of other theoretical positions or traditions. For instance, in a 1975 volume I proposed the following traditions of leisure:[13]

> The humanistic tradition that sees leisure as an end
> The therapeutic tradition, with leisure as means
> The quantitative tradition, or "time left over . . ."
> The institutional tradition, distinguishing leisure from religion, marriage, education, politics
> The epistomological tradition, relating one's views of the world to assumptive, analytic, and aesthetic
> The sociological tradition, with leisure as a construct of elements

Neither in the original presentation or here will be found the full relationship of these assumptions in traditions to age or maturity among scholars. The complete absence of reaction to these categories among my colleagues since their proposal in 1975 leads me more anxiously toward such analysis on my own, but as the eighth decade of life takes over, my violin is more tempting than my pen. As long as accuracy remains a penchant of the young,

12: APOSTLES OF ACCURACY, EXPLORATION, SIGNIFICANCE 167

I do not expect an analysis by the new generation. I suspect, however, that personal maturity leads to an affinity for the humanistic, institutional, and sociological traditions. Permit some rationale for this hypothesis.

Looking back privately, it was possible to obtain the doctorate from a world-famous department of sociology in 1951 without one course in statistics. Almost a decade later, there were only 11 computers in Japan, 265 in all of Europe, and a little more than 2,000 in the United States. Two decades later we still had less than half a million here. By 1990, *40 million* office workers in our country alone sat in front of a monitor all day. Where I live now, in rural Georgia, an elementary school class without an Apple feels deprived, and our supermarket provides one free whenever the mothers turn in sufficient purchase receipts. Yet, I note again that, even though a science involving mathematics and its application to statistical disciplines or demography had existed for centuries, the doctorate in our social science ignored this quantitative tradition.

Add to this another personal note or caveat—call it what you will. I now have a $6.00 RadioShack calculator, used for such idiosyncratic computations as discovering that my fourscore years had encompassed 4,160 weeks, 29,120 days, 698,880 hours, about 87,360 meals; that about 2,000 university classes had reached or bored over 75,000 students. Yes, those figures are trivia, suggesting that one is not anti-technological by nature or by choice, but also that several millions of words can be composed to demonstrate that a few ideas may emerge *sans computers.* Such a scholar-relic, along with his pen, scissors, wastebasket, and yellow pad, is comforted by the model of past eminent contributors who had access to ideas long before anyone had access to Fortran.

In the late 1950s and early 1960s we read Simmel, Weber, Spencer, Pieper, and Aristotle without the convenience of anthologies. In the 1960s we became familiar with Dumazedier's *Toward a Society of Leisure,* with Pieper's *Leisure: The Basis of Culture,*[14] with de Grazia's *Of Time, Work and Leisure,* with a major essay by Bennett Berger, "The Sociology of Leisure,"[15] with Tillich's "The Person in Technological Society,"[16] and with Gabor's *Inventing the Future.*[17] In 1969 we came back from Hungary with the Academy of Science polemic on *Civilization at the Crossroads.*[18] Indeed, that same decade, just before our current crop of young leisure scholars was out of preparatory schools, became a fertile decade for systematic grappling with the future; from it came forty-one references out of fifty listings provided by Alvin Toffler on one of his volumes on the future.[19]

Thus the "old" scholars of leisure may be thought of as *The Apostles of Significance.*

For an illustration we can turn to almost any page in the large contribution of Joffre Dumazedier. He has proved his worth as a close scholar of specific situations, even of whole towns and societies. But one need go no further than the first page of his *Sociology of Leisure* to taste the comprehensive mind of an Apostle of Significance.[20]

> Prophecies of doom greeted the approach of the year One Thousand: the end of the world has alleged to be at hand. As the year Two Thousand draws near, our prophets are rather less than unanimous. Under cover of ideological critiques, of futurology, of utopian speculations, of science fiction or even of 'sociology,' forecasts are ventured, ranging from the rosy to the bleak. However, bleakness tends to prevail and, as a result, scientific observation, exploration, and forecasting lose out.
>
> This attitude has impinged on the study of leisure, which may well be peculiarly vulnerable to the delusions of prophesizing. The indefiniteness of its scope, the heterogeneousness of its forms, the elusiveness of its far-reaching implications, the emotional undertones conjured up by some of its current or unusual, lawful or forbidden practices, prompt either enthusiasm or spite—which are equally incompatible with rigorous study. In addition, epistomological difficulties slowing down the development and dissemination of scientific knowledge spring from the overt or hidden resistance to the old ideologies centering on work or study, on family duties or political committment, to the distrusted values embodied in leisure.

Observations

Of course, the elements of accuracy, exploration and significance are all basic to the scientific process. There are several reasons to suppose that the association of each with the generation of scholars will be less possible in the decades ahead.

1. All students of today receive training in numbers and machines; thus the "old" of tomorrow will not have been deprived in these regards.
2. While the concept and reality of biological "generations" will always be with us, their cultural roles will not follow traditional

patterns. Increasingly, we can decide how "old" we want to be in terms of where we place our interests,[21] and the problem of "ageism" may decline as the life span enlarges and such outdated practices as mandatory retirement are eliminated.

3. If, indeed, for budgetary or other reasons, training in the social sciences becomes more policy-oriented, significance as a goal will become more closely integrated with other elements of research. Already, some departments of sociology have been eliminated because they cannot demonstrate the same degree of acceptance in the marketplace or policy as can graduates in psychology or economics.

There remains the undisputable fact that by our temperament, scholars in the leisure field are led to the paths of empiricism, intellectual adventure, or integrated forms of understanding. In my own case, the lack of training in numbers was in pleasant keeping with my penchant for generalizing; thus, a simultaneous activity in the musical world escaped a schizophrenic confusion. It is not a sad thing that our field has treasured such diverse temperaments as a Szalai and a De Grazia, or a Dumazedier and a Grushin.

Perhaps the most appropriate observation from these musings of an old man is that as the studies of leisure confront the complexities of the new century, there may emerge a greater totality in our perspective and our science; in some quarters of the public need there will be an emphasis on consumer expenditures and comparisons of hours; others will zero in on human satisfactions and needs. All serious scholarship will be in demand. For if there is no longer sense in such discrete categories as economics, sociology, and the like, except for items in university catalogues, then even new physics has something to say to us. In the past we envied it for its exactitude, and much of sociological mythology about accuracy and objectivity reflects our envy of data beyond our control. Now, as indeed we may hope for a reconciliation or fusion between accuracy, exploration and significance, we see that physics and the other hard sciences are creating a unified approach of organic and inorganic, or reality and simulation, of numerical and symbolic values. We should demand no less of ourselves.

13
Sociology and Music Education (University of Oklahoma conference, spring 1995)

THE title of the Oklahoma conference was "Symposium '95; the Sociology of Music Education. Theoretical Underpinnings and Practical Applications." Papers were read by scholars from Maryland, Wisconsin, Colorado, Texas, Oklahoma, Ontario, Minnesota, and England (Liverpool). A second keynote paper was presented by the distinguished Christopher Small, critic and musicologist, now living in Spain.

A conference on the same theme was held several months later at the University of Indiana. However, the Oklahoma symposium, as a pioneer in bringing these two disciplines together, illustrates the current tendency—in other parts of the campus as well—for the overlapping or interfacing of seemingly disparate disciplines. This is one direction for the free academic.

This essay is reproduced with the kind permission of the School of Music of the University of Oklahoma and Associate Professor Roger Rideout.

A week after the brochure announcing the symposium, a letter came from another university, inviting my participation in a collection of chapters on precisely the same topic. I was struck, and at first irritated, by the statement that until now, sociologists had only "dabbled" in the area of music education. "Dabbled?" We are a serious bunch, quite dull, and do not dabble. Perhaps we complicate, obfuscate, and confuse (especially sophomores). If the Right is to be heard, we even deceive the public, in company of the eastern liberals.

On second thought, I realized that the letter writer was quite right, but also unaware of the nature of sociology. Music education is part of the general process of music as a whole. Our purpose, with all society as our general canvas, is to provide interconnections, as in the "social institution" or "culture." We leave it to the practitioners of music education to draw upon these interconnections for their own purposes.

I cannot speak for all sociologists, even for those who have delved deeply into the arts—Arnold Hauser, Peter Etzkorn, T. W. Adorno, Max Weber, and many others. I invite you to share my very personal approach, which originated from my background as a musician, a violinist whose first love is the string quartet. The career turned to sociology and, for some forty years, to the study of leisure. The two fields, vastly different, might have produced an academic schizophrenia; however, I found common ground, each field enlarging the possibilities of the other. The result, after many years of "dabbling" was the construction of a comprehensive model, one that enables the investigator to put all social institutions into a total view of society.

My hesitation in presenting a visual model, neatly organized into sixteen "elements," is that it may suggest a mechanistic view that is at odds with the nature, the purpose, or the actual way in which art works. "God the mathematician" comes to mind, or from the critical analysis of western science, the imperialistic position that only science ultimately knows all.

In actuality, the arts provide one substantive challenge to science as a form of truth. Therefore, in a 1966 volume, *Foundations and Frontiers of Music Education*, I proposed that we might consider three types or sources of knowledge about the world, which I called the assumptive, the analytic, and the aesthetic:

> The assumptive is the kind that reaches into past generations. It is therefore believed, affirmed, legendized, poetized, dramatized, embraced with enthusiasm, prayed to, immortalized in song, reaffirmed in salute. The analytic source of knowledge is best illustrated by the sciences. It is a knowledge based on objectivity, evaluation, examination, doubt, tests and experiments. The aesthetic kind of knowledge is based on the existence of originality, in putting together things, objects, ideas, sounds, forms, and time and space relations in ways that have not been done before, but on the principle of beauty.[1]

Rather than refine this trinity, I shall pose a more difficult intellectual experiment, crossing the parameters of the analytic and the aesthetic. Joseph Haydn did it in perfecting the string quartet. A full century before the sociological pioneer, Herbert Spencer,

Haydn posed the symbolic issue of the relation of the one to the group, and secondly, the relation of the homogeneous to the heterogeneous. In this sense, I hereby nominate Haydn to the front ranks of symbolic sociology.

The model I propose now is a juxtaposition of four quartets, or a grand quartet of what in our lingo we might call "four closed systems." I trust this explanation will soften the accusation of a mechanistic model, contrary to the free principle of beauty and creativity (see page 79 of this volume for the model).

That model, first created for leisure studies, was published by a research group in Prague, funded by UNESCO and the Czech Academy of Science, before it appeared in my 1975 volume, *Leisure: Theory and Policy*.[2] In one of my trips to that city, a call came from the ministry of culture of Iran. Would I visit Teheran to see if the scheme could be applied to the arts, and specifically, to that nation? This resulted in several visits to consult with the shah's team of young national planners. They had been assigned to develop a five-year economic and cultural plan. Their objective was to develop a contemporary industrial nation that would combine contemporary life with the best of the rich Persian traditions. One major project would be the creation of Farrabee University, devoted entirely to postgraduate studies in the arts. The shah's wife, sponsor of this project, had put aside one hundred million dollars of the new oil money. Students would come from Iran, all Asia and the U.S.S.R. Three curricula would be offered: skills from both the past and the present in the creation and technical mastery of the performing and exhibiting arts, skills in the political administration of the arts as national policy, and skills in analyzing and reporting arts data and activity. This trio of offerings went far beyond any other program in the arts, especially the provision that every student would have experience in each of the three tracks, while specializing in one. My responsibility was to direct the third curriculum: training faculty, charting directions, recording and assessing national activity in music, dance, theater, painting and weaving, and poetry reading. The model I bring to you now was officially accepted by the ministry; the implications for music education are extracted for this symposium, with the precautionary note that models—this one, or those popular in circles of business and information theory, are not intended to provide solutions; they merely create possibilities for relevant relationships by noting pertinent elements and configurations. This model of four quartets moves outwardly from more to less specific. The innermost quartet defines whether our subject for research is leisure, or science, or law, or family, or anything else. In each case, the elements or "members" of the first quartet will differ. Before exposing the model to critical colleagues here and abroad in the 1970s, I had experimented in several fields for conference papers, as in the fields of aging and industrial design. The members or elements of our present quartet for the arts are creators, distributors, the publics, and educators. Obviously, as a sociologist, I am speaking here of the arts as a social process.

Music educators are, of course, concerned with creativity. One of your concerns is the nature of such concepts as sensitivity, talent, originality. We are all familiar with the work of Sigmund Freud, Arthur Koestler, A. L. Kroeber, Arnold Toynbee, and others. One of our major inputs as sociologists is in the nature-nurture argument, revived in a recent book, *The Bell Curve*.[3] In a playful mood, I wrote the following words in a 1991 volume, *The Arts: A Social Perspective:*

> Some day an imaginative novelist . . . will imagine the world as foreseen by an embryo in the womb of a woman, just before birth. This embryo has already decided to be an artist, and wonders about the kind of world it wants when its eyes open and it utters the first cry of celebration. Those eyes might open in some Indian village, in a hut in Thailand, or a mountain town in Italy. What, instead, if it were to be a motel in Sausalito, a hospital bed in St. Paul, or a modest cottage in Gadsden, Alabama? What difference would it make to the life chances for this bundle of creative energy, destined to become a 170-pound sculptor?[4]

Our hope is that the American community and its classrooms can provide one of those favorable environments for our future scholar, or composer, or painter. The democratic ethos that prevails—MENC's motto, "Music for all"—is simultaneously a watchful mechanism for the unusual talent and an experience for the less outstanding. We have undoubtedly the best network in the world for discovering and encouraging young creative persons in all the arts, from elementary schools through great university and conservatory programs. The development of magnet schools on the high school level has solved some of the debate on the discovery of and training for creative youth. The performing groups we hear in our national and regional conferences suggest preprofessional standards, largely unknown by the public at large and unreported by the media. I had something to do with the beginnings of the Greater Boston Youth Symphony Orchestra, a project every bit as exciting, aesthetically, as my consultative experience with the Lincoln Center in New York. I stress the environmental, socially supportive aspect of music education in part because of the controversial volume, *The Bell Curve*, by Richard Herrnstein and Charles Murray, published toward the end of 1994. The volume employs a unilateral concept of "intelligence," as a static, stable measure and predictor of achievement. In the argument that the social sciences have witnessed for decades—between nature and nurture—music education has provided ongoing evidence for placing musical instruction at the disposal of everyone. As a social theorist who seeks to lay the basis for statistically oriented researchers, I find more sophisticated the "multiple intelligences" approach taken by Howard Gardner,[5] who suggests the existence of a variety of intelligences—linguistic, musical, logical-mathematical, spatial, bodily-kinesthetic, intrapersonal, and interpersonal in nature.

My volume on the arts notes several kinds of distributors, each related to the various purposes of the arts. We are dealing with complicated connections, indeed, but for our purpose let us take another direction, suggested by Peter Etzkorn, the University of Missouri-St. Louis sociologist-ethnomusicologist. In his contribution to a recent book on the Barber shop singers, Etzkorn draws attention to what has been called the age of "mediamorphosis." Making qualitative distinctions between mediated and live music, he writes:

> Anyone making a survey of musical life in the United States will be challenged by the tremendous quantity of musical sounds that will be encountered. Most of these, however, will not come from a live musical source . . . whether it is classified as classic, popular, jazz, or even religious . . . most musical sounds, instead, will come from loudspeakers. Indeed, some of these occur at such levels of volume that their presence may cause physical damage to hearing organs not unlike other noises characteristic of our technological age.[6]

We do not often think of how precious it is that many of our children—not all—sing songs in school at a time when singing in the home is rare. In the past twenty years, sales for audio and video in the home went up from less than 9 to over 56 billion dollars. Not only did music-making go down correspondingly, the sale of tickets to musical and theatrical events in the same period after 1970 went up by only a small margin, from 4.2 billion to 4.9 billion. Further, the making of live music by adult amateurs, as in community choruses, is far from what it was in my youth, when immigrants from Europe brought with them such institutions as the *Singverein* among the Germans, often meeting in the back room of a saloon or in the social headquarters of their groups. The Czechs, Romanians, and Hungarians stand out in my memory. The classroom singing of today is also a link to the past, of which I will have more to say later. As to the relation of music education to live audiences, all of your performing groups have that in mind. A dramatic example was my experience as a consultant to Lincoln Center for the Performing Arts. They had a large fund to bring the center into direct contact with students of the New York area. The theoretical issue arose, with a large expenditure at stake, as to this simple question: what are the relative advantages of bringing an inner-city student to hear the Philharmonic only once, thus reaching more children, rather than limiting the numbers to bring each student several times? The issue is part of the larger problem, how are musical audiences built?

II

Quartet II proposes four additional elements in the society that surrounds music and the arts: person-family, group-subculture, community-region, world-nation. In each of these profound changes are taking place, and continuous upheavals may be expected in the next century. The traditional family of mother, father, and children is already a thing of the past, and no discussions of "family values" will automatically bring it back. The single parent may not be the norm in A.D. 2050, for new combinations of group living may come about. Even the kibbutz in Israel has undergone changes in its policy on raising children outside the home. We may find, in the decades ahead, new patterns in the nature of neighborhoods, the meanings of suburbia, and the pooling of resources among unrelated family units. Or there may be a swing of the social pendulum, with a return to nineteenth-century values. As to groups and subcultures, we need hardly be reminded of the movement toward the identity and the rights of minorities. Relationships between the subcultures are changing—in the courts, the streets, the workplace, the schools. The multilingual arguments are alive. How this has already affected your thinking and your classrooms, I do not know. Michael Mark notes that

The nature of American society has been such that nonwhite heritages were sublimated for generations. It was widely accepted that they were less worthy of attention than European heritages. This is ironic, because American society has been deeply influenced by the black heritage.[7]

That attitude could not escape the force and logic of the civil rights movement and the reaching out of the black people for their own definition of who they are and want to be. The Tanglewood Symposium happened to come at the height of the struggle. I remember that in the midst of our deliberations, the representative of the United Auto Workers left suddenly for Detroit when riots broke out there. It was no idle question that the symposium put to the profession:

Separate musics have separated functions . . . There are happenings all around us, on the street corners, in churches, events both social and political. They pose the problem of value judgments, not only of the quality of the music, but quality within the function of the music as well. Can we and should we assign a hierarchy to various musics?[8]

I need not belabor the expectation that during the professional careers of every graduate student, especially those who will teach in large cities, this question will be relevant. The growing presence and importance of Latin Americans will further press the matter. Community-region (II-C) is the third element of the quartet, and is a major factor in your planning in respect to the tax base, the political power center, the support of the press, the cultural traditions of the region, the population composition, the degree of stability and movement, the religious flavor, the occupational ranges. Finally, in a nation and a world of new highways of communication, no community, no school, no subject matter exists in a vacuum, free of national fads and fashions. The mass media see to that. Children everywhere, rural or urban, surrounded by cows or by cars, are exposed to the same commercial jingles. A single televised performance by the Metropolitan Opera may have as many viewers, young and old, as its accumulated live audiences for a generation of time in the past. Thus, it seems to me, stands the issue of textbooks and lesson plans aimed at the mass of Americans vis-à-vis the more indigenous literature of regions. Has the Foxfire experience in Georgia had an impact on music education? On the worldwide level, the literature of music and its instruction have always been partly international.

Has the surge in ethnomusicology brought the Asiatic, African, and other cultural areas alongside eastern and western Europe?

III

Our third quartet moves us to even wider vistas. By the "energy system" (III-A) I refer to our economy, where the most dramatic change, because of technology, is the new nature of work. Farming was the first great occupation affected by automation, beginning a virtual revolution. Many studies have been conducted on the nature of work since muscles were replaced by machines. In manufacturing, the small machine became larger, Taylorism and the assembly line took over, before the remarkable processes of computer robotics led to the impersonality of the workplace, a technical impersonality that has now led to the absence of human relationships between corporations and employees. Meantime, led by central European nations, time patterns of work came under scrutiny, for technological apparatus is free of vacation demands, coffee breaks, or fatigue. Thus the concept of flexitime arose, and is now having its impact on American personnel practices as well. Our CEOs have been slow to study their workers, and unable or unwilling to grasp the elementary fact that workers do best in time frames they prefer for psychological or family reasons. These changes were behind the all-year school concept, or more accurately, a school schedule more closely geared to other members of the family. And aside from the presence of more women in the workforce, easy communication makes the so-called cottage industry as feasible here as it is in Japan. But for music educators, the major input of the new work is the new priority of nonwork, or leisure. By now, perhaps more in Europe, leisure concerns, measurements and national policy have demanded official attention. Our network of leisure scholars is truly worldwide, with a separate research commission as part of the International Sociological Association. The live arts remain significant in Europe, even with the death of Communist funding. The famous Russian Male Chorus remains intact, searching for support to visit our country. Here, without seeing it as such, the National Endowment for the Arts has been a contributing factor to our leisure patterns. Every hour of music education is a potential contribution to the leisure destiny of your students for the rest of their lives. Although violins and clarinets now in use in our performing groups may gather dust later, they have opened alternatives to the invasion of the home by technical gadgets.

IV

Permit me to address the remainder of the model as a whole, especially the outermost quartet. It speaks of various social orders, the conquest pre-industrial, the kilowatt-industrial, the cogno and the cultivated. Here we put music and music education—and all the arts—into the largest perspective. Among the specific issues implicit here is the place of the arts in revolutionary periods and in periods of turmoil. My interest in this large picture is that the arts may have a number of functions, identified in my book as a form of knowledge, a collective possession, a personal experience, a form of therapy, a moral and symbolic force, an incidental commodity, a forerunner of social change, and a link between the past, the present, and scenarios of the future. It is the last of these functions that I would apply to these social orders.

In the volume on the arts, I note:

> our revolutionary time seems to move not in a straight line, but back and forth between the scientific and the humanistic-aesthetic. The fact that the arts contain elements of science and that science cannot do without creative aspects of the arts makes this alternative possible, even desirable. It is the subjective nature of the arts, and its accumulative nature as part of every culture, that gives it the unique stability to which the scientist may turn for his own sense of stability in his objective, experimental world. The current generation of computers, to be sure, will be replaced; the Beethoven Ninth will not be, and it will be heard in the year 2089 A.D. Other specific works of art that we now enjoy and prize will be heard, seen, and enjoyed then. Thus the function of art as a link is indisputable, and in spite of the myths in some educational circles, makes it a basic form of knowledge and a major cultural value.[9]

You may think that in your classroom you are insignificant, one teacher of music among thousands. Not so. Every thoughtful priest is conscious of his place in the history of his church; every judge, as he puts on his robe, knows that he is a symbol in the link with past centuries of law and order. Itzhak Perlman, thoughtful as he is, lifts his Guarnerius to his shoulder, awake to his linkage with the tradition of Viotti, Paganini, Kreisler, and Heifetz. The music teacher is likewise a link, a historic role, generally hidden from public view, but there. There is a job to be done, a responsibility to fulfill, a continuity to be maintained.

I return here to my experience in Iran. Here was a society highly conscious of its contemporary lifestyle, but without surrendering its cultural past. As a dictatorship, decisions were simple. In one room I met with about twenty-five planners, all highly educated in Europe or America. Compare that with the body of legislators in our Congress, beset with personal agendas and ninety thousand lobbyists.

The links between past and present in Iran were visible. There were, in one neighborhood that I visited, great craftsmen on life stipends, working with apprentices in making musical instruments (including harps), creating magnificent furniture, and keeping the Persian art of weaving alive, mostly with depictions of the shah. We too have visible links with the past in museums, in public buildings, in homes, in libraries.

Here I find a remarkable thing, in other cultures as well as in our own. You are aware of the ongoing discussion in music education as to its justification on the tax rolls: the argument between the importance of ancillary, or social reasons, such as national pride and personal growth on the one hand, and the belief that art rests on its own values, difficult to articulate, especially for the general level of school boards.

Yet, as I see the matter, the linkage conception of the arts *satisfies both the ancillary and the aesthetic function.* Musicians play Bach and Barber on the same concert as a normal aesthetic mix; sociologically considered, they are keeping alive the sounds of vastly differing societies. Thus, without a conscious agenda, your natural conduct in the classroom or on the stage acquaints the child, the family, and the audience with the sounds and the spirit of many civilizations.

With respect for your patience on a Saturday evening, my suggestions for issues from the model were indeed cursory on significant issues of talent and creativity, live and mediated music in distribution, the building of audiences, the changing family, power among subcultures, the new community, the changing economy and the new leisure ethic, and finally, the arts as continuity from one social order to another.

I submit that, in one way or another, I saw these issues as appropriate to Iran in the 1970s as I see them now among us in the 1990s. In Iran, for instance, the 225 national planners for the shah had a clear mandate in their third year of a five-year plan, to devise and to forge links between the Persian traditions and the post-industrial order that immense oil profits might create. Believe it or not, even in that society that consists largely of villages, we were asked to plan a world conference on leisure and the arts as a feature of the Farabee University opening ceremony.

Yet in both controlled and a free society, there is one issue that goes beyond anything I have mentioned. It emerges from the basic dichotomy of all social studies—the relation of person to society, individual to group, the "I" to the "other." This connection penetrates law, social survival, the structure as a whole, all fundamental blocks in any culture and civilization, whether of ancient Greece, medieval Europe, or the contemporary United States. The individual-social equation penetrates all educational policy, including the periodic meetings of a Norman, Oklahoma school board.

It did not take Sputnik to justify the sciences and mathematics. School boards had already accepted these areas as essential to the military and economic systems, just as civics courses were essential for the body politic. Little needed to be said of science as a mental discipline for the student. But the same board and the 104th Congress do not approach the arts in the same way. Now the emphasis turns to the emotions, to personal sensitivity and to the individual. Indeed, the advocacy for this emphasis is often deficient and less than articulate.

An observation about the Kodály system of music education may be pertinent here. My wife, Barbara, is an expert in that field, as are several members of the faculty on this campus. As you know, the whole Hungarian music program was deeply affected by the philosophy and activity of the great composer, researcher, and educator Zoltán Kodály; sufficient national resources were provided for Kodály institutes and academies, demonstration programs, even international exchanges. While Kodály was still alive, the country, liberated from Nazi domination by Communist troops, was subjected to a new political regime. What was the justification with which the new "rulers" decided to carry on with further resources for the program? As I noted in my introduction to a collection of writings on the meaning and emergence of the system:

> pure Marxism was fundamentally sympathetic to urban values; yet Kodály—whose life and educational work spanned the political metamorphosis in Hungary—was accepted in part because the orientation of his program to peasant life served to enrich national consciousness and to link personal growth among all segments of the population.[10]

13: SOCIOLOGY AND MUSIC EDUCATION

On other grounds, but with a similar duality, the sociologist would also emphasize the personal and social duality. Michael Mark notes that:

> The philosophy of music education is not a philosophy of music. It is a philosophy of education. To be credible it must also recognize the benefits to society of having an aesthetically developed population.

The pervasive message of the cultural concept in the social sciences is that the person is society "writ small" and that society is the individual "writ large." In short, music educators need not engage in the perennial, artificial dichotomy of aesthetic versus social functions. They serve both.

In the past century, the issue has been accentuated by the advent of a galloping technology, a phenomenon so pervasive that Jacques Ellul argues that it has superseded all other values. Technology, he writes, is its own value, its own meaning, and aside from its substance—the space age, the computer age, the information age, the "eco-system, the Third Age"—reveres change for the sake of change. Discoveries in the physical and life sciences that were until recently unimaginable may now be found on an inside page of the newspaper. So recent is all this that about ninety percent of all experimental scientists in the history of the world are still alive.

In such areas as work, commerce, and entertainment, impersonality has replaced human relationships. The mom-and-pop grocery of my youth is now a Kroger or Safeway; the vaudeville theater that entertained our family is now the nightly TV schedule; the collegial partnerships in the factory are replaced by robots or by button-pushers at a computer terminal. In a perceptive piece on our identity crisis in the *U.S. News and World Report* of five weeks ago, Wray Herbert speaks of our "current economic and emotional rootlessness, cultural tribalism and a rampant market-driven individualism that is corroding family and neighborhood."[11]

This has special meaning for one of my age, alive, entirely healthy and curious at eighty-three. These eyes have witnessed fire engines drawn by horses, foods delivered from the corner grocer, radios built with oatmeal boxes and "cat's whiskers" from Woolworth, a home without telephone or car. Even at the time of graduate studies, it was possible to function as a young scholar and technician without passing a single course in statistics, and of course the Internet was unknown to us. But from our reading of the original giants in our field—Max Weber, Herbert Spencer, Georg Simmel—we developed a feel for the meaning of the time, meaning for the person, meaning for the community. Perhaps never before have we so much needed that clarification of meaning. Instead, as we approach a new century, one sees a time of increasing cynicism, crime, alienation, indignity—a sad and strange age of suspicion.

We distrust the medical profession, the legal profession, large corporations, the mass media, politicians, the police. Children sue their parents; elementary school corridors house policemen; filibusters become standard weapons in Congress; a sports hero accused of a double murder is idolized by many; talk shows delight in dirt; guns and drugs are for sale everywhere. My generation is afraid to be on the streets.

Yet there are elements of hope, stability, even beauty among us—less publicized, but quietly influential. True, children have ready access to drugs; but attend any conference of music educators to hear their choruses and orchestras. I can never forget the remarkable sounds of the national chorus brought together by the Kodály conference in Chattanooga in 1994. No headlines. No reporting.

So it is more than an historic or cross-cultural link that stamps your efforts. It is also that of cultural anchor and meaning to life in a time of transition. This cannot be measured or visualized by the social sciences. It comes down to faith on your part, a faith in music and children as strong as your faith in God.

Perhaps I do not stray too far from my function as a sociologist-musician in concluding with some prescriptions.

You must look beyond your special purposes and techniques. You must become more literate and articulate. You must be able to represent, even to argue, your case for public support on both the aesthetic and social level. You must be ready to work with educators in other fields. You must maintain your own creativity. You must—well, I respectfully recommend—occasionally read the *New York Times*.

Respect your aesthetic tradition, respect your pioneers, respect your students and your colleagues. Mostly, respect yourselves. To reach out to another universe of tradition—sociology—is an evidence of security. And for you to reach out to one of my generation is more a tribute to your sense of continuity than to my experience. People provide links and anchors. The university is to be congratulated for these explorations; these can but strengthen your own purposes and contribute to music education everywhere.

14

Las Colinas: Plans for an Experiment in Puerto Rico

(*Planning a tourist-recreation region for the age of leisure* third annual workshop on Planning and Utilization of Leisure Resources, Appalachian State University, Boone, North Carolina, 18–19 March 1974)

THE "free academic" is available to both profit and nonpublic or semipublic agencies and programs. Some universities set both time and fee limits on the first.

The case of Las Colinas was unique in that this utopian community was designed as a commercial enterprise by a planner-contractor, but simultaneously as a vision for the good, creative life, with strong educational and cultural elements. Had the project succeeded in surmounting its financial condition, the author might have moved to Puerto Rico to nurture and observe this experiment.

I. HISTORY

Puerto Rico is one hundred miles long, thirty-five miles wide; this area is about a third smaller than Connecticut, but in many ways—historically, culturally, politically, in its status as a commonwealth, and in the exodus of several hundred thousand of its residents to the mainland—it is unlike anything else in the United States. As the George Washington of Puerto Rico, former governor Luis Muñoz Marin likes to say, it is "a group of islands—the main one being Puerto Rico, the others being the offshore islands of Vieques, Culebra, Manhattan, Brooklyn, Staten Island."

In 1960 a young, highly intelligent developer named Vigdor Schreibman acquired bits and pieces of property on its northeastern corner, near the town of Fajardo; when he got through he owned eight hundred magnificent acres of hills, valleys, and a half-mile of beach. The hills, in translation, took on the name Las Colinas, and would be Schreibman's resort community of three thousand units (homes and condominiums). When eighty of these were at various stages of building, his financier closed in on technicalities, bringing the project to a temporary halt. The real estate man decided to study finance and property laws, and spent every day of the next eight years in the library. However, with lawyers at his side, he lost a series of cases in the lower courts, finally presented his own case to the Supreme Court, and won the decision two years ago.

Meanwhile, property values had gone up as Puerto Rico's famous Bootstrap Plan nurtured its economy; the value of Las Colinas, simply as real estate, has multiplied many times.

This time there was no problem getting backing from a major financier on a vast scale. But by now Schreibman had as a person moved toward a serious concern for development of the whole human being; his general readings, during the years while he read the law, had convinced him that a community dedicated to the theme "self-discovery through leisure" could contribute to the solution of a serious problem, and at the same time tap a large market of people who were searching for satisfactions beyond material comfort. Here I lay down the principle—to be used again later—that long-range humanistic concerns need not be incompatible with profits. Schreibman abandoned his earlier plans for Las Colinas, determined now to leave more than half of it in its natural state, with a creative staff and consultants to develop facilities and programs for the harbor and beach, for an aviary, for creative arts, for conferences, for ferry service to nearby islands, for relationships to the entire island (especially through the arts), and so on. The corporation turned to us in Tampa for help in articulating the leisure theme in its full community and personal sense; the upshot was that a Leisure Studies Institute will be organized as a nonprofit corporation, perhaps to begin next September. Permit a short resume of this institute, as we view it now, before turning to basic issues for planning and research.

Full funding for the institute will come from the corporation. Supplementary income may come from publications, conferences, or outside grants, but the institute will not count on these. Physical facilities will be constructed for the institute, and perhaps for living and working quarters for visiting scholars and interns. The "visiting scholars" program will bring authorities in leisure from around the world, to stay with us for short periods up to two months, to consult with us, lecture, work with other scholars on the island, observe, write,—and fish. "Interns" will be students from all parts of the world, coming and leaving on their own schedules and at their own expense, to attend our seminars, to participate in observations in Las Colinas or elsewhere on the island, to obtain credit when they can relate to a university, or to follow their own program if they are on sabbatical leave from an institution.

Aside from serving all the planners and activities of the new community as built-in consultants, we will continue many of the activities that have until now constituted the Leisure Studies Program at the University of South Florida, presenting lectures, sponsoring conferences, continuing relationships with UNESCO, serving as world headquarters for the International Program for Films on Leisure (with a film festival planned for 1976), developing a major working library, serving a wide public as spokesmen on the subject, working with the seven-nation team within the International Sociological Society, and consulting with the World Leisure and Recreation Association as well as with governmental and private groups.

II. Leisure in the Dynamic of Las Colinas

Four main tasks would seem to await us that deal directly with residents and visitors in the community; these will refer to *people, program, evaluation,* and *generalization*.

A. People

The first task is to anticipate who such persons are likely to be; then after they come, to study them as deeply as we can and as they permit. Sociological, psychological, and perhaps a limited level of psychiatric tools would be in order. Ultimately, what we seek are the external influences—health, education, work background, etc.—as well as the aspirations and attitudes that explain the person's present and potential leisure behavior. We may anticipate several common characteristics among residents and visitors to Las Colinas, such as ample financial means, high educational background and social status, and most interesting, the common value of curiosity, personal adventure, and quest.

There will obviously emerge a set of paradoxes as well. A case in point is the degree of poverty interspersed among the hillsides, which are within rock-throwing distance of the symbols of great abundance, as exemplified by elegant hotels and high-rise condominiums. The particular strains that may evolve from this awareness is interesting enough, but combined with the strong Hispanic agrarian value structure of the island residents, there is indeed a model riddled with paradoxical possibilities. On the one hand it is possible that the present residents will look at Las Colinas as a nest of social and economic enemies; on the other hand, as a new cultural resource with which they will engage in cooperative experiences. We trust that the selection of residents in the new community will help to create some balanced formulas between community privacy and openness.

B. Program

The second consideration, or question, is *how* can we, with this foundation, develop a program of systematic/spontaneous leisure counseling when, at present, there exists very little in the literature that is applicable? With a consultant psychiatrist already on the Puerto Rican project—one with long prior experience with NIMH—there will exist a mood for interdisciplinary conceptualization. Certainly, a counseling program seems to be a natural part of such a community as this, so that its purpose of "self-discovery" can be more clearly articulated and its fulfillment or failure studied. We come, therefore, to:

C. Evaluation

The third function of our institute is therefore the ongoing evaluation of the progress of residents—individuals, families, or groups—towards the goals established in the conceptualization of the community, and goals that need to be constantly reexamined.

Given the setting of the community, all the equipment, the program and the leadership, how can such a goal be used as an ideal in a realistic testing?

If, indeed, a change can be detected by residents through guided introspection, or by analysts through tests, questionnaires, interviews, diaries, or observations of behavior, will be able to isolate the precise sources of change.

It is in this sense that we may look upon Las Colinas as a social "experiment."

D. Generalization

Finally, we may define our commitment to the relatively new field of "leisureology": can our observations—however arrived at—with residents and visitors to a community of several thousand, *be generalized and integrated into the larger body of social science?* There is no time here to develop the outlines of what leisure is, or how it can be studied.

III. Leisure in the Culture of Puerto Rico

Three subsections will be useful in placing leisure against the total perspective of this Commonwealth: *culture, class,* and *community.*

A. Culture

Two major aspects of Puerto Rico as a culture bear potentially close relationship to leisure, those that link Puerto Rico to other parts of the world through mass media, tourism, educational levels, trade, or participation in war, and those that are based on the Hispanic tradition.

As to the first, dramatic factors especially applicable to Puerto Rico are the exodus of its residents to the mainland, especially New York City, and its participation, through television, in Marshall McLuhan's "world village." The Hispanic tradition provides the indigenous identity and shelter from the external turbulence. Traceable to this heritage, shared with other Latin American nations, are such items as the Spanish language, male dominance, the paseo (comparable to the *korso* in eastern Europe) and, according to anthropologist Julian Steward—the lottery, cockfighting, Spanish styles of music, literature, art, architecture, emphasis upon spiritual and human rather than commercial values, interest in poetry, literature, and philosophy rather than in science and industry, and emphasis upon hospitality and interpersonal relations rather than upon competitive individualism.[1]

There are models, at least illustrations, of lifestyles in this island that have something to say to a construction of ideals for leisure; and the basic issue, as with all other humanistic models, whether in Japan, Turkey, or any developing culture undergoing industrialization, is whether the major elements of such lifestyle can remain secure under technology. This theme will be reopened later.

Further, as the prospect for technological and urban growth occurs, the traditional values and institutions of the agrarian heritage are increasingly challenged. Traditionally, there has been a respect for the values among and within homogeneous communities. To develop into a heterogeneous whole with diversity is a much more difficult task, especially when some of the elements in a Spanish-oriented culture take on American elements. Europe provides case studies of suspicion about Americanization as a price of industrialization.

B. Class

The class structure of Puerto Rico is one of the most interesting phenomenon precisely because of this nonmaterialistic ideology or set of values. Indeed, if we rely—as we will until we can pursue our own primary studies—on the intensive investigation of social class and social change by Melvin Tumin, we find something that contradicts traditional sociology. Academic research into social stratification tells us that in a growing, industrializing society, the mark and self-worth of a man comes from his personal possessions and, in respect to leisure, from what Veblen called conspicuous consumption. In Puerto Rico, Tumin finds the poor are entirely aware of their lack of education, occupational opportunity, and relatively low income. Yet they act, he reports, that "as if these objective indices of social position had little or nothing to do with social worthiness" (p. 452). He sees this as an index of social strain, as an ongoing conflict between an older, more traditional society and an emerging, rapidly changing, money-mad ethos. It will be interesting for us to see if the *independistas*—the 5 to 10 percent who work and vote for complete separation from the United States—do so on purely political grounds, or whether in part they prefer to remain poorer economically, but freer to cling to their old Hispanic culture. As students of leisure, we can observe which games, festivals, art forms, or types of sociable relations—as in family groups or neighborhoods—are considered to be integrative and which are prized and kept somewhat pure from "outside" impurities. In this respect, the uses made of the mass media might prove a crucial, almost the decisive instrument of leisure, which becomes on the one hand a tool for membership in the "world village" and on the other hand, an instrument of cultural individuality (as in the dominance of Spanish as the main TV language).

There will be many other observations of leisure that will center on social class. Puerto Rico, in spite of the success of Operation Bootstrap, remains an area of dramatic economic and social disparities.

In 1972, the per capita average income for the U.S.A.—excluding Puerto Rico—was $4,500; the average income in Puerto Rico per person was only $1,500. Even this last figure is more than double the average for Latin American countries, and over ten times what the figure was on the island itself two decades ago. Yet, the luxury apartments in San Juan probably compare with the best in any major city of the world. And the tourists, whom Puerto Rican domestics serve in such places as El Conquistador (a few miles from Las Colinas) for $90 per day, are seen by the residents. Again, the question arises as to perceptions of what is leisure among the rich and the poor, and how they approach it, value it, aspire toward it, fear it, and bring of their traditions to it. Oscar Lewis's volume *La Vida*, with his conceptualization of "the culture of poverty" can, in precisely the setting for his classic anthropological inquiry, provide rich clues, hypotheses, and surprises for the student of leisure.

C. Community

The third concern of the new Leisure Studies Institute, centered as it will be in a small community at one end of the island, is the potential interconnection between the leisure within the planned community and the whole island. Three general models might be followed.

First, the traditional model would be for the programs within Las Colinas to be geared fundamentally to the enjoyment of life within the village. Whatever exists in the rest of the island would be for the residents or short-term visitor to enjoy, such as going into San Juan for a movie or a night club. A perfect model of this kind is the community (Palmas del Mar) that recently opened just a few miles to the south of Las Colinas, a community financed by owners of the Sea Pines Plantation at Hilton Head Island, South Carolina.

A second model is its opposite, a community not unlike many neighborhoods, suburbs, or small towns in the nation that has a minimum of its own resources; its residents, therefore, have to rely for entertainment, art sports, adult education, etc., on resources outside, as in the nearby metropolitan center.

The third model, of course, is between these two. The leadership and the program in such a situation provides substantive activities, but serves also as a bridge to larger or more varied resources, as in San Juan, the national forest of El Yunque, the festivals of villages throughout the island, the many services to the future.

However, now we must probe a little more deeply into the relationship of a leisure community to its regional content.

IV. INTERRELATIONSHIPS OF COMMUNITY TO REGION: PHILOSOPHY

Immediately it is necessary to expose a very large issue as a criteria of everything that has been said thus far and a brief comparison of Las Colinas and Disney World as the data for a hypothesis.

The issue has been stated by many observers of industrialization, and has become a crucial concern about the nature of the so-called Post-Industrial Society. It was well put by Henry Thoreau when he wondered whether technological man is such a genius at creating tools that, quite unknowingly, he surrenders his humanity and becomes the tool of his tools. U Thant, with the United Nations then, put the question another way when he observed that yesterday our decision-makers would measure their available resources, then set their goals; today, as with the Space Age, they declare their goals, appropriate the funds, then invent the necessary resources. In the second case, how are the goals arrived at, and does the invention itself become the goal? Jacques Ellul's gloomy masterpiece, *The Technological Society*, systematically raises the same question. Heilbronner, the political scientist, only a few weeks ago in the *New York Review of Books* restated the issue in a brilliant analysis of man's prospects, looking far beyond Watergate, inflation, or energy crises.

Now the point here is that a resort area is a small experiment along these lines, a state or region such as these counties in North Carolina, as Florida, California, Arizona, Puerto Rico, southern Italy, Greece, or the lower coastline of Yugoslavia, are also historical "experiments" in the various balances between, on one hand, comfort, relaxation, play, sunshine, beach, outdoor recreation, and on the other hand, significant confrontation of the mind, the creative arts, or rich human relationship.

We have been told, quite rightly, by Professor Sessoms that the familiar lines between work and leisure are fading, as seen in such developments as the four-day week, flexitime, early retirement, or longer weekends. We seek to live closer now to our play spaces than to our work places. Thus there has been a spiritual cosmological relocation whereby Heaven has been lowered to Earth in a leisure revolution brought about by the mass accessibility to TV, ideas, people, distances, physical equipment, learning, the arts, or sports—to the good life, which was once the right and aspiration of only the rich. Leisure's passkey to Heaven on Earth is the new time, the new classlessness, and most magical of all, the credit card that makes possible a trip around the world—in eighty payments.

Those of us who live in these perpetual resort syndromes like Florida, North Carolina, or Puerto Rico—even the intellectuals and ascetics—must admit that there is validity in comfort, sunshine, or beaches; but can those of us in this mileau also have access to museums, symphony concerts, well-stocked bookstores or libraries? For the public policy of leisure and of community or of regional quality of life must seriously consider this principle of policy. As a hypothesis, to be more cautious, we might consider the ideal region or the ideal lifestyle within it as that which (1) permits alternatives in values, leisure, and work patterns, (2) which educates its residents to know themselves and to be confident and guiltless in their selections of leisure, and (3) which permits their democratic access to the choices they make.

V. Two "Experiments": Las Colinas and Disney World

With this broad statement of goals and hypotheses, we may turn to Las Colinas and Disney World as relevant case studies for philosophy, policy, and planning. Note first some striking similarities.

Both projects were the creations of individuals with vision, skill in implementation, qualities of persistence and leadership in attracting others to their dreams. Walter Disney and Vigdor Schreibman were such men, both self-made.

Second, both Puerto Rico and Florida are "experiments" in the historical sense noted earlier. Blessed with good weather, lush growth, natural beauty, both have become symbols of play and paradise, of gracious living and painless aging. The images of both, were John Hunt's tests to be applied, would undoubtedly be clear, and indicate a decided ignorance by outsiders of universities, symphony orchestras, or serious values—an ignorance reinforced by the travel literature emanating from those regions or from advertisements by interested airlines.

Finally, both Florida and Puerto Rico are now deeply involved with ongoing debates within and across circles of business, government, education, and labor on precisely the issues raised above, that is, whether in respect to density control through zoning, the kind of areas they wish to be vis-à-vis 2000 A.D.; the kinds of persons or industries they wish to attract, their relationship to the rest of the nation, or in sum, the nature of their collective identities and desirable quality of life.

Thus, Las Colinas and Disney World come upon their respective and somewhat similar contexts at a critical historical time. They represent diametrically opposite approaches to the resolution of the dilemma of synthesizing various leisure worlds of coequal validity.

Consider, now, some distinctions.

Although both projects emanate from private corporations, the Florida group is geared to the concept of immediate profit for each type of activity, with short life for any red-entry. The Puerto Rican enterprise, having decided that its half-mile of harbor should not be converted into a marina—no matter how profitable—brought in water-life experts who developed an inventory of the underwater areas as far out as the island called Vieques, leading to plans for a marine museum on the Las Colinas beach.

Second, whereas both projects are rooted in the idea of contemporary leisure, one is creating in its infant stages a nonprofit institute as an instrument of mature thought, research, education on a worldwide basis, and as a supplementary planning and evaluative instrument. Disney World, and indeed its California predecessor, have not yet recognized a need for such articulation.

There is no evidence that Disney World, in all of its ingenious, internal planning, has shown—at least until now—the slightest interest in its impact upon the region, accepting the American premise of economic growth as its own rationale. Nor, as a consequence, has it involved any of the state's governmental or educational resources, or the leadership of other community resources, in planning the program within its boundaries, or in relating the project to recreational or other interests of the region except on a purely business level. Hence, with short-run profits as the only

14: LAS COLINAS

guiding principle, the corporation—so imaginative in mechanical and marketing directions—has demonstrated a complete indifference to or ignorance of relationships and carryover techniques to home life, school life, or community life of its clients. The implicit confidence in the immortality of Mickey Mouse may have some basis in the decades ahead, but when its revenues will rely on repeat visitations, the unending revitalization so well described yesterday by Kevin Donnelly may wear thin next to such conceivable techniques as a built-in instruction in the arts for visiting children, or the sponsorship of exhibitions or concerts by real community organizations of the region rather than wasting two million dollars on an ersatz of bad symphony orchestra created for only two concerts, by Arthur Fiedler, with the shabby gimmick of musicians selected from many nations of the world.

Finally, consider the major hypothesis from above, as it applies dramatically to our comparison. Florida, as the "experiment" for evaluating the critiques of Thoreau, Ellul, Mumford, Torraine, or Eric Fromm about technological society, has given to it a half-billion-dollar project, marvelously designed, highly entertaining in non-Tivoli and somewhat mechanical format, and bringing another ten million visitors per year. Tourist businesses to the south, as in Miami, complain about the reduction in average tourist stays from a week to three days with the genius of Disney to drain the family vacation budget; there are the criticisms of environmentalists like Dr. Gade yesterday, the astronomical inflation of land values recently, the coming glut of gasoline stations and the transformation of such communities as Orlando. All that is the American way, and the Disney planners cannot be faulted for these by-products. We can change the capitalistic system, but Florida will never take the lead, with a history of land chicanery and pollution that long antedates anything here discussed. Further, there is need in life for fantasy, and the Disney project in Florida is only an extension of what has been profitable to the corporation, but is not without enormous contribution to the imaginative life of the entire world.

What is lamentable, and perhaps not beyond repair, is that for its own profit interests in the long run, and for the parallel good of the region, the Disney World planners kept themselves too busy to involve its neighbors in developing the bridges and the mutually beneficial exchanges (especially with the schools) that are one mark of alert and bold, and yet necessarily humble and human planning principles.

Our present and growing involvement as a leisure planning

group with Las Colinas has already become evident early in this paper. Our observations about Disney World are also based on involvement—or sincere attempts at involvement. A short distance away, the Disney World officers knew they had available—at no cost to them—the only American fulltime think tank on leisure issues, one with close ties throughout the world. They had given to them documentation offering to plan and even raise the funds for such proposals as a children's miniature Lincoln Center for the Performing Arts, for which we had been consultants in New York. They ignored requests for such simple matters as tours through the project by the leading leisure scholars of the world who came to our team meeting in 1971. But these are details and afford only as partial evidence that the critique is based on some experience.

Nor, in conclusion, will Florida's or Puerto Rico's destiny be finally determined by the planners of either Las Colinas or Disney World. The latter, with a second more youthful generation of successors to the genius of Walt Disney, have a remarkable opportunity ahead to develop creative ties by redirecting the imagination they so clearly possess, and becoming a psychological part of the region. Las Colinas, on the other hand, still has before it the crystallization of its present hopes, and may falter in its own way within the rapid change and the internal excitement that marks the commonwealth to the south. Indeed, one hope for all such projects is precisely the kind of interchange we have here, if carried on with good will, and attuned to the vast changes in life and leisure made evident in the conference.

15
Leisure: Toward a Theory and Policy for Israel

THE title of this paper was also the title of an international seminar held 11–14 June 1979, in Jerusalem. It was sponsored by several groups: the Israel Leisure and Recreation Association, the European Leisure and Recreation Association, The Hebrew University of Jerusalem, Department of Physical Education and Recreation, and the City of Jerusalem, Department of Youth, Sports and Social Activities. Dr. Hillel Ruskin was the initiator and chairman. The seminar was closely observed by the national governing body, the Knesset, waiting for recommendations. Aside from serving with other scholars from Canada, the U.S.A., Belgium, and Israel, I had the opportunity for personal observations following the seminar.

Ten years after the Jerusalem meetings, I was invited by Dr. Hillel and the City of Jerusalem to return for an evaluation of the impact made by the consultants on programs adopted by the government and Jerusalem (which has special funds for acting independently). For personal reasons, I did not go, but I am aware of developments in this unusual nation. Cultural developments there have reached a high point within the singular political and economic conditions in that part of the world.

It is not often that a consultant is recalled to review past recommendations. Another such opportunity in my experience was the invitation by the National Guild of Community Schools of the Arts, in the United States, a year or more after I had visited many of their music schools in various parts of the country. I had prepared a book-length report for the guild in the mid-sixties, commenting on the schools, but also proposing many implementations. In the '90s I am again in communication with the guild, one of the most significant programs in music education, for all ages, for all social classes. I look forward to ongoing relationships, even to another opportunity to check on the sense of my recommendations a full generation after they were made.

It is appropriate that this conference opens with a tribute to the late Norman Lourie. For many years he lived here and breathed Israel's history, growth, and visions. He carried with him to the end a private dream of creating a project combining the elements of religion, philosophy, and leisure. In his capacity as vice-chairman of the World Leisure & Recreation Association we worked together closely, and I had to take his measure. Never a scholar, Norman was open to ideas as WLRA entered a period of major rethinking about its international purposes and programs. Whether we spoke of the Third World War, Japan, the United States, the European nations, or Israel, he spoke of leisure always with reference to personal enrichment, creativity, and democratic institutions. Norman would have wanted a living memorial such as this conference and its aftermath. And I knew him well enough to know that he would have subscribed to the duality, first that:

1. The study of leisure in Israel is of the highest importance to our understanding of leisure everywhere, for while the nation shares many characteristics with other societies, it exhibits several unique characteristics.
2. Within Israel, public leisure policy will become increasingly important in the next few decades; indeed, the directions of such policy will serve as one indicator of national meaning and success.

Israel shares with all industrialized nations the recent miracles of instantaneous communications with the world; an interdependence in its economy and politics with events outside its borders; contemporary insights through the physical and social sciences, consequences of rapid modernization upon traditions, values, and social institutions.

There are also several elements here that are unique and may have a direct bearing upon leisure as an area of pertinent study and policy:

1. Israel's strong historical roots, a gathering of 3 million whose religious, cultural, communal, and family traditions speak directly to meanings of life beyond survival;
2. Since 15 May 1948, Israel has been involved in major wars and ongoing attacks, thus raising issues of leisure as morale, therapy, instrument of personal strength and internal renewal, or as contributor to positive values.

3. Israel's social and cultural heterogeneity is visible everywhere, with residents from over one hundred nations, representing over eighty languages and dialects, raising policy issues of ethnic independence vis-à-vis national cultural identity and cohesion.

Israel provides itself and the world with a series of remarkable conditions for research, as on the position of women, the proximity of kibbutz and private lifestyles, and above all, the processes of social change in the dramatic interplay of the old and the new.

Now add to this inventory the newest factor, the tangible beginnings of a creative relationship to Egypt and perhaps a new hope for some regional constructive integration. Given the panorama as the cultural setting in which this conference commences, we dare not begin with a modest, safe, simplistic conception of leisure.

If, for example, by leisure we mean small, fragmented bits and pieces—a chess game, a TV show, a restless car trip—then the topic remains internally disjointed and nationally irrelevant. If, on the other hand, leisure is approached holistically, emanating from and contributing to personal and collective values, it is immediately enmeshed with the national world culture, with dreams, images, social disguises, and a variety of realities, with therapeutic tools for escape and emotional rehabilitation; with self-discovery or realization. The gamut, after all, includes such large prototypes as physical, social, aesthetic, intellectual, and civic activity. Barzini of Italy speaks of national play symbols to cover up national sadness; Huizinga analyzes play elements in arts, war and law; Pieper sees in leisure a basis of civilization; Dumazedier views leisure as a major indicator and value of the post-industrial society; Piaget, Sorokin, Aristotle, F. S. C. Northrup, Max Weber, Freud, Marx, Simmel—they and others have taken us far beyond the surface of play, or pleasure, or sociability, or the aesthetic, or travel, and far into the world of man's meanings, the human condition, and—at least in my writings—the relocation of heaven to earth in a kind of Judaic reordering of the cosmos through leisure.

The fact is that many levels of culture have always intermingled in Jewish history. Visiting Auschwitz, I saw a picture of the symphony orchestra formed by prisoners; in New York at the turn of the century, as Irving Howe reports in *World of our Fathers*, the theater and other arts thrived amidst the poverty and adaptations to a strange society; in Israel itself, a rich creative and aesthetic life has flourished throughout its recent decades of turbulence.

A new era of comprehensive rapport with your neighbor nation can only underscore the search for meanings of life, as well as of death. But the difference vis-à-vis the past thirty years is that knowledge and insights have accumulated during that time, by which mankind everywhere can think and act in the light of new technology, a holistic social science, and a social philosophy that is enmeshed with the new physics. It is more than an interesting coincidence that the treaty was signed, and this conference takes place, in the one hundredth year of Albert Einstein's birth. His largest dream, as yet unfulfilled, was of a quantum theory by which we could perceive the ultimate interrelationships of all the fragments and elements of being. The "new physics" is a holistic approach to the world, so that the ying and yang, the animals and plants, the chemical and the geological, the social and the physical, the processes of birth and death, are found within the other, one needing the other, and both essential to the whole. Various expressions of the groping toward an integrated conception are found in such constructions as the oriental and occidental, socialistic and capitalistic, or the functionalist anthropology of Malinowski and the structural-functional approach of Talcott Parsons.

Similarly, the study of leisure can be understood only in the comprehensive framework of the *total* society. That is, indeed, the first significant implication of this conference: that leisure and recreation in Israel are central, not peripheral, issues.

However, the integrality of leisure/recreation to national cultural theory and policy requires a formidable, comprehensive, holistic working model to set out a series of potential relationships. I need hardly note here that there is little consensus on the international scene on a formalized conception of leisure; nor, given the nature of social science, does there have to be. Each of us constructs his own tools, sometimes forgetting that they are *tools*, not gems of truth. In 1971 our Leisure Studies Program, then in Tampa, called a special conference of experts from many nations, including the socialist countries, devoting three full days entirely to the concept. Of course, afterwards each of us went his own way. But there is more need for some consensus here; the outsider has the feeling that both local and national officials in Israel are listening. Your educational leaders have gone through major reorganization. They at least will ask, what is a reasonable characterization of leisure so that they may proceed on more than an ad hoc level?

With a few notable exceptions, such as my colleague Joffre Du-

15: LEISURE: TOWARD A POLICY FOR ISRAEL

mazedier in Paris, or the Czech scholar Zuzanik, now in Canada, Kenneth Roberts in England, Phillip Bosserman in the United States, and Herald Swedner in Sweden, leisure scholars have not had much to contribute to creative thinking on the cultural level. The reverse has been more to the point: studies of such cultural policy institutions as UNESCO and the Council of Europe have themselves turned to the leisure concept. This direction among cultural policy-makers was inevitable as, in recent years, these international bodies realized that "culture" was more than the right of the elites.

The conception I have reached is a Weberian construct of elements. I find that all attempts to distinguish neat packages which are called "work," "religion," "science," "family," "education," and so forth only feed the myths or unrealities that constitute some contemporary social science. None of these institutions exists within clear-cut boundaries; each consists of very general elements that often overlap. "Work" may have "social" aspects; "religion" and the "state" are enriched with symbols. The daily realities of living do not go on in neat categories, because that is the way in sociological studies in university catalogues. My mentor and colleague in Illinois, Florian Znaniecki, used the term "human coefficient" to emphasize the need for scientists to see through the eyes of those whom they are studying, rather than through their a priori categories of human action and meaning.

Thus, I view leisure as a relatively self-determined activity experience *that falls into one's economically free-time roles, that is seen as leisure by participants, that is psychologically pleasant in anticipation and recollection, that potentially covers the whole range of commitment and intensity, that contains characteristic norms and constraints, and that provides opportunities for recreation, personal growth, and service to others.*[1]

The next question in theory is to relate our characterization to a larger set of elements in the society. The strategy in creating the model was to construct four subsystems that could be equally useful in providing a context of relationships for religion, science, education, or anything else. Thus, by putting "leisure" into the center position, we automatically elevate that subject to an institutional level, open to the same strict analytic standards. As a string quartet player, I am comfortable with the fourfold construction. Its purpose, of course, is fully realized only through the interplay of the instrumental elements; my 1975 volume should be judged on that basis.[2] Here I proposed a far simpler plan—to extract one issue from each subsystem with special applications to Israel. (see page 79 for model.)

I

The first subsystem suggests that to develop either analysis or policy, we begin with concrete, objective, measurable items such as age, income, education, residential location, health, and discretionary time. My last volume, issued a few months ago, dealt entirely with the age factor. Permit here some comments on time structure, for the Katz-Gurevitch volume, undoubtedly familiar to everyone here, notes the trend toward adoption of the five-day week, and some debate has been going on as to which should be the additional day of rest. It is clear that here, as in all Western societies, time has become a value in itself, an aspiration of all social classes for understandable purposes of personal use, relaxation from work routines, extended trips, and so on—and not as Veblen observed, merely as emulation of upper classes. In the United States there is now considerable talk of the four-day work week, and Poland in 1974 moved in that direction by doubling the number of "free" Saturdays from six to twelve per year. But these ideas are now replaced, at least supplemented, by the intriguing and sensible concept of a work-time structure based on individual tests and lifestyles, moderated of course by exigencies of the particular job or its interpenetration into the work of others.

One-third of all workers in West Germany are now on flexitime. O.E.C.D. in Paris, several years ago, devoted a full conference to new work-time structures. The idea has recently been seized upon in the United States, especially by the California Senate, as offering one way of finding part-time jobs for unemployed, for the research finds that many are willing to reduce their own work hours with the consequent surrender of some income. The new trade-off stems from the simultaneous decline in the real value of the dollar, mark, or pound, and the rising value of the hour with the growth of alternatives for its use and better material facilities to implement the selection, as in transportation.

Supporting evidence on the potential of flextime and flexible arrangements of working years is provided in the states by our National Commission for Manpower Policy, especially in the researches by Fred Best. The familiar "linear" work life has, indeed, reduced our work week from sixty to less than forty in the course of this century, and the work hours have been largely compressed into the middle portion of the lifespan. In a national sampling survey of 1978, Best found that 45 percent of workers were willing to reduce their work to part-time, with a corresponding loss of income.[3]

Obviously, the feasibility of flexitime depends on the type and structure of the job. Dr. Bernhard Teriet of West Germany holds that flexitime is "practical and applicable for up to 50–60 percent of all employees."[4]

It may be that Israel offers a unique set of circumstances for such experiments. Here the Sabbath observance by almost all provides an anchor in the weekly rhythm without the need for an arbitrary selection of a second free day. Further, your growing problem of more elderly persons, as among us, can be approached in part by reducing work time a few years before retirement. Not only can governmental services and offices adjust to flexitime with their own flexibilities, leisure services would do so as well. The gasoline shortage in the United States now introduces another motivation toward flexible work schedules and fewer working days.

The outsider may, therefore, hope that Israel will move beyond traditional time-thinking, especially when individualism and creative thinking are so characteristic of Jewish community life.

If, as Heschel holds, Judaism itself is an innovation in the "architecture of time"—with its introduction of the Sabbath—then Israel's work, and therefore, its nonwork structure, could serve as a model of social engineering with the flexible time resource as a major input. Computer techniques have made such flexible time-use more feasible to manpower and inventory controls.

For the recreation profession, flexibility then becomes both a response and a stimulus for breaking traditional benefits for what is called the "delivery of recreational services." Diana Dunn notes that in the United States, not one city of over half a million provides public recreation in its facilities from midnight to 8 A.M.[5] Yet in Bucharest I have seen a public library, well-stocked with books in half a dozen languages, open all night in a public park.

Obviously, flexibility in space goes with time. In the United States presently, from a combination of inflation, a Watergate legacy of suspicion of all government, and the "Proposition 13" mentality that now dominates all political concerns, new interest is being shown in the private or commercial sector as the coming job market for recreation graduate students (more than thirty-seven thousand in our country). Israel, in this regard, could become a laboratory for other nations if its policy permitted these flexibilities for between work and leisure time.

II

From the second subsystem there are again a multitude of revelant issues. Permit a few comments on II-B, subcultures, for the ethnic issue is central to Israeli cultural and educational policy.

As far back as 1953, AVODAH KEHILATIT, or community work, was established as a program to overcome dependency among the immigrants in twenty-one new towns; by 1968 the program had fifty staff persons in thirty-five localities under the sponsorship of SAAD, the Ministry of Social Welfare, and AMIDAR, the national housing corporation. Among the several goals, one has been "To bring different ethnic and religious groups together to improve their social relationships and to develop citizen participation."[6] The result, apparently, is a mixed picture. Katz and Gurevith conclude from their studies of leisure that "the extent of normative integration in the society . . . is very striking."[7] Yet they report that all groups, whatever their age or education, wish to maintain a national policy of cultural pluralism. Serious differences still exist among class and ethnic groups. Among the few world scholars who have related leisure seriously to cultural policy, Joffre Dumazedier suggests that the purpose of cultural planning is "merely to apply more rationally to cultural development as a function of each individual's, each group's, each class's, and each society's needs."[8]

Repeatedly, the administrators of Israel raise the question, how is a balance to be sought between national identity and ethnic variety? There are many levels of this so-called balance. In respect to proportions of population, less than 15 percent of Israel's population was of Eastern, or non-Ashkenazi origin, subdivided between what Professor Avineri of Hebrew University calls the Sephardic patriciate, the Sephardic masses and the Yemenites; by 1973 the proportion of Sephardic and all Orientals had gone to 60 percent. The Orientals have grown in political talent and power, especially in the smaller communities. The issues here are the cultural patterns among the subgroups, or more precisely, whether the European educational, recreational, and aesthetic traditions will continue to dominate in spite of new population proportions. There are forces underlying all of this, including the growing economic equality among these subcultures. The purpose of policy is to promote both the traditional and the innovative elements of the new relationships. In the past year we have seen the price paid when innovation was too rapid for part of the society. This was one of the factors in the fall of the shah in Iran. As a consultant to his ministry of culture, I met with his social planners in their attempts to preserve Islamic arts. His recent five-year plans, unsuccessful as they turned out to be, were very explicit in their search for a blend of the old and the new. Currently, in Israel, a strategy of great subtlety and potential impact is taking place in the field of music education. It stems from the method for teaching music to children through their own folksongs, and reaching forward into the most contemporary of sounds and understanding. Unable to go themselves to Hungary until now, music educators at Tel Aviv University called upon my wife, Dr. Barbara Kaplan, and her long residency in Hungary to introduce the system developed there by Zoltán Kodály. Here, then, is a simultaneous reliance upon innovation and tradition.

The field of leisure, if interpreted to cover the whole range of self-chosen activity, provides an unending laboratory for preserving and innovating—in the arts, education on all levels, the content of television, and so on. Innovations addressed to everyone can remain on the level of distribution of the mass media, or in the opportunities given to the blind, deaf, elderly, and to villages of the country. But the policy can simultaneously respect the dignity of traditions found among the subcultures. One would hope that recreation leaders and cultural policy-makers here are drawn from a broad base of population. The Council of Europe has in recent years produced conferences and reports on this point. The contrast they make is between the "democratization of culture" and "cultural democracy." The first phrase is an implicit evaluation of elite culture that should be spread among the "disadvantaged"; the second was stimulated in the anthropological literature by Oscar Lewis, and calls attention to what he termed the "culture of poverty," or the dignity of life even among the materially disadvantaged. No one would argue that minorities are culturally deprived, yet in the American society this was for a long time the educational attitude toward the blacks, and remains our policy toward our Indian children.

The purpose of leisure amidst these many ethnic groups must not be to erase differences but to feed them and therefore bring the differences in lifestyle to a state of consciousness; leadership in the recreational realm therefore performs the function of channeling the area of pluralism away from the conflict areas of politics to the areas of play. In politics, conflicts are disruptive; in play, they serve creative purposes.

III

Permit a brief discussion of leisure as a "social system," a component of the third subsystem on the model. Chapter 13 of my 1975 volume treats various prototypes of leisure as social systems, familiar originally in the work of Joffre Dumazedier as the physical, social, intellectual, aesthetic, and civic. As social systems, each of these types has its respective roles, symbols, spaces, attitudes, times, skills, functions, and restraints. It is a far different approach to activities than a mere tabulation of numbers who participate and their expenditures, or even of correlations with education or income. This nation is fortunate to have, since 1976, the studies by one of our conferees, Professor Elihu Katz of Hebrew University, and his colleague in England, Professor Michael Gurevitch; both are sociologists. The title of their volume already reveals their central conclusion—*The Secularization of Leisure: Culture and Communication in Israel.* The data is plentiful. In the rhythms of work and leisure, Israel is like other industrial societies. Sociability, time for reading and for child care rank high. Most meaningful of the major holidays is Israel's Independence Day. Yom Kippur, traditionally the most sacred of days, is now "meaningless" to sixteen of every twenty Israelis—surely, a contributing item toward the theme of secularization. Among fifty-five communities sampled by the interviewers, the kibbutzim contain the richest variety and quality of leisure resources; new settlements have the least. Trips to theaters, museums, and public parks are frequent. Educational background is most influential in the choice of daytime activities, age, for night activities. As throughout Europe, visits to the coffeehouse and walking remain important in Israel. Visiting with friends continues as a frequent activity, with one's education as the main influence on content of conversation. About half of all free time goes to television. TV programs are now broadcast on Friday night as well as Saturday, after what must have been a lively controversy; expectedly, news programs are most popular, followed by light entertainment. Finally, as the outsider would expect for a population with a strong value on the mind and the book, reading and study are esteemed for their own value and as "an important connection to Jewish tradition." Beyond these empirical findings, Katz and Gurevitch go farther than many students of the field in relating and interpreting their observations to large issues of culture and national policy. We shall anticipate eagerly the next volume in which they promise to make these policy implications more explicit.

Religious patterns and education are major variables in time-use differences. The Sabbath—both Friday evening and Saturday—is given to much family visiting, trips and rest. Television is largely a family affair. The ethic of work remains strong. As in the United States, the better educated are more content with their work and play, and would like more free time.

Among the issues these authors raise is the place of these patterns to the "attributes of the Jewish people." Their book title flows from the finding that ethnic attributes far exceed those of a religious nature. "What's more, the young people are as likely as their elders to emphasize the importance of the ethical and the ethnic, and are *less* likely than their elders to agree that religious beliefs and practices are characteristic."[9]

The purpose of this portion of my statement is to suggest the need for a theoretical analysis of activity prototypes in relation to social symbols, needs, and the uniqueness of both national and subcultural patterns. This serves the purpose of leisure counselling and education; it clarifies the needs of persons who are being served; programming takes on the dimension of conscious purpose. The preparation of recreation leaders, therefore, calls upon social-psychological awareness of activities as well as of people. Among the special studies reported in the Katz-Gurevitch volume, the place of mass media is especially important. In your country as well as mine, movies, radio, newspapers, and television represent important use of time, both in quantity and impact. But the questions asked by these scholars—both expert in the field of communications—go beyond a simple counting of the public and ask "What do people do with the media?" Contrary to Marshall McLuhan, their functional technique of research "argues that people bind the media to their needs more readily then the media overpowers them." They begin with an attempt to identify the felt needs of the population and of subgroups; then the extent to which the media fills those needs. There is no time or necessity here to examine their results in detail. Perhaps the most significant for the conference is the fivefold grouping of socio-psychological needs among the Israelis (Arab residents were excluded from the survey).

1. Needs related to strengthening information, knowledge, and understanding . . .

2. Needs related to strengthening aesthetic, pleasurable, and emotional experience . . .
3. Needs related to strengthening credibility, confidence, stability, status . . .
4. Needs related to strengthening contact with family, friends, and the world . . .
5. Needs related to escape or tension-release . . .

Comfort for the recreation profession can derive from their first conclusion, that "For all needs examined, the nonmedia sources (combined) were deemed more gratifying than the mass media. Friends, holidays, lectures, and work were often said to be more important sources of gratification than the media." For example, "friends are more important than the mass media in needs having to do with self-gratification, even 'to be entertained.'"

Some comments on our current situation in the U.S.A. may be of interest. Until recently, inflation was the new focus of our leisure research. The issue was pertinent everywhere in terms of changing lifestyles, but especially to the South and states like Florida. The index of tourism became a crucial indication. To the surprise of many newspaper columnist and politicians, tourism kept expanding. Disney World in Florida had exceeded attendence expectations by several millions in the 60s in its first years, and May 1979 saw a 13 percent increase over May of 1978—and this in the face of both inflation and our newest fear—the real or manipulated shortage of gasoline. However, the near panic over oil shortage did result in deserted highways in many states, especially California, over our recent Memorial Day weekend. If, in fact, the fear continues, or a real shortage is confirmed, a far-reaching change in American life may be expected: shorter trips for pleasure and vacation, more use of community and neighborhood facilities, and more home-centered activity. On the last of these, television's impact will be interesting to observe, for a recent national survey for the *Washington Post* indicated a lowering use of TV, largely because of growing disgust with commercials and the quality of programs. The revolution going on in electronic communications is the key to the future of much leisure in the United States. For example, if pay-TV grows in popularity and within this, freedom—at a price—to eliminate commercials and select a higher offer of levels—one result may be direct broadcasts of concerts, as from Lincoln Center, and an enormous economic boom for the arts. Already, federal subsidy for the arts has gone from seven to over two hundred million since 1965; as a nation we already spend annually about eight billion more for attendance at professional arts than for all sports. Our total national expenditure for recreation in recent years exceeds the cost of national defense. There are other significant leisure trends in the United States, but that is not our fundamental issue here. I have mentioned some of our issues in the hope that when Professor Katz and his colleagues relate their findings here to broad cultural issues, they will treat Israel as a case study among other technological societies as well as for its uniquenesses.

It would appear that in both societies the race between education and technology, envisioned by H. G. Wells, is not yet a black-and-white issue; nor, as Jacques Ellul fears, a clear victory for technological values. Even in Israel, we are told, women are knitting, men are engaged in sports, games, and collecting; and many more of both sexes than we supposed are involved with the arts.

The Israeli school system is understandably focused on the issue of "integration" since your State Education Act of 1953 and the reforms following the Prawer committees in the mid-1960s. Those attempts at reform, successful or not, sought to restructure the schools, to do something about the existing social and economic stratification among its people.

Perhaps, with the rethinking in your new political and cultural situation, the time has come for another look at your schools in reference to substantive issues on quality of life. This is a more difficult issue than structural reform for a pluralistic and democratical goal.

This conference and profession might consider its role in the initiation of a new educational initiative. The United States has a similar need to consider a widening of its purposes, and to enlarge the current demand for a return to the "basics." By that is meant usually the skills of reading, writing and arithmetic as tools for making a living. The need now is to convince our policymakers that skills in the nature of leisure commitments are equally basic. Educators, however, will react only if the point is made by the society as a whole.

In all industrial societies then, the need for educational institutions to prepare for leisure and ultimately retirement is well founded. One of my classes was visibly moved a few weeks ago as we discussed lifestyles in the postindustrial society. In the United States, the current twenty-year old can—by present time-use—anticipate a minimum of 35 hours of "free time" every week; even without vacations and the anticipated reduction of work hours per year, this comes to 1750 free hours per year, and 87,500 over fifty years. That is, by the age of seventy, our current college sophomore will have had an equivalent of almost thirty *years* of free time at the rate of eight hours per day! That is the reason that the LEAP program was developed in Indianapolis several years ago—Leisure Education Advancement Project—limited to the public schools and funded by a private foundation.

IV

We come to the last subsystem of the model, and here I prefer to end with some general comments touching all four components. It is clear that, to an unusual, even to a dramatic degree, Israel is a "social order" that contains the first three, perhaps also the fourth component. Among its residents are some who live as their forebears did centuries ago. They differ from examples in other societies in that they comprise a part of a modern environment, but the force of tradition or religion are strong as among Arab, Oriental, or gypsy groups.

The second, so-called Kilowatt type of social order is shared here with industrial societies in Western Europe and parts of the communist bloc and Japan: technological processes, middle classes, high literacy, rapid change and so on.

The Cogno-Social Order is transitional, seeking to understand its roots as well as its goals and direction. The Cultivated order, finally, differs from Daniel Bell's more familiar "post-industrial," by paving the way for a blending of moralistic utopias with scenarios that are grounded in realities and trends.

Thus, the model is not devised as an historical order, and that is why I avoid the sequential categories—preindustrial, industrial, and postindustrial. Bell and others have attempted to establish criteria for the last category, with evidences from the United States, Japan, and Sweden.

The assumption to guide policies for Israel's future is that the country will continue to be a state of flux, change and self-evaluation, typifying the so-called Cogno-Social Order. For a long time to come, no matter what its external political or military circumstances, social and cultural stability are unrealistic scenarios. Elements from the past will always remain dominant, and mixed in a unique way with Western science, technology, and thought. Both educational and leisure policy, to be realistic, must prepare for and reflect this permanent dynamic.

The first principle for leisure policy is both flexibility in program and depth of content. Even more than in the relatively stable situations of Europe and the United States, people here become the focus, rather than formulae for organization or programs. The training of recreation and community workers in such a changing content must be humanistic as well as technical, grounded in philosophy and history, conscious of community structure and social heterogeneity. For example, the evaluation of the recreation program is mistaken if in the words of a recent letter to me from the Ontario Recreation Society, it seeks to find indices to measure the so-called "soft" assessments where they are—on the internal, private, indefinable level. I am not anti-science; I am concerned that science recognize its limitations. That aspect of recreation and leisure had best be treated through such instruments of language and emotion familiar in aesthetic or humanistic and poetic discourse." This approach requires leaders who are secure individuals, working for flexible but secure administrators.

A second derivative principle with a Cogno-Social Order is that the leisure-recreation profession is highly interdependent with other agencies and institutions of the community or nation, and even close to international bodies. On the world level, the curriculum for leisure and recreation students should know the series of UNESCO cultural policy reports from more than twenty countries, and the 1978 reports from the Council of Europe on "Socio-Cultural Animation." Within the communities to which they are sent for field experiences, young leaders should know the full cultural resources—libraries, theaters, ethnic activities, and so on. If, as is often the case, the national or local government bodies are overly decompartmentalized, the leisure-recreational proponents are in a favorable position to cross times; their impact upon the schools can help provide a cultural focus. Still in its humanistic role, this profession is also interested in the work context and its improvement. But overall, we may accept for leisure-recreation the concept of responsibilities defined by a 1973 report of the European Foundation for Cultural Development.

> Animation may be defined as that stimulus to the mental, physical and emotional life of people in an area which moves them to undertake a range of experiences through which they find a greater degree of self-realization, self-expression and awareness of belonging to a community over the development of which they can excercise an influence.

Returning, finally, to this association, several directions seem desirable:

1. That this association explore the possibilities of a permanent alliance, perhaps in the form of a joint committee with your ministries of culture and education, based on a resolution from these proceedings. Its purpose would be a comprehensive exploration of common issues and strategies. The mood vis-à-vis the United States may now be ripe for interchange with American authorities and agencies, and through your affiliation with ELRA and its worldwide umbrella, WLRA, for permanent interchange with educators and recreators of other nations.

2. That this association explore a permanent relationship with relevant groups and training institutions in Egypt. Following the thinking of the Israeli business community, it is important to pursue a policy of joint action. A statement from Mr. Uzia Galil, president of an electronics firm in Haifa, is worthy of more. "It's more important that the first things we do must be successful. The image of success is vital . . . It's also terribly important that we create a spirit of partnership. We should try to look for Egyptian areas of strength. The worst thing we can do is to try to appear as teachers."

3. That this association join with other agencies of Israel to design the future. My view is that a major result of futurology is that the criteria of its success is, in large part, a different attitude toward the present. The major challenge in all industrial societies is to rethink and restructure their attitudes toward work and nonwork. In my last book, published in April, I raise some questions about the actuality of a work ethic. Did it ever exist? Or rather, did this ethic serve as a convenient myth for the industrial age? For if work per se is a fundamental motivation, why does it need a theological rationale? Why is a heavenly reward necessary? And indeed, a reading of English history in the early decades of the Industrial Revolution indicates that villagers and families did not flow to Manchester, London, or Liverpool to reach Heaven sooner; nor did they hurry to the factories in response to a work instinct. They went to make money. Even with this earthly reward, some had to be recruited or dragooned by force and false promises.

There is a more serious objection to the view that the work ethic is our primary value or drive: it is after all, a means: Heaven represents the end. Can work be both means and end? This logical fallacy has been repeated endlessly, yet the paradox exists. Further, what is Heaven? A forty-hour week, or any number of hours? The fuzzy concept of Heaven, accepted with little elaboration, is that in Heaven there is no work and the chosen are forever free to gambol, converse, or in Sebastian de Grazia's articulation of the Greek view of PAIDIA, to be led to "beauty, to the wonder of man and nature, to its contemplation and its recreation, in word and song, to be serenely objective . . ." Let us submit a more realistic hypothesis, more in line with the evidence all around us: *the primary value of mankind in industrial societies is leisure.* This is what work permits and frees us to do. In preindustrial societies there is a difference, for then one's work is holistic; the whole farm is cultivated, whole shoes and whole dresses are made. The preindustrial worker does not find himself in an assembly line, with fragmented responsibility and only a fragmented car fender to guide through a machine process under technology's Saint Taylor.[10]

Two cautions may be pertinent. One is from our French colleague, Dumazedier, in his 1974 volume: "Those who support cultural planning do not intend to turn rationality in general, and service in particular, into a preferred context for cultural development . . . An official culture by those in power. It is merely to apply more rationality to cultural development as a function of each individual's, each group's, each class's, and each society's needs."[11]

A second warning comes from your renowned authority in policy-planning, Prof. Y. Dror of the Hebrew University, in his characterization of the social sciences. Among them he notes: "(a) oscillation between idiographic microstudies and 'grand theory'; (b) a priori commitment to equilibrium and structural-functional concepts, which result in do-nothing, or at best, incremental-change recommendations; (c) timidity in falling into social issues and in handling taboo subjects; (d) perfectionism which causes withdrawal from problems with time-constraints, that is, all significant policy issues; (e) deep feelings of guilt about getting involved in applications that go beyond 'value-free,' 'pure,' 'factual,' and 'behavioral' research."[12]

These several directions for goals have only begun to lay some base for more specific considerations of leisure in educational, communal and labor frameworks. This conference, therefore, is not grafted on to your national life, with leisure only a minor consideration in a larger struggle for economic growth, internal political stability, and peace; the conference can make explicit a philosophical and policy tool of high importance—no less than a framework for unity, comprehensiveness, balance, interrelatedness and the eternal flow from the "I" to the "thou," from the one to the many, from rationalism to existentialism.

A few days ago, I was interviewed in Tel Aviv by a young journalist writing for one of the Tel Aviv evening newspapers. We spoke broadly of many issues; she is disturbed about the antiwork attitudes here, the difficulty of obtaining sustained dedicated work. My response could hardly be on a factual level. As an outsider, I told her that the material goods are apparently going forward—buildings, highways, new communities. But to me that surprising achievement is not the material foundation of society, or even its ability to survive. These are means, and testify to efficiency, good intelligence, the will to live, and as everywhere are only the means. But the ends are exemplified or symbolized by the superb chamber orchestra I listened to in rehearsal in Shevayyin, made up of thirty fine musicians from kibbutzim around the country, playing Mozart, Handel, and a contemporary Israeli work; or the dance festival at Dahlia, or the fine pictures, sculptures, and jewelry we saw in the art galleries of Tel Aviv and Ein Harod. It is this threefold synthesis or juxtaposition of creative life, the struggle for survival, and natural national growth that is the real miracle. This synthesis needs constant articulation research, celebration, and nurturing. This, I suggest, is perhaps your contribution.

Epilogue

THUS, some strands of one life, one lifestyle. Now, in eighty-four years, perhaps a web can be discerned. It must go beyond summary, and attempt more than a subjective summary, hopefully honest. Other issues will be treated to contribute to the whole work.

Who was it that wrote, "The life that is not examined is not worth living"? At any moment the miraculous brain system that each of us possesses can immediately bring into focus our mother, our father, a specific small event, or an emotion of many years past. It makes no difference, the age we are for the moment. Now in my 80s, I can see father coming home on his free Saturday with a bag of taffy for the boys; or, without any more effort, Prof. Znaniecki in a graduate seminar, as in his Polish accent he explains his version of "social role"; or suddenly in my mind I find myself again at an elegant party in Rome, everyone jabbering in rapid Italian.

Similarly, all I have written of maturing, teaching, consulting, fiddling, and writing are with me. I need no mouse in this personal Internet. It is all there.

The ultimate issue is not *presence*, but *essence*. Now, approaching the end of life, what has this web meant? Does it reveal a pattern? A person?

Obviously, there are unities or consistencies in each life. My first self-inventory seeks out those consistencies. I find, then, a person who gives evidence of the Hellenic-Judaic manner of mind, who is in some ways insecure and in other ways very certain, who makes much of the "if" factor—judging his past decisions; who is both a realist and a romantic—an idealist and a pragmatist; who is both detached from the world and yet a modest creative force; finally, one who, approaching the end has a feeling of just beginning to see himself in the total web of the society, just beginning to understand even the issues of which he has written and taught to students and the public.

In short, the key to this man is revealed by the unity that Sorokin called his "key role" as an academic, in juxtaposition with the adventures as extra-campus consultant, as citizen, fiddler, and writer. The central characteristic that runs through this manage in the presence of the family, first, an immigrant family.

All in all, this has prepared me to leave the earth with both a troubled and a settled mind.

Do not expect that I will illustrate every item above. They are what I know. Take the Hellenic-Judaic matter. I know definitely that my mind—therefore the writing and teaching—definitely leans toward categories and generalizations rather than to details. For example, an interesting year was spent as the academic dean of Bennett College in Millbrook, N.Y. This private institution for privileged girls, now defunct, did not benefit from an expected mastery of details on such matters as schedules, allocation of credits, and the like. Even in a small institution, such items are the skeleton of good administration and protection for the student. The writing throughout illustrated the Germanic kind of mind, such as in the disassociation of "leisure" from specific activities (sports, arts, travel), relating leisure as a part of the social process in the manifestation of sociability, association, movement, and immobility. Again, the turn toward consultation stems from the need or the tendency for generalizations: the role of the consultant to others is more inclined to avoiding details in the attempt to get at the goals and policies of others.

How can it be that in his eighth decade, a scholar is just "beginning?" Indeed, that is both the joy of the intellectual life and its limitations. The subject widens more as we study it. In part this is a dilemma of his depth. This must be a problem for the architect who passes a building that he devised, and wished he could redo it, or the painter who would like to repaint the picture of his that hangs permanently in a gallery.

Recently I decided to reread the two-volume work by the historian, Daniel Boorstin, on the discoverers and the creators. Aside from its rich substance, Boorstin takes the trouble, on pages 687–713 of the first volume, to comment on the sources he had found valuable. That supplementary section was written to induce further reading, and it succeeds in producing historic appetite. Boorstin's level of detail as a seminal historian is beyond the reach of one like myself, the incomplete sociologist.

It is useful to know one's limitations, but also one's potential. The musical part of my life added to the sociological, providing one kind of truth. The teaching part of the career helped to cultivate the expressive or creative element of the "scientific."

Now, toward the end, I can accept this strange polarity. With every day or month that I am inactive as a creator of ideas or as analyst of readings, I feel myself in a position of more than disengagement, indeed, of a slowing, comfortable exit from the web of the total life situation or existence. My family—unto three great-children—grows in importance, and I bow to the humility of one's contribution to the tradition of knowledge.

What I have had to say about spirituality or the place of religion in my life is perhaps implicit in the picture of the family. I prefer the term "tradition" rather than "theology." Were a label essential, Mordecai Kaplan's "Reconstructionism" would be my choice. As one commentator writes,

> Even though he dropped belief in God as Jews had understood the term for three thousand years, Kaplan never considered dropping his Jewish affiliation. Basic to the Reconstructionist ideology that he developed was the conviction that Judaism is an 'evolving religious civilization' in which religious teachings, ritual observances, peoplehood, and culture all play a part . . . the most important book, *Judaism as a Civilization.*

Over the many years, the community experience of the Jews added up to a history of adaptations. One result was that the direction of its philosophy was earthbound. Its concept of heaven was perhaps developed or needed in other religions. The result was a Judaic conception of the good life as one of earthly service, ongoing education, strong community and family life.

Yet, as important as a life may be in relation to spiritual, moral, or religious values and concepts, I return to the fact that this one life came at a highly unique time of human history. Teaching and writing are, after all, forms of communication. My life has bridged the long continuum from handwritten letters to typewriters to e-mail. I, for one, have not entered the computer age directly—a dinosaur of the past. Now, in the 1990s, I become increasingly aware of this as I find difficulty in locating typewriter ribbons for my IBM. . . .

One can be intellectually aware of "cyberspace," be affected by it, and yet not be "into" it. I have never used a fax, and can hardly digest the miracle of e-mail. My daughter, her husband, and both of their daughters each possess a Casio gadget, small enough for pocket or purse, that is a portable office. It subsumes a calculator system, records addresses, reminds one of tasks for the day, takes notes of conversations, notes expenditures and income . . . perhaps more. I have no need for such a gadget, would probably misplace it constantly around the house, and distrust my intelligence in its mastery. I am a misfit for Casio.

I am not sure that cyberspace will produce a better world. It makes for less individuality, even as total strangers become worldwide correspondants. The possibility of airborne destructiveness is enhanced, even producing filth in the form of pornography. Amid the many advantages for communications of every kind, ways will be found by unscrupulous agents to profit from dishonesty. Of course, this giant technical direction cannot be stopped. This is no time for Luddites. This is the new "technopoly" of Neil Postman.

As much as cyberspace forces us to deal with human values, technopoly brings our society to face survival on its deepest levels: first, the potential for an *"end of work"* as we know it because of cybernation/automation/robotization/computerization; second, the *end of community* because of the impersonal nature of the new technology.

Joseph Schumpeter, some time ago, argued that capitalism will eventually fail or be seriously modified precisely because of its successes. His prophecy seems to be taking place now, with capitalism as we know it going through a dramatic revolution. The change is spelled out in a recent dramatic examination by Jeremy Rifkin in his volume *The End of Work*.[2]

> On the eve of the third millenium, civilization finds itself straddling two very different worlds, one utopian and full of promise, the other distopian and rife with perils. At issue is the very concept of work itself. How does humanity begin to prepare for a future in which most formal work will have passed from human being to machines? Our political institutions, social covenants, and economic relationships are based on human beings selling their labor as a commodity in the open marketplace. Now that the commodity value of that labor is becoming increasingly unimportant in the production and distribution of goods and services, new approaches to providing income and purchasing power will need to be implemented. Alternatives to formal work will have to be devised to engage the energies and talents of future generations. In the period of transition to a new order, the hundreds of millions of workers affected by the re-engineering of the global economy will have to be counseled and cared for. Their plight will require immediate and sustained attention if we are to avoid social conflict on a global scale.

Rifkin provides a wealth of data to support this thesis that "the triumph of technology appears more a bitter curse, a requiem for those who will be made redundant by the new economy and the breathtaking advances in automation that are eliminating so many human beings from the economic process." He notes that already eight hundred million persons in the world are unemployed or unemployable.[3] The Third Industrial Revolution is substitution software for workers, while *raising* the productive capacity of America, Europe, and Asia, "Reengineering" can reduce or eliminate between one and 2.5 million workers in the United States as the workerless factory becomes the goal.[4] Peter Drucker estimates that there will be a drop from 33 percent of United States workers engaged in manufacturing in the 1950s to less than 12 percent in the next decade,[5] calling this disappearance of labor the "unfinished business of capitalist society."[6]

Rifkin derides the familiar theory of "trickle down" benefits brought on by that . . . trickle down to the masses of workers in the form of cheaper goods, greater purchasing power and more jobs.[7]

The one hundred million computers presently in use throughout the world, says Rifkin, will become more than one billion in a few years—computers more advanced, of course, than the present generation in respect to "intelligence."[8]

Special attention is paid in the volume to the situation of African-Americans and to farmers. He ends with proposals for the shorter work-week, increased volunteerism to fill the enlarged portions of leisure, public works programs, and other steps for the "independent sector." The future, concludes this economist, must center in "human relationships, or feelings of intimacy, on companionship, fraternal bonds, and stewardship—qualities not easily reducible to or replacable by machines. This end of work could spell a death sentence for civilization as we have come to know it . . . could also signal a beginning of a great social transformation, a rebirth of the human spirit."[9]

Alas, I will not live long enough to witness the directions predicted for the Third Industrial Revolution. As a "possibilist," I rely on the changing nature of human values; as a Dewey-ite, I rely on the intelligence of the coming generations. As one who has spent a career on the theory of leisure as both a set of actions and a source of values, I recognize more than ever before that my worldwide colleagues and I have been engaged in thinking through one of the major solutions offered by Rifkin. His analysis confirms my deep-seated conviction that we have just begun to explore the possibilities of the workless segments of the present and future generations. We trust it has been a solid beginning, without thousands of publications, numerous conferences in all parts of the world, and serious research.

Second, technology both symbolizes and realizes an end of individuality, a large step toward the primacy of secondary human relationships. The matter is well put by Joel L. Swerdlow in his piece in the *National Geographic:*[10]

> Often the changes that accompany new information technologies are subtle we barely notice them. Before the written word, people relied on their memories. Before telephones, more people knew the pleasure of writing and receiving letters, the small joy of finding a handwritten envelope in the mailbox from a friend or a relative. Before television and computers, people had a stronger sense of community, a greater attachment to neighborhoods and families.
>
> Television has glued us to our homes, isolating us from other human beings. Only one-quarter of all Americans know their next-door neighbors. Our communities will become less intimate and more isolated as we earn college credits, begin romances, and gossip on the internet, a worldwide system that allows computers to communicate with one another. The Age of Software will offer more games, home banking, electronic shopping, video on demand, and a host of other services that unplug us from physical contact.

I return to the question, would I want to relive the life that is implicit in the description of these writings?

It has been the life of an educator, within a university framework, structured within the discipline and tradition of sociology, narrowed around the special issues of leisure, the arts and society, and gerontology. All of this, in turn, was intimately linked to my origins of immigrants in a democracy new to them, to an identity with Judaism, to family patterns, to the unique historical circumstances of an evolving "technological society" (Ellul), the "end of ideology" (Bell), an inundation of a Third Wave (Toffler), and the impact of a mass-oriented "other directedness" (Riesman).

Clear lines cannot be drawn between particularistic and general influences upon any of us as persons, or between those aspects of our lives that come from our own decisions as subjective participants vis-à-vis decisions made for us by persons even unknown to us.

Many years ago I was deeply affected by a silent movie. An older Chinese gentleman backs into a wall and is killed by a sharp abutting nail. As he dies, three short scenarios rush through his mind. The first two depict the lives that might have been lived had he followed different paths in his choice of mate and career.

EPILOGUE 219

The third depicts the life that actually took place. His final flashes of thought accept his real life course as the most ideal.

For one in his youth, this movie raised the eternal "if" question. Some of us daydream repeatedly on the "if" level. Others, like President Truman, could make a fateful decision on dropping the Bomb, then sleep soundly that night.

With all the "ifs" in the back of my mind over the years, a final evaluation validates my career as it actually took shape.

My Jewishness, based far more on values and common pride than on theology, was nourished by the realization that leisure at its best is ultimately a search and symbol of a "heaven on earth."[11]

My concerns for creativity, self-expression, and internal freedom were met in my studies of the arts as a way of confronting the world.[12]

My conviction about the contemporary elderly—my generation now—that Old is Triumphant was verified in observations of current activism and even greater potential.[13]

Overreaching such intellectual concerns, the ultimate conclusion by the Chinese gentleman in his final moments and my own in the final years, must rest on a visceral feeling that it has been a good life. I have touched thousands of young minds. A few concepts have been suggested to colleagues; there has been direct access to agencies, governments, and colleagues in many parts of the world as well as in my own country; performances as a violinist have come from the same hands that scribbled generously on yellow pads. Perhaps most importantly, these concerns and writings have dealt with some realities of a changing world.

Who knows how any of this has changed the world?

But can anyone have asked for more?

But—can that be all? There were other lives—a life of teaching, of fathering, of traveling, of organizing, of citizen-ing. Can one of these be isolated from the other? Of course not, for "life" is not divisible, except for a moment, for a specific purpose. So I look back, after finishing those pages, to the autobiography that I wrote for my grandchildren, taking the life up to the move from Florida (Tampa) to Alabama (Auburn) in 1979. One of the dramatic years in that account is as academic dean at a small two-year college for daughters of the rich in a feudal part of New York state—a drama that opened my thoughts to the "soul" of such an institution. In the document, I recall some of the trips into eastern and western nations during the period of the 1970s and the early 1980s, trips that exhibited the place of scholarship-political brews in the academic centers of Communist Poland,

Hungary, Czechoslovakia, and Yugoslavia. And in the same work for the six girls I am led to very private observations as a consultant to Lincoln Center in its formative years, and of the birth of a great youth orchestra in Boston.

With these adventures in mind, among many others, I realize how narrow was the portion of my life as depicted in the short essays about this book or that book. Indeed, even as these commentaries were in preparation, I found myself, perhaps an index of advancing age, reading some remarkable histories: Howard Sachar's *History of the Jews in America*. David McCullough's *Truman*, Albert Hourani's *A History of the Arab Peoples*, Simon Schama's *Citizens, A Chronicle of the French Revolution,* Daniel Boorstin's *The Creators, a History of Heroes of the Imagination*.

Never have I encouraged such a wealth of true scholarship in a few months time. Such a standard by these authors is hardly approached by any of the twenty-six works in my catalog. Indeed, they confirm my conviction that even in the most serious among them—perhaps the books of 1961, 1975, 1991, 1992—I have only begun to recognize and treat the subjects that took my attention. In that sense, my studies have been no more than introductions for younger and better scholars to pursue.

And yet I am aware of the differences in the traditions of historiography and sociology. Even among the giants of the second discipline—Max Weber, Herbert Spencer, Talcott Parsons, and others—while there is evidence of historical grasp, the essence is unique. Social science is not the narration and interpretation of mankind's story, but the construction of systems of analysis toward the understanding of social processes and institutions. The rest of us in this discipline have done no more than to open a few doors and windows. This had to be done in the early stages of the study of leisure. Little more could be hoped for among the early generation of these students than to attempt some conceptualizations, propose some categories, or suggest some relationships to the larger patterns of work, family, church, or community. It was especially necessary because the first group of policy-makers and frontliners in the leisure area came from the world of recreation; it has, until lately, been a world not known for its concern with the abstract and the theoretical. For better or for worse, sociology dominated this body of theory, and since the European sociologists were better equipped than we in a type of sociology that incorporated philosophy, history, and literature, such men as Joffre Dumazedier of France, together with his countrymen, Georges Gurevitch and Jacques Ellul, perceived the significance of the phenomenon. It was the first of these, in Paris, who had the connections with UNESCO to bring action into play; and thus, we in the other nations had to think on international levels to be realistic.

This was a heady world which the son of immigrant Lithuanians had taken as his own. Yet there was a leavening influence, music, which had been a legacy from that family, to which the violin lessons for one of its sons was a symbol of their new freedom; the fiddler, as Yehudi Menuhin makes clear in his Preface to Boris Schwart's *Great Masters of the Violin*,[14] "always played the violin to express the joys and sorrows of the Russian villages . . . the violin was the passport, purse, and path to the summits of society." Just as the life of scholarship, especially in the new field of leisure, was amorphous, often vague, and always required a justification among the uninitiated, so the violin and music in general were accepted everywhere, relatively precise, and included such built-in objective measures of accomplishment as the execution of the Bach solo sonatas and partitas. At any time in my life, including the present, I take a whack at the great Chaconne, and can instantly and precisely know for myself the condition I am in, both left and right hand. This is impossible in writing a book, an article, or teaching a lesson for university sophomores. The book of 1975 is not necessarily better—"better"—than the one on the same subject of 1961. Indeed, the second is more often quoted than the first. It was, I am sure, this combination of music and sociology in one life that brought some sanity rather than potential schizophrenia.

Further, there is a hypothesis that I may pursue some day: That the study of music provides a "truth," a stability, while the study of sociology provides a position for laughing at the foibles of our time. The arts are close to theology; the social sciences, to psychiatry and comedy.

Notes

Prologue

1. Eric Trist, in *Main Trends in the Social and Human Sciences* Part I. (Paris, The Hague: Mouton/UNESCO, 1970).
2. Yehezkel Dror, *Ventures in Policy Sciences, Concepts and Applications* (New York: Elsevier, 1971), Ch. 2.
3. Gunnar Myrdal, *Asian Drama, an Inquiry Into the Poverty of Nations* (New York: Pantheon, 1968), Vol. I.

Part One: Life. Introduction

1. Max Kaplan, *Essays on Leisure: Human and Policy Issues, An approach to leisure studies: origins and influences.* (Madison, N.J.: Fairleigh-Dickinson University Press, 1991), p. 23.

Chapter 1. Maturing

1. Abraham Shulman, *The Old Country: The Lost World of East European Jewry* (New York: Scribners Sons, 1974.)
2. Irving Howe, *World of Our Fathers* (New York: Harcourt Brace, Jovanovich, 1976.)
3. W. I. Thomas and Florian Znaniecki, *The Polish Peasant in Europe and America* (New York: Dover Publications, Inc., 1958), Introduction, p. 308.
4. Isaac Metzker, editor, *A Bintel Brief*, vol. ii, *Letters to the Jewish Daily Forward*, 1950–1980, Introduction. (New York: The Viking Press) See also, Irving Howe, *World of Our Fathers*, pp. 533–37.
5. Irving Howe, *World of Our Fathers*, p. 359.
6. Ibid., p. 358.
7. Max Lerner, *America as a Civilization*, vol. 1. (New York: Simon and Schuster, 1957), pp. 21–22.
8. Mark Twain, What Paul Bourget thinks of us, *Collected Tales, Sketches, Speeches and Essays* (New York: The Library of America, 1992), pp. 168–169.
9. Alvin Toffler, *The Third Wave* (New York: William Morrow and Company, Inc., 1980).
10. Paul Kennedy, *Preparing for the Twenty-First Century* (New York: Random House, 1933).
11. Jacques Ellul, *The Technological Society* (New York: Vintage Books, 1964), Chapter 2, pp. 61–147.
12. Robert Morison, Visions, in *Technology and the Future*, Albert H. Teich, editor. (New York: St. Martin's Press, 1986), p. 9.

13. John Naisbitt, *Megatrends* (New York: Warner Books, 1982), pp. 30–31, 35–52.
14. John Condry, *Daedalus* (Winter 1993).
15. Mark Twain, Corn-Pone Opinions, in *Collected Tales, Sketches, Speeches, and Essays*, 1891–1910, pp. 507–11.
16. Max Kaplan, An approach to leisure studies—origins and influences, *Loisir et Société*, vol 3. no. 2, November 1980.
17. Max Kaplan, *Leisure: Theory and Policy* (New York: John Wiley and Sons, Inc., 1975), Chapter 18.
18. Arthur Koestler, *The Act of Creation* (New York: Dell Publishing Co., 1967), pp 231–33.

Chapter 2. Teaching

1. Daniel Boorstin, *The Discoverers* (New York: Random House, 1983), p. 322.
2. Allan Bloom, *The Closing of the American Mind* (New York: Simon and Schuster, 1987).
3. Michel de Montaigne, *Essays* (New York: Heritage Press, 1946). Of custom, and the undesirability of changing established laws, p. 145.
4. Pitirim Sorokin, *Contemporary Sociological Theories* (New York: Harper and Brothers, 1928).
5. Florian Znaniecki, *Cultural Sciences, Their Origin and Development* (Urbana: University of Illinois Press, 1953).
6. Gunnar Myrdal, *Asian Drama, An Inquiry into the Poverty of Nations* (New York: Pantheon, 1968), Vol. 1, p. 32.)
7. John Neulinger, *Leisure Information*.

Chapter 4. Writing

1. Gunnar Myrdal, *An American Dilemma* (New York: Harper and Brothers, 1944), vol. 11, pp. 982–86.
2. David Riesman, *The Lonely Crowd, A Study of the Changing American Character* (New Haven: Yale University Press, 1950).
3. Joseph Pieper, *Leisure, the Basis of Culture* (London: Faber, 1962).
4. Jacques Ellul, *The Technological Society* (New York: Vintage Books, 1964).
5. Sebastian de Grazia, *Of Time, Work, and Leisure* (New York: Twentieth Century Fund, 1962).
6. Morris Ernst, *Utopia* (New York: Rinehart, 1955).
7. Ibid., p. 15.
8. M. Kaplan, *Music in Recreation* (Champaign, IL: Stipes Publishing Co., 1955).
9. M. Kaplan, *Leisure in America: a Social Inquiry* (New York: John Wiley and Sons, Inc., 1960).
10. Ibid., Preface.
11. Ibid., p. 304.
12. *From Max Weber: Essays in Sociology.* H. H. Gerth and C. Wright Mills, eds. (New York: Oxford University Press, 1946), p. 59 f, 294, 323 f. Also, Talcott

Parsons, *The Structure of Social Action* (Glencoe, Illinois: The Free Press, 1949, pp. 601–609.
13. M. Kaplan, *Leisure Theory and Policy*, p. 26.

Chapter 5. Modeling

1. John Neulinger, *The Psychology of Leisure: Research Approaches to the Study of Leisure.* (Springfield IL: Charles C. Thomas. 1974, 1981), p. 14.
2. Max Kaplan, *Leisure, Theory and Policy*, pp 26–33.

Chapter 6. Fiddling

1. Yehudi Menuhin, Preface, Boris Schwartz, *Great Masters of the Violin* (New York: Simon and Schuster, 1983).
2. Michael Mark, *Contemporary Music Education* (New York: Schirmer Books, 1986), p. 3.
3. John Mueller, *The American Symphony Orchestra* (Bloomington: Indiana University Press, 1951), p. 17.

Chapter 7. Ending

1. Heshel Jaffe, James Rudin, Marcia Rudin. *Why Me? Why Anyone?* (New York. St. Martins Press. 1986, 1994), pp 182–83.

Part Two: Vision. Introduction

1. Daniel Bell, The future as present expectation, in *The Futurists*, Alvin Toffler, ed. (New York: Random House, 1972), p. 258.
2. Alvin Toffler, *The Third Wave*, p. 25.
3. Bell, The future as present expectation, p. 259.
4. Arthur C. Clarke, Hazards of Prophecy, in *The Futurist*, Alvin Toffler, ed., (New York: Random House, 1972), p. 135.
5. Ibid., p. 145.

Chapter 8. Roles: Prophets, Activists, Scientists

1. R. Lynd and H. M., *Middletown* (New York: Harcourt, Brace and Co., 1929); *Middletown in Transition* (New York: Harcourt, Brace, 1937).
2. George Sarton, *A History of Science* (New York: W. W. Norton and Co., Inc. 1952).
3. Charles Singer et al, editors, *A History of Technology* (New York and London: Oxford University Press, 1954), vol 1–5.
4. Daniel Boorstin, *The Creators, a History of Heroes of the Imagination.* (New York: Random House, 1992).
5. Jacques Ellul, *The Technological Society* (New York: Vintage Books, 1964).
6. M. Kaplan and Paul Lazarsfeld, The mass media and man's orientation

to nature. Report 22, *Outdoor Recreation Resources Review Commission* (U.S. Government Printing Office, 1962), 187–214.
   8. Jeremy Rifkin, *The End of Work* (New York. G. P. Putnam, 1995), pp. 216–17.
   9. Ibid., p. 26.
   10. Ibid., XV.
   11. Ibid., p. 7.
   12. Ibid., p. 8.
   13. Ibid., p. 12.
   14. Ibid., p. 15.
   15. Ibid., p. 61.

CHAPTER 9. FLEXIBILITIES: LIFESTYLE, TIME AND PLACE, WORK

   1. Alvin Toffler, *The Third Wave*.
   2. Joffre Dumazedier, *Toward a Society of Leisure* (New York, The Free Press, 1969).

CHAPTER 10. LEISURE AND THE GENERAL PROCESS OF THEORY/POLICY

   1. Max Kaplan and Attias-Donfut, Claudine, editors, *Educational and Leisure Time Activities of the Elderly* (Prague: European Centre for Leisure and Education, 1973).
   2. James Coleman, *American Psychological Association Monitor*, February 1973.
   3. *Annotated Bibliography on Leisure: Poland (1960–1970)*. Bibliographic Series No. 3. (Prague: European Centre for Leisure and Education, 1971).
   4. Foreign Trade Agency. *Polish Economy Survey*. Warsawa, 1974, II (296), p. 7. Polish Interpress Agency. *Panorama of Polish Industry, 1944–1974*.
   5. Stein Rokkan, "Cross-Cultural, Cross-Societal and Cross-National Research." *Main Trends of Research in the Social and Human Sciences* (Paris, The Hague: UNESCO, Mouton, 1970), Chapter X.
   6. Jan Szydlak, Speech to national conference, Warsaw, January 8, 1973.
   7. Edmund Wnuk'-Lipinski, "Job Satisfaction and the Quality of Working Life: The Polish Experience." *International Labour Review* 115; January–February 1977.
   8. Joffre Dumazedier, *Toward a Society of Leisure*, pp. 169–73.
   9. *Cultural Affairs* 1: 1–2. Bulletin of the Department of Cultural Research and Planning, Ministry of Culture and Art, Baharesten, Tehran, Iran. October 1974.
   10. Joffre Dumazedier, *Toward a Society of Leisure*, p. 166.
   11. Radovan Richta, editor, Civilization at the Crossroads (Prague: Hungarian Academy of Sciences, 1969)
   12. Daniel Bell, *The Coming of Post-Industrial Society*, op. cit.

CHAPTER 11. LEISURE AND ETHICS: CONNECTIONS AND JUDGMENTS

   1. Sebastian de Grazia, *Of Time, Work and Leisure*.
   2. Johann Huizinga, *Homo Ludens: A Study of the Play Element in Culture*. (Boston: Beacon, 1950).

3. S. R. Parker, *The Future of Work and Leisure* (London: MacGibbon and Kee, 1971).
4. David Macarov, *Work and Welfare, the Unholy Alliance*. (Beverly Hills, CA: Sage Publications, 1980). *Worker Productivity* (Beverly Hills, CA: Sage 1982).
5. C. Wright Mills, *The Sociological Imagination*. (New York: Oxford, 1959). Pitirim Sorokin, *Fads and Foibles in Modern Sociology* (New York: Regnery, 1956). Howard Becker, *Through Values to Social Interpretation* (Durham, NC: Duke University Press, 1950).
6. Max Weber, Science as a vocation, in *From Max Weber: Essays in Sociology*.
7. Florian Znaniecki, *The Method of Sociology* (New York: Farrar and Rinehart, 1934); *The Social Role of the Man of Knowledge* (New York: Columbia University Press, 1940); *Cultural Sciences: Their Origin and Development*.
8. Norberto Valentini and Clara di Meglio, *Sex and the Confessional* (London: Hutchinson and Co., 1974).
9. Martin Buber, *I and Thou*, translated by R. G. Smith. (Edinburgh: T. Clark, 1937).
10. For a commentary on "pairings" that prevail in our own society, see pp. 22–23 of Robert Bierstedt's *The Social Order* (New York: McGraw-Hill, 1957).
11. E. A. Jordan, *The Good Life* (Chicago: The University of Chicago Press, 1949).
12. Florian Znaniecki, *The Social Roles of the Man of Knowledge*.
13. Joffre Dumazedier. Among his many important writings, see *Toward a Society of Leisure* (Paris, Editions V Seuil, 1962); *The Sociology of Leisure* (New York: Elsevier, 1974); *The Study of Leisure*, (New York: The Free Press, 1967).
14. M. Kaplan, *Leisure: Theory and Policy*. (New York: John Wiley, 1975), and (Springfield, IL: Charles Thomas, 1985).
15. A. J. Heschel, *Man is Not Alone: A Philosophy of Religion*. (New York: Jewish Publication Society, 1951), pp. 28–29.
16. *Trends in American Living and Outdoor Recreation*. Outdoor Recreation Resources Review Commission, U.S. Government Printing Office, 1962.
17. *A Literature Review*, The President's Commission on Americans Outdoors. U.S. Government Printing Office, 1987.
18. M. Kaplan, *Leisure: Theory and Policy*, 1975, p. 284.
19. Alexander Szalai, *The Use of Time: Daily Activities of Urban and Suburban Populations in Twelve Countries* (The Hague: Mouton, 1972).
20. *Employment Issues in Recreation for the Elderly*, U.S. Department of Labor. Bureau of Labor Statistics, 1979.
21. Ronald Riggins, Social Responsibility and the Public Sector Entrepeneur, *Journal of Physical Education, Recreation and Dance*, October 1988 Vol. 59, 8.
22. *Work in America*, Report of the Special Task Force to the Secretary of Health, Education and Welfare, James O'Toole, Chairman. (Cambridge: MA: MIT Press, 1971).

Chapter 12. Apostles of Accuracy, Exploration, Significance

1. Alexander Szalai, editor, *The Use of Time*.
2. Ford Foundation, *The Finances of the Performing Arts: Survey of the Characteristics and Audiences for Theatre, Opera, and Ballet in 12 U.S. Cities* (New York, 1974).

3. A. C. Johnson and E. A. Prieve, *Older Americans: the Unrealized Audience for the Arts*. Graduate School of Business, University of Wisconsin, Madison, 1977.

4. Rhona and Robert N. Rapoport, *Leisure and the Family Life Cycle*. (London: Routledge and Kegan Paul, 1975).

5. Ibid, Chapter 3.

6. Youngkill Lee and Kathleen J. Helberg, An exploratory study of college students' perceptions in leisure and shyness, *Leisure Sciences*, vol. II, 217–27. 1989.

7. Youngkill Lee, Immediate leisure experiences: a phenomenological approach, Leisure Research Symposium, National Recreation and Park Association, 1990, Sociological Aspects of Leisure Research.

8. Rapoports, *Leisure and the Family Life Cycle*, p. 186.

9. Joffre Dumazedier, *Toward a Society of Leisure*.

10. Sebastian de Grazia, *Of Time, Work and Leisure*, p. 365.

11. Franz Werfel, The calendar of sleep, *Poems*. (Princeton: Princeton University Press, 1945).

12. Holmes Rolston II, Beyond recreational values and the greater outdoors preservation-related and environmental benefits, *A Literature Review, The President's Commission on Americans Outdoors*, 1986, Values, 104.

13. Max Kaplan, *Leisure: Theory and Policy*, 1975, pp. 18–19.

14. Joseph Pieper, *Leisure, the Basis of Culture* (London: Faber, 1962).

15. Bennett Berger, The sociology of leisure: some suggestions, *Industrial Relations*, (February, 1962): 31–35.

16. Paul Tillich, The person in a technological society, *Varieties of Modern Social Theory* H. M Ruitenbeek, ed. (New York: E. P. Dutton, 1963).

17. Dennis Gabor, *Inventing the Future* (New York: Penguin Books, 1963).

18. Radovan Richta, ed., *Civilization at the Crossroads* (Prague, Hungarian Academy of Sciences, 1969).

19. Alvin Toffler, editor, *The Futurists*.

20. Joffre Dumazedier, *Sociology of Leisure*. (Amsterdam: Elsevier, 1974, Introduction, p. 1.)

21. Max Kaplan, Implications for gerontology from a general theory of leisure. *Leisure and the 3rd Age* (Paris: Centre International de Gerontologie Sociale, Dubrovnik Proceedings, 1972).

CHAPTER 13. SOCIOLOGY AND MUSIC EDUCATION

1. Max Kaplan, *Foundations and Frontiers of Music Education*. (New York: Holt, Rinehart and Winston, Inc. 1966), pp. 19–20.

2. Max Kaplan, *Leisure Theory and Policy*, 1975.

3. R. Herrnstein and C. Murray, *The Bell Curve* (New York: Simon, 1994).

4. Max Kaplan, *The Arts: A Social Perspective*. (Cranbury, NJ: Associated University Presses, 1990).

5. Howard Gardner, *Frames of Mind: The Theory of Multiple Intelligences* (New York: Basic Books, 1983).

6. Peter Etzkorn, "Barbershoppers as Vestige of the Past and Promise for the Future" in Max Kaplan, *Barbershopping: Musical and Social Harmony*. (Cranbury, NJ: Associated University Presses, 1993).

7. Michael L. Mark. *Contemporary Music Education* (New York: Schirmer Books, 1978), p. 226.

8. Robert Choate, ed., *Documentary Report of the Tanglewood Symposium* (Washington, D.C.: Music Educators National Conference, 1968).
9. Max Kaplan. *The Arts*, p. 37.
10. László Vikár, ed., *Reflections on Kodály* (Budapest: International Kodály Society, 1985).
11. Wray Herbert, "Our identity crisis," *U.S. News and World Report*, (March 6, 1995): 83.

Chapter 14. Las Colinas: Plans for an Experiment in Puerto Rico

1. Julian H. Steward, et al. *The People of Puerto Rico*. (Urbana, University of Illinois Press, 1972).

Chapter 15. Leisure: Toward a Theory and Policy for Israel

1. M. Kaplan, *Leisure: Theory & Policy*, 1975, p. 26.
2. Ibid., Chapter 2. See Chapter 5 of the present volume.
3. Fred Best, "The future of retirement & lifetime distribution of work," based on testimony before the Subcommittee on Human Services, Select Committee on Aging, U.S. House of Representatives, 3 May 1978, p. 2.
4. Bernhard Tereit, "The flexible time, an object for the future," *RPCCNTRES Europeenness* Du Care de Vie, Paris, Dec. 6.
5. Diana R. Dunn, "Urban recreation", chapter 2, in T. Todbet, *Recreation, Park & Leisure Services: Foundations, Organization, Administration* (Philadelphia: W. B. Saunders Co., 1978), p. 47.
6. Ralph M. Kramer, "Urban community development," in *Israel: Social Structure & Change*, M. Curtis & M. Chertoff, ed., (New Brunswick. Books, 1973).
7. Elihu Katz and Michael Gurevitch, *The Socialization of Leisure: Culture & Communication in Israel* (London: Faber & Faber, 1976), p. 262.
8. Joffre Dumazedier, *Sociology of Leisure*, p. 161.
9. Ibid., p. 254
10. M. Kaplan, *Leisure: Lifestyle & Lifespan—Perspective for Geronotology* (Philadelphia: W. B. Saunders Co., 1979), pp. 16–17.
11. J. Dumazedier, *Sociology of Leisure*, p. 161.
12. Yehezkel Dror, *Design for Policy Sciences* (New York, Elsevier, 1971), p. 9.

Epilogue

1. Joseph Telushkin, *Jewish Literacy* (New York, William Morrow, 1991).
2. Jeremy Rifkin, *The End of Work*, pp. 216–217.
3. Ibid, p. xv.
4. Ibid, p. 7.
5. Ibid, p. 8.
6. Ibid, p. 12.
7. Ibid, p. 15.

8. Ibid, p. 61.
9. Ibid, p. 293.
10. Joel Swerdlow, Information Revolution, *National Geographic* vol. 188, no. 4, (October 1995): 6.
11. Max Kaplan, *Leisure in America, a Social Inquiry* (New York: John Wiley and Sons, Inc., 1960), pp. 101–6.
12. Max Kaplan, *The Arts.* Chapter 2.
13. Max Kaplan, *Leisure: Lifestyle and Lifespan, Perspectives for Gerontology,* Chapters 15–20.
14. Boris Schwartz, *Great masters of the Violin* (New York, Simon and Schuster, 1983).